Radical Hospitality

Radical Hospitality

American Policy, Media, and Immigration

NOUR HALABI

Rutgers University Press

New Brunswick, Camden, and Newark, New Jersey, and London

Library of Congress Cataloging-in-Publication Data

Names: Halabi, Nour, author.
Title: Radical hospitality : American media and regulatory stances towards immigration & travel bans / Nour Halabi.
Description: New Brunswick, New Jersey : Rutgers University Press, [2023] | Includes bibliographical references and index.
Identifiers: LCCN 2022009350 | ISBN 9781978827738 (hardback) | ISBN 9781978827721 (paperback) | ISBN 9781978827745 (epub) | ISBN 9781978827752 (pdf)
Subjects: LCSH: Emigration and immigration law—United States—History. | Emigration and immigration in mass media. | Immigrants in mass media. | Discrimination in mass media. | Mass media—Political aspects—United States. | United States—Emigration and immigration—Government policy. | United States—Race relations—History.
Classification: LCC JV6483 .H35 2023 | DDC 325.73—dc23/eng/20220803
LC record available at https://lccn.loc.gov/2022009350

A British Cataloging-in-Publication record for this book is available from the British Library.

References to internet websites (URLs) were accurate at the time of writing. Neither the author nor Rutgers University Press is responsible for URLs that may have expired or changed since the manuscript was prepared.

∞ The paper used in this publication meets the requirements of the American National Standard for Information Sciences—Permanence of Paper for Printed Library Materials, ANSI Z39.48-1992.

www.rutgersuniversitypress.org

Manufactured in the United States of America

In ancient Greek, *xenia* describes the relationship between a guest and his or her host. It is a relationship governed by Zeus "the protector of guests." In extending hospitality, humans "demonstrate their virtue or piety by extending hospitality to a humble stranger (xenos), who may turn out to be a disguised deity (theos) with the capacity to bestow rewards."

The violation of the laws of *xenia*—represented by the abduction of Helen of Sparta—is often portrayed as the *casus belli* of the Trojan War at the center of the *Iliad*.
—Erwin F. Cook, "Homeric Reciprocities"

Contents

Radical Hospitality

1

The Case for Hospitality

• •

In July 2019, two speeches—one by a law professor at an Ivy League university and my then-institutional home, and another by the then-president of the United States—presented ethical inflection points in American immigration politics, media coverage, and the public and academic discourse of immigration. After firing off a series of tweets on Sunday, July 14, 2019, suggesting that several minority congresswomen should go back to their countries of origin, President Donald Trump quietly smiled for thirteen seconds while the crowd at a North Carolina reelection rally chanted, "Send her back," referring to the former Somali refugee and Muslim Democratic congresswoman Ilhan Omar.

A few days earlier, at a Conservative Law Convention in Washington, D.C., University of Pennsylvania law professor Amy Wax delivered a speech in a panel titled "American Greatness and Immigration: The Case for Low and Slow." Wax suggested that "*our country* will be better off with more whites and fewer nonwhites" (Hermann 2019; my italics). She argued that this position is not racist, because "the problem" with these immigrants was cultural rather than racial; they are "loud," and they contribute to an increase in "litter." Her speech at the conference was not the first time Wax had espoused racist and eugenicist views; a year earlier, she suggested that Black students "rarely graduate in the top quarter of the class and rarely, rarely in the top half" (Lamon 2018).

At the core of these two public pronouncements of immigration and belonging, one addressed to the Republican base and another aimed at legal scholars and policymakers, lies a fundamental crisis in American immigration discourse. Both declarations imply that non-White immigrants originating from the Global South are racially and culturally distinct and unassimilable. They do not belong in *our* nation, as both speakers remind us. Nor do they possess the intelligence, work ethic, or presumed family planning capacities that enable them to meaningfully contribute to the nation's universities and workforce. According to this racist, White supremacist, eugenicist logic, it follows that their importation into the body politic should be "low and slow" if at all (Hermann 2019). Indeed, even when non-White immigrants enter the American citizenry, their belonging and that of their children continue to be called into question, as the actions at presidential nominee Donald Trump's July 2019 rally suggest.

These speeches (and especially the actions of the U.S. president) reverberated in the academic community and news media discourse both in the United States and around the world. They highlighted an insidious contradiction at the core of American politics and media: immigration and naturalization are fundamental elements of the American political system, enshrined in both the Declaration of Independence and the Constitution (Article I, Section 8, Clause 4, respectively); yet, the United States possesses a long-standing record of restrictive, racially discriminatory, and unwelcoming American immigration policies and media coverage. It is this contradiction that my book confronts, and for good reason.

The second contradiction that this book addresses is the positionality of the migrant and foreigner at the intersection of media and immigration studies. Although immigrants are impacted by immigration policies and represented to the public in national media, immigrants remain excluded from the legislative, administrative, and judicial bodies impacting their lives. As legal aliens, they have little say in the policies that impact their lives and futures. They are also subject to multiple intersecting obstacles, from linguistic barriers to access to professional networks, that would grant them the power to define how the media represents them to the public.

As such, this book draws on the experience of researching immigration while simultaneously navigating the intricacies of the immigration system. The seed for this book began while I was a Syrian PhD student at the very same university that employs Amy Wax. This research also began as a comparative international project, which morphed in scope as a travel ban limited my ability to travel and safely return to my studies in the United States. As the restrictive policy affected other fields as well, the isolationist nature of the executive order transformed this project into a much-needed introspective look at the policies and discourses surrounding immigration to the United States. As a graduate student, I juggled comprehensive exams with speaking to immigration lawyers and arranging my parents' application for asylum in this country, and thus this book embraces the position of the foreigner and stranger as an authoritative rather than marginalized voice within immigration and media studies.

My firsthand experience with the U.S. immigration processing system throughout the writing of this book reaffirmed the complexity and impenetrability of what Sara McKinnon has called the "modality of access" to the American public that is often predicated on "dense applications, court hearings, medical examinations, [and] interviews, all shrouded in technical and legal language that can be the difference between access and deportation" (McKinnon 2010, 131). As McKinnon notes, even immigrants and asylum seekers who are denied access "are unswervingly constituted by the publics (and states) that exclude them" (135). I experienced this exclusion firsthand, as I simultaneously researched and navigated the legal labyrinth of the American immigration system. Inscrutable and complex immigration policies, as well as biased media coverage of immigration in the United States, simultaneously offer the conditions that exclude the stranger from the "public" while defining and constituting the figure of the migrant. The multilayered injustice that this combination represents calls for a study that considers both the legal and media language of hospitality and exclusion.

Scholars in immigration studies have published numerous reflections addressing the racially discriminatory nature of immigration policy during the Trump administration, connecting contemporary discrimination with echoes of earlier waves. For a comprehensive analysis of this continuum, Erika Lee's *America for Americans: A History of Xenophobia in the United States* (2019) offers a particularly insightful record that traces the "echoes of past" xenophobia (Lee 2020) in contemporary American immigration policy. A number of studies have also sought to articulate the racial dimensions of access to the American public for visible minorities, from Mae Ngai's *Impossible Subjects*, which explores immigration policy from 1924 onward (Ngai 2014), to scholars who have turned a critical lens toward the immigration of various ethnic groups (Olzak 1989; Goldberg 2003). Yet another group, including Alixa Naff, Sarah Gualtieri, and Neda Maghbouleh, has attended to the tensions underlying Arab and Middle Eastern immigration in particular, as this group's immigration and pathway to "whiteness" highlighted and at times capitalized on the racially discriminatory foundations of belonging and citizenship (Ajrouch and Jamal, 2007; Naff 1993; Gualtieri 2009; Maghbouleh 2017).

This book is not a definitive and comprehensive record of discriminatory policies and discourses in itself. Instead, it hopes to make a unique contribution to the existing literature on U.S. immigration history and media by putting these two fields into conversation within a *normkritisk, or norm-critical, framework*. As Henriksson observes, norm-critical frameworks engage with Foucault's notion of enunciative modalities in that they critically examine the "positions, sites and relation to the object of discourse that are which give us a picture of the manifold subject that is allowed to 'speak the discourse'" (Foucault 1972, as cited in Henriksson 2017, 150). In fact, as Derrida tells us, the immigrant is a foreigner to legal and social discourse surrounding their moral rights (Derrida 2000, 19). Thus, I ask, how does the positionality of the scholar who is simultaneously excluded from the body politic and who is navigating this exclusion provide a fruitful vantage point to denaturalizing the ideologies underlying American immigration and its media coverage? Moreover, how could this vantage point provide concrete reflections grounded in the reality of American belonging and immigrant home-building rather than in its theoretical or legal treatment? I therefore wish to add a deeply personal and unique perspective on the history and contemporary politics of U.S. immigration by writing this book from the position of a Syrian immigrant in the United States and from the perspective of the daughter of asylum-applicant parents during a Trump presidency. I wrote this book as I navigated the complex immigration process for myself and for my family, in the hope that this perspective could enrich our understanding of the lived experience of U.S. immigrants. My hope is equally that this book draws our collective attention to the moral responsibility that host populations, and specifically policymakers and media professionals, owe to the immigrant who arrives at the nation's door.

Finally, this book combines the legal and historical analysis of American immigration with a critical discourse analysis of representations of immigration in the media. In so doing, it hopes to introduce an intersectional and interdisciplinary perspective that considers the combined impact of both media and policy in shaping the immigrant experience and the degree of welcome they encounter in host countries. I argue that by introducing the concepts of regulatory and media hospitality as crucial ethical frameworks through which the issue of immigration may be examined, we may begin to observe the convergence of these factors at work.

The Question of the Stranger

> Between me and the other world there is ever an unasked question: unasked by some through feelings of delicacy; by others through the difficulty of rightly framing it. All, nevertheless, flutter round it. They approach me in a half-hesitant sort of way, eye me curiously or compassionately, and then, instead of saying directly, How does it feel to be a problem? they say, I know an excellent colored man in my town.
> —W. E. B. Du Bois, *The Souls of Black Folk*

During the first presidential debate of the 2020 election, Chris Wallace, the debate moderator, asked the candidates, "Why should voters trust you, rather than your opponent, to deal with the race issues facing this country over the next four years?" (TGRANE 2020).[1] The wording of Wallace's question reflects the problematic ways in which both entertainment and news media in the United States frame issues of race and difference to policymakers and to the wider public. Rather than asking the candidates about the issue of racism, the moderator's question misguidedly frames race as the root of the tensions facing the nation. This pattern echoes the prescient observation Du Bois made in his 1903 book *The Souls of Black Folk*, in which he asked, "How does it feel to be a problem?" (Du Bois 1903).[2] Over a century later, Paul Lawrie reiterates Du Bois's observation, saying, "The conception of blackness as problem . . . is inherently inimical or at best incidental to the imperatives of modern American capitalism for much of the twentieth century" (2016, 169). The construction of difference as an inevitable problem also dominates news and entertainment media. Indeed, this trend is echoed in the work of scholars addressing the representation of multiple minorities: Sasha Torres's study of American television demonstrates how the media portrays race and particularly Blackness "as a problem." Torres notes in particular how American television has tied its depiction of "raced bodies [and] African-American bodies to particular social conditions which are considered undesirable and inextricably linked to racially marked communities" (Torres 2005, 396). Equally, in her influential study of the media representation of Asian Americans, Nancy Wang Yuen laments the racialization and racially tinged typecasting of Asian Americans in American entertainment industries (2017, 71–72).

Framing racial tensions as a problem of race rather than racism diverts moral responsibility from the individual and institutional vectors of systematic racism to the victims of (often) deadly racial discrimination. Particularly within the context of a presidential debate witnessed by sixty-three million viewers in the United States ("Media Advisory" 2020) and many more across the world, the question put to the candidates misses a crucial opportunity to reckon with the issue of systematic racism facing multiple areas of American society, from education and employment to health care and criminal justice. If Chris Wallace had instead asked candidates, "Why should voters trust you, rather than your opponent, to deal with the problem of *systemic racism* facing this country?" could this framing that is grounded in a hospitality framework have shifted our focus toward a collective reimagining of a more just political discourse?

The treatment of immigration follows a similar pattern as that of race. In fact, we can trace a thread directly from Du Bois's provocative question on Blackness almost a century earlier to Derrida's question on the position of the immigrant in "question of the stranger." Derrida asks, "Isn't the question of the foreigner/stranger a foreigner's question? Coming from the foreigner, from abroad?" (2000, 3). Here Derrida's eloquent observation hinges on the shared word that weaves these interrelated themes together: *étranger*, which in its adjective form describes all that "does not belong to the nation" and in its noun form translates to "foreigner," "stranger," and "abroad" (Larousse 2020). Linguistically, as Derrida's formulation calls to mind, the term draws together all that is distant, strange, and foreign and distances it from the nation, cementing its permanent belonging elsewhere. Thus, when the "question of the foreigner" arises, it naturally follows that it is a question that comes from elsewhere, an imposition onto the nation. The question of the *étranger* is in fact embodied in the person of the immigrant. Just as the treatment of difference concerning race often places the responsibility on the racialized persons, who seem to raise the matter by virtue of merely existing, policymaking and media coverage of migration often presents the "issue of immigration" and the foreigner as problems raised by the immigrant, instigated by their arrival at the nation's borders.

One reason for the tendency to focus on race rather than racism is what Du Bois acknowledges as the perceived indelicacy of addressing racism and discrimination, particularly given the moral reprehensibility of racism itself (1903). Nigerian philosopher Polycarp Ikuenobe notes that racism is widely considered morally reprehensible "because it is an attitude that is manifested in one's bad actions and behaviors that are unjust, discriminatory, degrading, and disrespectful of some people solely because of their racial designation" (Ikuenobe 2011, 162). In spite of the widespread acceptance of the moral reprehensibleness of racism, the inability to address it directly engenders "a great deal of confusion surrounding the meaning of 'racism' and 'racist'" that leaves plenty of room for racism to unfold without the racist being called out. Only one thing is clear, he adds, "Few people wish to be, or to be thought of as, 'racists'" (Blum 2002, 204).

Hospitality in many ways mirrors the discourse on racism and antiracism in that hospitality occupies "a universal normatively positive position," whether its motivations come from cultural, religious, philosophical, or other discourses (Bulley 2016, 3). Just as shifting our focus from race to racism reframes the moral framework surrounding racism in society, hospitality replaces the discourse surrounding the "issue of immigration" with a discourse that examines the degree of welcome extended to the Other in media and regulation. This paradigmatic shift reascribes moral responsibility for the discord that immigration appears to present from the body of the *étranger* to the host society. Thus, the focus on race and immigration being the "problem" places moral responsibility on the victims of injustice, while a discourse of racism and hospitality / racism and hostility place moral responsibility on the communities that may practice racism or xenophobia or instead extend their welcome and hospitality to newcomers.

Hospitality is often evoked in multiple religious traditions as an indicator of righteousness: In Islam, a religion practiced by around 1.8 billion people worldwide (Lipka and Hackett 2017), hospitality is equated with the core beliefs of the faith. As prophet Mohammed (PBUH) stated, "He who believes in God and the last day should honor his guest" (Khan 1995, Hadith 5673). Similarly, hospitality is evoked in Christianity to justify the need to "make room" (Pohl 1999) and "welcome the stranger at one's door" (Soerens, Yang, and Anderson 2018), while in the Indic traditions—Hindu, Buddhist, and Jain—hospitality reflects one's "relationship with the divine," where the "guest is God" (Rotman 2011, 115). Moreover, *Dana*, a key concept within the religious ethics of all Indic religions, represents the importance of the religious gift that "flows from the giver, usually a householder, to a worthy recipient, with no expectation whatsoever of return" (Eck 2013).[3] Hospitality also appears in cultural forms: "*Karam al-Arab*," or Arab hospitality, is a source of great pride throughout Arab societies (Shryock 2004).

In each manifestation across religious and cultural traditions, hospitality evokes an engagement with notions of morality and "goodness" (Rosello 2001a, 32), wherein the good treatment of a guest is seen as a reflection of the morality of the host. Thus, centering a study of immigration policy and discourse on hospitality as an ethical ideal not only achieves a more just grounding in moral responsibility; it also situates the treatment of migration squarely within a postcolonial conceptual frame (Rosello 2001a) that speaks to global publics from east to west and from north to south.

Hospitality and immigration in the context of the settler-colonial multiracial United States cannot be fully understood without taking race into account. As Mae Ngai notes, American immigration policies were not only informed by discriminatory race-based and eugenicist logics but also central to the creation, transformation, and codification of official racial categories and knowledge (Ngai 1999, 69). Of course, race operates as *one* variable among others in influencing immigration exclusion. For instance, as Catherine Lee notes in her study of Chinese exclusion, the act emerged from a confluence of race making, ethnic differentiation, and gender construction that centered on the construction of Chinese women as a threat to the sanctity of American families (Lee 2010, 248–249). Yet the history of American immigration illustrates junctures of hospitality and exclusion, influenced by perceptions of the races and national origins of migrant flows. It is therefore necessary to discuss immigration policy and media discourse with an eye for how racialized hierarchies influence the levels of welcome shown to migrants. Hospitality provides a language and framework to gauge how race impacts the degree of welcome shown to different immigrant groups.

Moreover, particularly as forced migration continues to grow, the condition of the immigrant increasingly mirrors that of the racialized Other in the sense that one cannot choose the color of their skin any more than they can choose to be born in an affluent, secure nation where one can safely live and prosper without the need to escape. Introducing immigrants into a nation also introduces racial, linguistic, religious, and cultural differences into the body politic, by virtue of being *étranger*. As such, migration depends on hospitality, for mobility necessarily involves leaving places of belonging, entering alien spaces, and relying on policies, laws, and media coverage to provide a welcoming environment in the adopted nation. Existing research in other fields has recognized the usefulness of a hospitality lens, pointing to its usefulness, for instance, in literary analysis (Rosello 2001b). As Sara McKinnon observed in her study of asylum in the United States, hospitality provides a "fortuitous way to complicate constitutions of publics" (2010, 133). Drawing on Derrida's work on hospitality, I argue that hospitality is not only a valuable lens with which to consider immigration, but it is also a crucial intervening concept that unsettles assumptions about the belonging and sovereignty of a "native population" in the United States. It therefore allows scholars and members of the public to reflect upon the moral rights of the immigrant as addressed in policy and media debates.

Once I begin to make the case for hospitality as a practical lens through which to view immigration, it follows that I begin to define what I mean by the term. For this, I believe it is most constructive to move from the abstract to the concrete and from the universal to the individual. Beyond its abstract conceptualization, hospitality is a concrete act initiated by invitation or called upon in mobility, since all movement requires moving out of places of belonging—home, neighborhood, town, city, state, country, or continent—and entering spaces that belong to another. At the microlevel, hospitality involves (and indeed affirms) the ownership and belonging of the host to a place, and therefore, it entails an unequal relationship of spatially anchored power between the host and the guest. At the national level, the discourse of hospitality can refer to the population inhabiting a host state as "natives" and to the nation of settlement as a "host nation," highlighting the primacy of belonging and ownership of place while implying the existence of a sovereign authority (Bell 2010, 236–238). At the global level, ownership, belonging, and authority may be practiced through multiple domains or enacted legally through the issuing or rejection of visas, the granting of asylum, the normalization of political relations, and the presence of diplomatic representation. Moreover, transnational agreements signal the belonging of several populations to a region, such as the Schengen Territory agreement, which asserts the belonging of Europeans to agreed-upon boundaries of the European continent, or the Arab Gulf League, which asserts the free movement and belonging of Gulf citizens to that region of the Arab peninsula. Underscoring these legal frameworks is a primacy of belonging and attachment that validates the authority and control of spatially tied identities over places.

Once hospitality is extended, what does the act entail? Early notions of hospitality, drawn from Greek and Roman traditions, entailed "hosting a guest" with food and drink (Still 2006). In the commercial field, hospitality tends to be defined as the provision of "the holy trinity" of food, drink, and accommodation (Lynch et al. 2011, 4). In international relations, hospitality expands to "protecting a stranger who arrives at one's door" (Still 2006), entailing shelter and protection. More recently, the discourse surrounding hospitality has been intricately tied to the discourse on human rights, for hospitality involves acknowledging the "moral rights" of others whether or not they are inscribed in the law (Douzinas 2007, 9), an act that is considered the ultimate test of our humanity because "the right to have rights and to be part of humanity is expected in the modern world to be guaranteed by humanity itself" (Arendt 1973, 298). In this light, human rights cannot exist without hospitality, since the movement of a community that belongs to one place entails their arrival in the places of belonging of other communities, and the respect of the guest community's human rights rests upon hospitality. As Arendt argues, guarantees of recognizing the rights of the Other are not self-evident. Reflecting on Hitler's famous phrase, "What is right is what is good for the German people," Arendt demonstrates how the fascist dictator was able to commit atrocities and violate human rights while appealing to the national public by affording human rights only to those who, in his opinion, most rightfully belonged to the nation, thereby limiting hospitality (299). Hospitality therefore provides an intervention toward honoring our shared humanity and our responsibility to one another.

Thus, the host-guest relationship inherent to hospitality confronts the native population with an Other. It is defined by the mutual relationship between guests and hosts. For the host, hospitality rests on the host's willingness "to let passage to the other, the wholly other" (Derrida 1999, 80). Kuakkanen reaffirms this relationship, saying "Hospitality is an act of openness to the other that helps to bring guests temporarily within the sphere of family or group, even if they come as a stranger" (2003, 268). To him, hospitality goes beyond the material requirements of shelter and sustenance to the ideational "responsibility" of "openness" (280). Through openness, hospitality provides an opportunity for cultural as well as material exchange and allows the host to learn from the episteme of the Other. The guest is also reciprocally responsible for learning of and from his or her host. It is thus not surprising, for instance, that the genre of the *Bildungsroman* in literature consists of the narrative of the protagonist's travels in different terrains and cultures, each of which contributes to the *Bildung* or personal development of the character. The responsibility incumbent upon the guest is to learn and respect the host's culture and traditions (Cook 2006, 65). The edifying value of hospitality is also hailed in folklore, where "the Arkansas traveler" emblematizes an interaction of host and guest as an opportunity to unlearn prejudices and stereotypes (Bluestein 1962, 156).

Admittedly, hospitality is not without its limitations. Several scholars note that hospitality is a relationship of alterity (Sobh, Belk, and Wilson 2013, 446). Indeed, I argue that hospitality defines an unequal relationship of spatially anchored power. Scholars who recognize the importance of the concept to human rights advocacy often criticize its emphasis on difference and Otherness (Douzinas 2007, 9). However, as long as the Westphalian nation-state political system remains, immigration introduces a relationship of difference between the inhabitant of a state and the immigrant who arrives at its borders (Rudolph 2005). National citizenship and immigration regimes reinforce the belonging of the host population to the nation. Conversely, they classify and construct the figure of the immigrant as that of a non-citizen or "alien." This imbalance between the rights of the citizen and the lack of rights of the immigrant non-citizen therefore raises moral and ethical questions that we may elucidate and disentangle using hospitality as an ethical framework. If alterity cannot be evaded, it is how alterity is confronted that matters. Thus, it remains useful to confront what hospitality means in American society today and what it has meant over time.

As a lens through which to regard immigration, hospitality can also capture and make visible abuses of power by either party in the host-guest relationship. For instance, a host may mistreat or disrespect a guest or take the guest hostage, depriving him or her of expected shelter, food, openness, and even freedom and basic rights. At the same time, the guest may take advantage of a host's welcome, threatening the host or infringing upon his or her comfort or rights. Indeed, early conceptions of hospitality in Greek mythology required both host and guest to respect the sacred relationship they shared with one another. For hosts, the obligation to extend welcome and generosity springs from the solicitation of hospitality by the gods as tests of one's goodness and morality. In book XIV of the *Iliad*, Homer remarks, "For it is Zeus who sends to us all beggars and strangers" (Butler 1999, xiv). Similarly, guests are often shown to infringe on hosts' welcome as well. For example, the kidnapping of Helen of Sparta is an abuse of the hospitality of Agamemnon; another example is the numerous suitors Penelope received while Odysseus was traveling overstaying their welcome until Odysseus arrived and "planted the seed of death and slaughter for the suitors" (28). Thus, violations of the sanctity of the host-guest relationship by either party were portrayed as sacrilege punishable by the gods.

Drawing on these sources, I define hospitality as a relationship between a host who has developed an identity that is spatially anchored in a place—and is thus seen as belonging to a place and possessing authority over it—and a guest who enters the host's domain and whose identity is perceived as tied to other places. This relationship provides a lens through which to regard immigration as it combines notions of home and identity, host and belonging, and the guest and Other/stranger. Within this relationship, the host grants access to potential places of belonging, providing food, drink, and shelter while cultivating a relationship of openness and understanding (Kuakkanen 2003, 280). Meanwhile, the guest respects the traditions of his or her host. In the modern context, this relationship can be productively discerned in two environments: regulation and the media.

I apply the concept of hospitality to two environments pertinent to the immigrant experience—immigration policy and media discourse—distinguishing between two forms: what I call *regulatory hospitality* and *media hospitality*. The chapters of this book illustrate the interaction of policymaking and media coverage in three periods of immigration restriction: the 1880s, the 1920s, and the 2000s (post-9/11 period). Historicizing the American openness to immigration that I call *immigration hospitality*, this analysis provides a closer and more critical look at how and under what circumstances the United States extends hospitality toward immigrants and how media and policy interact to shape the immigrant experience.

Regulatory Hospitality

An important area of hospitality's relevance in the modern era is in immigration policy and the regulations that impact the lives of immigrants in their host countries. As such, regulatory hospitality is evident in the degree of welcome extended to immigrants in all "acts, treaties and conventions that relate to the immigration, exclusion, or expulsion of aliens" (Johnson 1921). It is also informed by other conditions that govern immigration and resettlement, such as constitutionally based rights, executive decisions, and the law enforcement environment. This is not to exclude conditions outside of the law that influence immigration decisions, such as the patterns of immigration in terms of demographic characteristics, countries of origin, and conditions of immigration.

As such, the first component of regulatory immigration hospitality concerns the barriers to entry set for immigrants and the degree of recognition accorded to the right of movement that is expressed by a country's laws. In the United States, the right of movement was enshrined in the nation's Constitution from its earliest moments, particularly in the law of naturalization, which anticipated the arrival of immigrants and their integration into the nation. Thus, the Constitution empowers Congress "to establish a uniform Rule of Naturalization" (Article I, Section 8, Clause 4), foreseeing immigration as a matter to be included in the foundational text of the United States. Immigration policies established in the first century of the republic's history did not present barriers to entry for incoming immigrants but rather required that they register their arrival on U.S. soil (Steerage Act 1819). The right to movement within the republic was also stressed in the Articles of Confederation, which stated that in order to "secure and perpetuate mutual friendship and intercourse among the people of the different States in this Union . . . the people of each State shall have free ingress and regress to and from any other State" (Article 5).

Second, recognizing the desire of immigrants to integrate into their host nation is another manifestation of regulatory hospitality. Just as the right to migrate was alluded to in the Declaration of Independence, the document also asserted that "all men are created equal" and "that they are endowed by their Creator with certain unalienable Rights, that among these are Life, Liberty and the pursuit of Happiness" (Declaration of Independence 1776). These arguments for life, liberty, and the pursuit of happiness, as extended to all "men" in the Declaration, suggest to immigrants the opportunity of attaining social and economic well-being in American society, an important component of successful home-building. The right of movement was thus fittingly connected in these texts to other socioeconomic activities—namely, the exchange of goods and services across borders—and it indirectly tied the international right of movement to the economic and social well-being of all residents, including immigrants.

Third, regulatory hospitality in a host nation is informed by the international conventions that impact the conditions of immigrants therein. These include international conventions such as the Geneva Convention, the Geneva Protocol, and the International Convention on Intervention and State Sovereignty (ICISS), as well as relevant executive actions and Supreme Court decisions that affect it (an issue of particular relevance to the first and second Muslim travel ban and the Supreme Court decision to allow its modified version in 2018). The Right to Protect Doctrine is also an orienting framework for U.S. political intervention in cases of humanitarian crises since the 1990s, assuring the displaced that they can take refuge in the United States and other signatory states. The ICISS, under the sponsorship of the government of Canada, issued the Responsibility to Protect Report in response to the "widely criticized humanitarian responses to crisis in the 1990s" (ICISS 2001, 1). The report stipulated the international sharing of responsibility for crisis response, and it enforced the Universal Declaration of Human Rights, the International Covenant on Civil and Political Rights, the Covenant on Economic and Social Rights, the Genocide Convention, the Geneva Conventions and additional protocols, and the Rome Statute of the International Criminal Court (2001, 3). Together, the global commitment toward enforcing these conventions—spearheaded by the United States and Canada—reframed the concept of hospitality within an international law framework. It is worthy of note that such applications of hospitality are yet again rooted in acknowledging the moral human rights of others.

Finally, regulatory hospitality interacts with the political and social environments that encourage policy responses to either extend or withhold hospitality. In these cases, the type of policy response, as well as a lack thereof, is also a manifestation of hospitality or inhospitality in the broader environment. That is to say that although regulatory hospitality rests foremost in regulatory frameworks, it has direct effect on cultural, social, and political movements taking shape beyond regulatory spheres.

In sum, regulatory hospitality is a concept that measures the degree of hospitality as manifested in national immigration policies and as a result of national policymaking, judicial decisions, and the ratification of international agreements that require a degree of hospitality toward particular groups of immigrants. The term *regulatory hospitality* signifies an overall openness to immigration that is demonstrated in a clearly outlined approach to immigration that may be navigated by an immigrant or potential immigrant with relative ease and that offers opportunities for arrival, settlement, and work in an adopted nation. When categories, races, or classes of people are excluded from such openness, hospitality is nonevident or evident to a lesser degree.

Media Hospitality

Hospitality requires a language through which it can be performed in the public sphere, and that is where media assume their role in extending hospitality toward immigrants and refugee communities. Media are ubiquitous, where "through their practices of selection, editing and production, [media] determine the kinds of news we receive about our nation" (Jiwani 1995, 738). Indeed, according to classic agenda-setting theory, editors, newsroom staff, journalists and broadcasters play an important role in shaping political reality by choosing and displaying what news is covered (McCombs and Shaw 1972). Thus, in selecting stories that portray immigrants as threats to the health, security, and cultural cohesion of a population, media shape the political reality that appears to the public.

Moreover, media coverage can frame the debate surrounding immigrants within a particular set of thematic issues that dictate a positive or negative portrayal of immigration. For example, by framing immigration and refugee policy as a matter of national security, humanitarian concern, economic opportunity, or labor market competition, media coverage contributes to how an issue is publicly viewed and discussed by policymakers (Weaver 2007). Silverstone elaborates on the responsibility of that role, as he defined media hospitality as a normative position where the media speaks not only to an empirical reality but to a moral interrelationship with the immigrant and refugee as an "Other" in social and cultural space ([2006] 2013, 100–101).

These representations have powerful repercussions for the rights of minority groups. As Gramsci pointed out, media provide a powerful tool for a majority group to exert influence by legitimizing its dominance in the representation of social and political reality (1971). For example, the "whiteness" of Hollywood impacts the marginalization and devaluation of the talent and life stories of non-White immigrants and racial minorities in the United States (Wang Yuen 2017). Similarly, media representations of immigrants and racial minorities can affirm or erase the complex experiences, contributions, and senses of belonging and place in the neighborhoods, communities, and countries in which they reside (Garcia et al. 2021).

Media representation is also significant to "home-building" within immigrant communities (Hage [1997] 2010); they bear a tangible impact on immigrants' sense of identity and sense of feeling at home in the host nation. In her analysis of Canadian mediated representations of minorities, Mahtani argued that "demeaning characterizations and an absence of nuanced representations" make immigrant communities "feel as if they do not belong" (Mahtani 2001, 3). The absence of visible minorities that are immigrants or descendants of immigrant parents is also significant because media coverage targets an imagined national "implied audience" (Livingstone 1998), thus denying the existence and belonging of minorities.

Media representations of marginalized groups affect a number of issues within their respective communities, from mental health (Collins 2000; Chae et al. 2017) to gender identity (Ward, Hansbrough, and Walker 2005) as well as opportunities for educational attainment, employment, access to capital, and other realms that affect socioeconomic well-being. Thus, the media's role in a majority group's representation of immigrants is critical, particularly in how such representations interact with immigration policies to create an environment that is either hospitable or hostile toward them.

I argue that media hospitality implies an openness to the Other through his or her inclusion in media portrayals and media professional spheres. If hospitality is "openness" to an Other (Kuakkanen 2003, 280), then learning the language, literature, idioms, and expressions of that Other indicates openness. Newsroom diversity, which introduces diverse linguistic skills into journalistic professional circles, may enhance the degree of hospitality shown to migrants in a host nation. By contrast, a lack of familiarity with the Other—as well as with his or her culture and language—suggests a lack of openness and an unwillingness to "do the homework" to accommodate other worldviews. The presence or absence of marginal voices in the national media ecology is another vector of media hospitality, because absence may suggest the lack of importance or even nonexistence of the Other (Mahtani 2001, 4).

The meanings and representations offered by the media define the experience of minority communities in society, suggesting that the valence of media portrayals is an important indicator of media hospitality. Conversely, the underrepresentation and misrepresentation (6) of immigrants and refugees in the media represent another obstacle to media hospitality.

In considering the impact of media representations of immigration on the migrant experience, I draw first and foremost on the work of Stuart Hall, who posits that the media is an important element of the "production and transformation of ideology," particularly racial ideologies that surround the social construction of race in society (1981, 18). Media construct their subjects, and they are powerful platforms through which both overt and inferential racism may circulate. The former, Hall argues, gives "open and favourable" coverage to openly racist statements, while the latter presents certain presumptions about race as natural and *unquestioned assumptions* (20). This book is also inspired by the writing of Roger Silverstone, whose reflections on media morality hone in on the representation of the Other in media coverage. Similarly, Stuart Hall's writing considers media messages to be reflections of the dominant cultural order (130–132). I therefore position the media as an important element that structures reality both for receiving populations—including policymakers—and for immigrants. To do so, the study undertakes a qualitative approach to media coverage that examines how the areas of media and policy interact, how they influence society's treatment of immigrants, and how they shape the contours of the immigrant experience.

As such, I define media hospitality as describing the degree of presence or absence of immigrant communities in the media as well as the valence of the representations of immigrant communities when they appear, taking into account misrepresentation in the form of stereotypes and otherwise. In parallel, media hospitality may be articulated directly through messages of welcome to immigrant communities and through emphasis being placed on the value of welcoming immigrants and refugees to national society.

A Working Definition of Hospitality

Hospitality describes a relationship between a host—who has developed an identity that is spatially anchored in a place and is thus associated with that place and seen to belong to it—and a guest whose identity is perceived as tied to other places and who enters the host's domain. This relationship combines notions of home and identity, host and belonging, and the guest and Other/stranger. The host grants the guest access to potential places of belonging—often providing food, drink, and shelter—and welcomes him or her by cultivating a relationship of "openness" and understanding (Kuakkanen 2003, 280). In the modern context, hospitality can be seen as present in immigration policy when clearly defined immigration guidelines provide opportunities for entry and settlement in a host nation. Similarly, hospitality can be seen as present in the media when immigrants are part of media coverage, when they have a positive representational valence, and when their presence is seen as valuable by the host society welcoming them.

The study of media hospitality is inextricably tied to that of regulatory hospitality, as media coverage bears an impact for policymaking and shapes the reception of policies by the public, helping to define the terminology in which policies are discussed. Bill Orme from the Ethical Journalism Network, for example, observed that the terms *alien* and *undocumented immigrants*, when used by media organizations, have different outcomes. In the first case, they normalize the Othering and criminalization of immigrants for the public; in the second, they focus objectively on the distinguishing legal situation of such immigrants (personal communication 2018). Media coverage also impacts the legislative process. As Henry notes, media "contribute[s] to the development of a negative image of racial communities, which are then marginalized and legislated against" (Henry 1999, vii). In light of these perspectives, regulatory and media hospitality act in tandem to affect the degree of welcome extended toward immigrants in each host country.

This book focuses on how the U.S. media and regulatory environments have approached the treatment of newcomers and what the systematic treatment of immigrants reveals about the value that society places not only on migrants' lives but also on the lives of the rest of the population. By examining policy and media coverage, this analysis provides a humanistic perspective of the combined role that these realms play in creating a hospitable environment for immigrants and shaping their experience arriving and settling in their adopted nation.

I treat regulatory regimes and media coverage of immigrants as observable manifestations of American immigration hospitality, drawing attention to the importance of hospitality as a moral, cultural, and symbolic framework through which to view immigration in media and politics. I show that extending welcome or withholding it cultivates an environment that is either hospitable or inhospitable to migrants, impacting immigrants' "home-building" efforts as they cultivate a sense of home in their adopted country (Hage 1997).

To conduct this analysis, I examine immigration legislation and its media coverage, focusing on three distinct periods of U.S. immigration history: the 1880s, the 1920s, and the 2000s period surrounding the passage of the Muslim travel ban. These periods are selected because they reflect specific historical moments in which media coverage and the regulatory environment focused on a category of immigrant Other within the U.S. public—Chinese, Eastern and Southern Europeans, and Muslims, respectively. Each period was analyzed by surveying the key legislation relevant to immigration of the period as well as its media coverage in the main news outlets of the time.

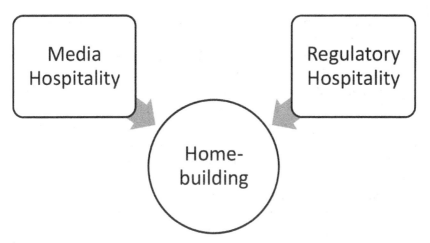

FIG. 1.1 The dual impact of media and regulatory hospitality on the immigrant experience. Created by the author.

The data collection adopted a twofold process to collect regulatory and media data. The analysis of regulatory hospitality includes all central acts, treaties, and conventions that relate to the immigration, exclusion, or expulsion of aliens during each time period, as well as relevant executive actions, legislation on constitutionally based rights, international conventions such as the Geneva Convention and the Geneva Protocol that require member states to adhere to a level of immigration hospitality, and relevant judicial and Supreme Court decisions that affect immigration. The parameters used to collect policies for analysis included key immigration documents from 1819 onward as well as other foundational legal texts influencing immigrants' lives, such as the Eighteenth Amendment and the Patriot Act.

I constructed a database of relevant immigration policies while doing archival research at the University of Pennsylvania Law Library between January and March of 2017, in the Thomas Jefferson and John Adams Papers at the Massachusetts Historical Society in April to May 2017 (for immigration debates of the postindependence era), in the Congressional Records at the CU–Boulder National Government Library in August to October 2017 (for immigration policy debates in Congress of the 1880s), and through the Congressional Record online database (1995–) as well as the United States Citizenship and Immigration Services online archives (for congressional immigration debates in the 2000s). Finally, the parameters for collecting information on international conventions were guided by the key documents available in the United Nations archive online, including the Geneva Convention and Geneva Protocol (1951). I also consulted the Treaties and Other International Acts

Series in the Department of State online archive for international and bilateral agreements that impact U.S. immigration regulation and administration.

For my analysis of media hospitality, I primarily relied on the *Wall Street Journal* (1889–), the *New York Times* (1851–), and the *Washington Post* (1877–) as primary sources of media coverage, because these publications reflected the breadth of the American ideological spectrum, and two of them were widely distributed newspapers that remained in circulation throughout all of the periods analyzed. Using ProQuest and each newspaper's subscription-based online archive, I analyzed a total of 223 news articles across the three central time periods discussed throughout the chapters of the book.

For the 1880s, I conducted a search for all articles published between January 1, 1880, and January 1, 1900, that used terms referencing Chinese immigrants, including "Chinese," "coolie," "immigrant," "Chinee," "immigration," and "cargo." I also searched for all articles that mentioned "Chinese exclusion," "immigration restriction," and "exclusion" in policy debates over immigration in the media. The search returned a total of forty-two articles, which form the basis of the analysis of the 1880s in chapter three. In light of the heightened importance of Chinese immigration for the West Coast in the 1880s, I also included West Coast publications such as the *San Francisco Tribune*, the *Oakland Tribune*, and the *Record-Union*, as well as select coverage from other publications. Moreover, as highlighted by journalistic historian Thomas Leonard, political cartoons and particularly the highly influential lithographs of Thomas Nast provided a mechanism of "visual thinking" in an environment of low literacy during the 1800s (Leonard 1986, 98, 127). As such, the sample incorporated the political cartoons dealing with immigration that appeared in *Harper's Weekly* and *The Wasp* during the same period.

In chapter four, the analysis of immigration policy during the 1920s draws on the *Wall Street Journal*, the *New York Times*, and the *Washington Post* online archives. I searched for all articles between January 1, 1920, and January 1, 1930, using the terms "immigration," "immigrant," "new immigrant," "immigrant stock," "refugee" and "refuge" as well as articles that reflected upon regulatory decisions that affected immigrant lives, including "prohibition," "wets," "drys," "temperance," "quota," "national origins," and "immigration law." I also searched for terms that related to particular immigrant communities targeted by restrictive policies, including but not restricted to "Italian," "Irish," "Greek," "Polish/Poles" "Russian," and "Jewish" as well as "southern European" and "eastern European." The search returned a total of ninety-eight articles that form the basis of the analysis in the chapter.

To conduct the analysis of media hospitality during the 2000s, I searched the archives for media coverage of immigration in the *New York Times*, the *Wall Street Journal*, and the *Washington Post* from 2001 to 2018, using the search terms "immigrant," "migrant," "refugee," and "asylum," as well as terms specific to coverage of immigration from Muslim-majority countries, including "Muslim," "Muslim-majority," and "Arab." A preliminary analysis of the dominant media tropes pointed to the widespread use of the terms "Muslim extremism," "radicalism," and "terrorism," as well as "soft targets," in security-minded coverage of immigration, requiring further searches for those terms. This search returned a total of eighty-three articles that form the basis of the analysis in chapter five. In addition, to reflect the widening of the media ecology of the twentieth and twenty-first centuries and the technological developments that have increased the number of media platforms available to politicians to publicize their views on immigration, the search also encompassed the Twitter accounts of key figures within the Trump administration, particularly those with significant input on immigration policy and discourse such as Mike Pence, Steve Bannon, Stephen Miller, Michael Flynn, and Jared Kushner. Finally, the study of online mobilization against the travel ban expanded to include discourse on social media, including the trending hashtags #MyMuslimAmericanFamily and #NoBanNoWall.

I argue that the history of the United States established a bifurcated environment for immigration from the earliest days as an imperial colony and subsequently as an independent republic. Within this environment, White, Protestant, primarily northern European immigrants were extended unlimited welcome while other immigrants were denied that same status and trapped within a host-hostage relationship.

This history shows that particular ethnic, racial, and religious communities have been systematically excluded from the embrace of American immigration hospitality. Chapter 2 addresses how a bifurcated immigration hospitality environment was built atop Native American and African American injustices. Chapter 3 highlights the factors that contributed to the discrimination of Chinese immigrants and brought about the Chinese Exclusion Act. Chapter 4 considers the factors that motivated discrimination in media and regulatory policies against southern and eastern European immigrants, culminating in the national origins quotas of the 1920s onward. Finally, chapter 5 examines the negative media and regulatory environment for Muslim immigrants in the aftermath of the September 2001 terrorist attacks.

Across these chapters, analysis has shown that American hospitality periodically and repeatedly shrinks and that the mechanisms of Othering and exclusion in regulation and media portrayals impact immigrants' ability to settle and feel "at home" in their new homes. To conclude this study of immigration hospitality, its past and its future, I turn to the most recent turning point in American immigration hospitality: the passage of the Muslim travel ban and the public, media, and regulatory responses to it. This conclusion points to one potential avenue in which hospitality may still have a future: public discourse that attests to the importance of the image of America as a nation of immigrants.

2
Poisoned Beginnings: The Birth of the (Immigrant) Nation

•••••••••••••••••••••

Research on immigration emphasizes international migration flows as emblematic of the modern condition and symptomatic of a new transnational understanding of home and belonging (Castells 1996; Anderson 2006). By and large, these accounts tend to frame global migration during the past few decades from a global perspective as defined by the crossing of international borders within the Westphalian political order. These perspectives take for granted how the nation and national identity have come to be in host nations and whether national identity has selectively privileged the belonging of one identity at the expense of others. As a result, such narratives of immigration may frame border crossing as a destabilizing force disrupting national identity, unmooring it from places of belonging and necessitating a reframing of identity to encompass newcomers (Alba and Nee 1997).

By adopting hospitality as an analytical framework with which we can consider American immigration, this chapter extends the temporal horizons governing narratives of immigration, complicating assumptions of belonging or the authority of presumed "native" populations who have in fact disrupted the relationship Indigenous communities have with their places of belonging. This is especially relevant to the study of settler-colonial societies. Secondly, by tracing couplets of host-guest relationships that encompass broad swaths of history, I shed light on abuses of hospitality that foreshadow and pave the way for future violations of this host-guest relationship.

The relevance of hospitality to American history dates to the earliest days of the American republic. The study of U.S. immigration hospitality must begin by first considering the legacy of Native American genocide and cultural erasure as well as the forced displacement and multiple forced internal migrations of Native American populations as they were relocated within the territory of the United States. Similarly, a study of immigration hospitality must consider the forced migration of African slaves. Both groups raise important questions about the resonance and validity of the claim of America as a nation of immigrants. Together, the inclusion of both groups complicates our vision of the history of American immigration hospitality's first host-guest relationships, foreshadowing the future of American immigration.

Adopting a timeline of immigration hospitality that encompasses all host-guest dyads is a particularly generative approach to the study of American immigration history and immigration history in other settler-colonial nations. Canonical texts that focus on immigration to the United States often begin in 1882 (Daniels 2004), a temporal focus that inadvertently neglects to acknowledge the history of the territories of the United States predating European colonization. Immigration scholars who examine settler-colonial nations' histories postcolonization thus continue to focus on the integration of newcomers into the taken-for-granted European identity of the settler-colonial state. This pattern is not only typical of the United States but common across other settler-colonial countries. For example, historical accounts of Canadian history begin with European colonization (Kelly and Trebilcock 1998) with little regard for the expropriation and displacement of First Nations who had established self-governing societies with their own languages, traditions, and spiritual beliefs alongside a deep-seated belonging to the territories they inhabited (Wilson and Peters 2005; Harris 2011; Kornelsen et al. 2010). Similarly, the study of Israeli history until recently centered on discussions that began with the arrival of settler immigrants to British mandate Palestine. Even texts that examined modes of Jewish "settlement" into Palestine failed to mention the existence of an Indigenous people in the region (Katz 1988). As a result, as Idith Zertal notes in *Israel's Holocaust and the Politics of Nationhood*, Israel continues to perceive itself as a victim of people who are living in untenable conditions under military occupation (Zertal 2005, 173). These examples demonstrate a marked trend of erasing and overlooking displaced communities in the immigration histories of settler-colonial nation-states. Nevertheless, the "creation" of settler-colonial nation-states, and the subsequent development of a sense of belonging for the populations residing therein, inevitably involves not only the voluntary migration to and between territories but also the forcible displacement of Indigenous peoples inhabiting the territories (Ahmed 2003, 1–3). They also implicate the importation of forced laborers needed to fuel the development of "new" worlds.

As such, while American immigration scholarship emphasizes that the "Great Migration" between 1630 and 1780 of an estimated 501,000 Europeans was pivotal for the nation's establishment, these accounts often fail to consider the forcible displacement of Indigenous peoples and African communities as foundational to this migration. A key indicator of this oversight lies in the portrayal of resident communities as "Native Americans," suggesting that their study only began once the political establishment of "America" was secured. This enabled the Indigenous communities inhabiting this territory to be called "Native Americans" rather than the self-ascribed tribal and other identities that predated settlement. Similarly, African American communities are addressed only insofar as they represent African arrivals to America, erasing the former countries, languages, and societies of enslaved people brought to the continent against their will.

In an effort to shed light on the poisoned beginnings of American immigration hospitality, this chapter attends to two particular communities whose treatment is indicative of the racially determined horizons of American hospitality: Indigenous peoples and African forced migrants brought to the United States during the slave trade.

Colonization of the "New World"

As a settler-colony, the immigrant history of the United States is an inevitable part of the nation's formation (Daniels 2016). As North America relied on the influx of primarily European settler-immigrants to populate the "New World," immigration was emphasized by the colonial powers as a critical component of the development of the region that would become the United States. As such, the region witnessed a high level of immigration during the eighteenth and nineteenth centuries, as fifty-five to sixty million Europeans sailed from the "Old World" to the North American continent (Akenson 2011, 5) in a historical period now referred to as the "Great Atlantic Migration."

As European settlers arrived in the United States, the settler population prioritized immigration and focused on encouraging incoming migration and naturalization. Later, promoting immigration would become one of the founding tenants of the Declaration of Independence and the foundation of the American nation. Thomas Jefferson listed immigration restrictions by England among the grievances of the American colonies against British colonial rule, lamenting that King George limited immigration to the United States and the naturalization of its newcomers, saying, "He has endeavoured to prevent the population of these States; for that purpose, obstructing the Laws for Naturalization of Foreigners; refusing to pass others to encourage their migrations hither, and raising the conditions of new Appropriations of Lands" (Declaration of Independence 1776).

This meant that the early European settlers and immigrants arriving on the continent in the eighteenth and nineteenth centuries encountered a high level of immigration hospitality at the expense of the native population. Immigrants arriving during the colonial era were also instantaneously recognized as imperial subjects upon arrival. As such, they were granted equal rights and responsibilities as the native population. This is telling given the significance of this period to painting an image of the origin story of the United States as one of high immigration hospitality that would endure far longer than the policies of this time.

During the republic's early history, an exceptionally high number of immigrants arrived in the country. Between 1820 and 1860, amid the "near-absence of federal legislation" on immigration (Zolberg 2006, 3), 5 million immigrants settled in the United States. The number rose to 13.5 million between 1860 and 1890—making one in every seven U.S. citizens foreign-born and earning the country a reputation as a "nation of immigrants" (4). This trend continued into the early twentieth century; an estimated 30 million people immigrated to the United States between 1836 and 1914.

The early period of the republic manifested many of the aspirations of Thomas Jefferson and the Founding Fathers in drafting the Declaration of Independence to "encourage migrations hither" (Declaration of Independence 1776).

Scholars in the twenty-first century attribute the early absence of immigration policy to an effort to preserve the sovereignty of individual states or to the relatively young regulatory infrastructure available (Zolberg 2006, 4).

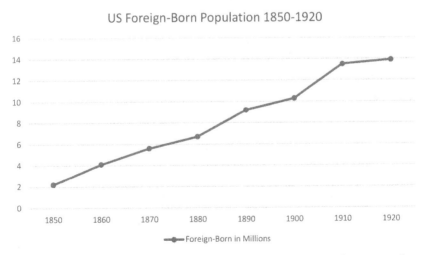

FIG. 2.1 U.S. foreign-born population (in millions). U.S. Census Bureau and Pew Research Center tabulations. Created by the author.

There are on board this Ship, all told, 50 persons. viz:-
Capt Winthrop Sears. — 1st 2d & 3 mates. — Carpenter,—
16 Able & Ordinary seamen. — 8 Boys (Green hands without regard to age)
among the latter is Cousin Wm S. Whitney. who has shipped before
the mast for the benefit of his eyes.
Steward. — Stewardess — assistant steward — & Cook.
and 17 Passengers.

                The passengers are as below
Revd   Hitchcock & wife   of Honolulu, Sandh Is.
        David Hitchcock   do
        Edward Hitchcock   do
Revd   Baldwin & wife bound to Lahaina. Sand Is.
Revd   Pierson & wife   Micronesia.
Mrs H.M. Whitney +2 children   of Honolulu. S.I.
Miss Celia P. Wright,   bound to Honolulu. S.I.
        Edwd Everett
        Chas H Lunt   } Bound to the Sandwich Islands and
        Edward M. Brewer } elsewhere in company, no particular plan made
        Alfred Tufts.   } beyond said islands.
        Geo F. Tufts

                December 7th 1855 Thursday.
Head wind. fine & mild weather
                        Position at noon Lat 34.28 N
Sailed 205 miles   Lon 44.38 W

                December 8th Friday.
Head wind. —
A Sail in sight   { Position at noon Lat 35.25 N
at 5 P.M. distant 6 or 8 miles   Lon 43.18 W
Sailed 92 miles

                December 9th Saturday
Head wind. — a pig died & was thrown overboard.
David Hitchcock & Alfred T. shooting with a rifle on qr deck.
                        Position at noon Lat 33.54 N
Sailed 90 miles.   Lon 43.36 W

FIG. 2.2 An example of a passenger list provided in accordance with the Steerage Act. Massachusetts Historical Society. Log of the bark *Frances Palmer*, 1855, Tufts Family Papers.

However, a closer examination of the evidence suggests that the absence of immigration policy was no oversight of policymakers of the time. During this same period, the young nation imposed several regulations to monitor immigration, revealing a regulatory willingness to legislate policy that did not curb immigration flows as well as an ability to legislate policy governing immigration. For example, the first congressional act governing immigration flows, the Steerage Act, simply required that ships provide information regarding immigrants on board and collect demographic information for the federal government (Steerage Act 1819). Thus, for over a century, immigrants flowed into the nation's receiving ports in Boston, Philadelphia, and New York with no barriers to their entry and a simple requirement of registering their passage to the United States.

Because hospitality involves not only welcoming the stranger but acknowledging the individual as an equal part of society, the transition of a "guest" into a citizen in immigration policy takes place through "naturalization," the process through which the United States grants citizenship to immigrant arrivals. As such, naturalization policy holds important implications for this study of immigration hospitality. Here, too, American immigration policy of the time demonstrated a high level of hospitality. Priority was granted to naturalization policy, with the centrality of immigration to the American experiment echoed in the Constitution, which enshrined the need for a uniform law of naturalization (Article I, Section 8, Clause 4). As such, recognizing the importance of incentivizing potential European migrants to populate the "New World," the framers inscribed immigration in the Constitution (Pfander and Wardon 2010, 367). During this period, European immigrants arrived with little regulation at the borders, as national regulations were sparse, granting states significant discretion to regulate immigrant arrivals. This in turn sustained the high rates of immigration of the period.

Under these conditions, immigration rose to historic levels according to immigration historians, earning the country a reputation as a "nation of immigrants" (Zolberg 2006, 4). As such, the origins of American immigration created an image of the United States as an "immigrant nation" possessing a high level of immigration hospitality. However, contemporary uses of the label "nation of immigrants" belie the less hospitable realities of early American immigration and obfuscate the injustices and contradictions underlying the myth of the immigrant nation. Overlooking this past has enabled statements across time that not only contradict but rewrite American immigration history. Consider the example of President John F. Kennedy's book *A Nation of Immigrants*, a laudatory account of the nation's immigrant past from a descendant of Irish immigrants whose ancestors endured significant discrimination for being "papists" and "bogtrotters," individuals destined to be "undigested, and indigestible" (Handlin 1991, 55).

In 1790, the U.S. Congress passed the Alien Naturalization Act, which stipulated that "any alien, being a free white person" who has resided lawfully in the United States for a period of two years may be "admitted to become a citizen" (Alien Naturalization Act 1790). In addition, as outlined in the definition of regulatory hospitality, the enforcement of immigration policies also offered avenues to assess immigration hospitality. As such, the relative ease of the naturalization process prior to 1906, when any court of record (municipal, county, state, or federal) could grant U.S. citizenship, demonstrated the effort of American policymakers to exhibit hospitality at all levels of the immigration process. This straightforward process stood in direct contrast to the complexity of immigration and naturalization processes in times of immigration restriction.

Judicial decisions also reaffirmed the right of immigrants to naturalization and citizenship. For instance, the Supreme Court decision of *United States v. Wong Kim Ark* stipulated that "the Fourteenth Amendment affirms the ancient and fundamental rule of citizenship by birth within the territory, in the allegiance and under the protection of the country, including all children here born of resident aliens, with the exceptions or qualifications (as old as the rule itself) of children of foreign sovereigns or their ministers, or born on foreign public ships, or of enemies within and during a hostile occupation of part of our territory" (*United States v. Wong Kim Ark* 1898). As such, hospitality extended to children born to foreign-born residents of the United States, seeing them as belonging to the nation and worthy of citizenship by birth (*Jus Soli*).

By enshrining the right to naturalization in the American Constitution and in allowing citizenship in the Alien Naturalization Act of 1790 to be granted to "any alien, being a free white person" who had resided lawfully in the United States for a period of two years (Alien Naturalization Act 1790), U.S. immigration laws thus exhibited a seemingly high degree of immigration hospitality in the early years of the nation's history.

However, the Naturalization Act of 1790 provided stark evidence of the racialized boundaries of American immigration hospitality. Even as the act granted a pathway to citizenship to White immigrants, it was also used to restrict the access of numerous groups of non-White immigrants to citizenship (Daniels 2004, 7). Thus, while U.S. immigration hospitality is widely noted in the literature on American immigration, its history of racialized exclusion is less noted. Nowhere is this bifurcated approach to hospitality clearer than in the starkly different experiences of European immigrants and other immigrant communities.

The Underside of American Hospitality: Indigenous and African Peoples

The high level of immigration hospitality in the United States was not without its contradictions. Hospitality toward European migrants aiming to populate the United States was coupled with the persecution of the Indigenous population referred to in the American context as Native Americans. I argue that the treatment of Indigenous people characterized the first degeneration of American hospitality relationships from those of host-guest to those of guest-hostage. Soon thereafter, immigration hospitality was denied in a similar fashion to African Americans who were brought to the country during the slave trade. The treatment of African forced migrants brought to the United States during the slave trade characterized the second degeneration of American hospitality from one of host-guest to one of host-hostage, wherein the incoming community lost their liberty and rights. This section briefly outlines the contradictions that these two populations posed and illustrates the importance such contradictions have in signaling future bifurcated approaches to hospitality in the American immigration environment.

The Guest/Host-Hostage Relationship: Indigenous Peoples and the "New World"

> In a world in which communications are nearly instantaneous and simultaneous experiences are possible, it must be spaces and places that distinguish us from one another, not time and history.
> —Vine Deloria Jr., *God Is Red*

As Roger Daniels observes, historians concerned with U.S. history "write as if the New World before the coming of the whites had been a *tabula rasa* or a virgin land for them to conquer and manipulate as they would" (2004, 5). Even historians who are aware of this bias position their histories of American immigration well after the establishment of the settler-colonial North American model and expropriation of the lands of Indigenous peoples (Daniels 2002). Indeed, canonical texts that focus on immigration to the United States often begin by emphasizing the "Great Migration" between 1630 and 1780 of an estimated 501,000 Europeans to the continent as a pivotal moment for the nation's immigration history. Nevertheless, these accounts often fail to consider the forcible displacement of Indigenous peoples and African communities as foundational to this migration.

As a result, historical treatments of U.S. immigration policy take for granted colonial assertions of belonging to and ownership of North America.

According to this Eurocentric perspective, the Euro-American "host" community could be seen to practice hospitality toward its newcomers with each coming wave of migration. A key indicator of this oversight lies in the portrayal of autochthonous people of the land as "Native Americans," suggesting that these complex tribes and nations can only be acknowledged insofar as they reaffirm the creation of "America," setting aside their preexisting tribal and other identities.

In fact, the settlement of North America took place around fifteen thousand years before the "discovery of the new world" in 1492 (Meltzer 2013). Indeed, archeologists estimate that northeastern Asians crossed the Bering Land Bridge between Asia and America during the Ice Ages (2013). A few even contend that these migrants may have arrived some 150,000 to 200,000 years earlier (Carter 1952). Whether this migration occurred 30,000 or 150,000 years earlier, these facts historically transform notions of the first migration to the North American continent, placing Native Americans in the region long before Europeans' arrival. This also places Indigenous communities at odds with the development of an immigration system that began with the establishment of the American nation-state.

Throughout several centuries of their inhabitation of North America and well before European contact began in the 1400s, the Indigenous peoples of North America had established belonging to the region due to their continuous inhabitation and cultivation of the land (Reich et al. 2012, 2). During this period, they also established distinct cultures and systems of governance in their territories. Most importantly, while enjoying a great deal of internal diversity, one common element of several Indigenous worldviews then and now is that they thrive on a strong and immutable relationship to land that transcends linear concepts of time and space and is therefore not easily erased with displacement. As Zimmerman reflects on Deloria's *God Is Red*, "For Indians (the term Deloria prefers), ideas of past, present, and future are often subsumed into present" (Zimmerman 1995, 298). As a result, the assumption of the alienation from places of belonging that underlies much of the scholarship on displacement does not easily apply to communities who perceive their belonging as squarely positioned outside of simplistic linear understandings of time. Deloria argues that the expansion of modern communications exacerbates the compression of time and space, saying, "It must be places that distinguish us . . . not time nor history" (2003, 64). This timeless relationship to land buttresses many of the movements that resist the depiction of Native Americans as relics of the past.

When European migration began—fostering the sensationalized portrayals of the "Great Transatlantic Migration" that continue to forefront contemporary treatments of American immigration—it brought with it a marked degree of chaos, so much so that scholars describe it as "one of the

truly freak phenomena in human history" (Akenson 2011, 5) because it produced "the greatest single period of land theft, cultural pillage and casual
genocide" in history (6). Others have noted this period as a singular period
of genocide, ecocide, and colonization (Churchill 2002). By and large, however, history overlooked the persecution and dispossession of the native
population produced by this migration. As a result, the racially driven discrimination and European imperialism that heavily accompanied it largely
escaped historical attention.

During this period, European settlers arriving in the United States colo-
nized the land with little regard for the societies and cultures that inhabited
it, operating with a sense of superiority as well as a religiously inspired mission to spread the empire of God westward (Daniels 2016, 4). The first European settlers had been given divine right to the territory of North America
by Pope Alexander VI in a papal bull on May 4, 1493 (Hanke 1937, 63).
Although some scholars suggest that the pope intended to protect Native
Americans—by suggesting that they be included in the populations and territory of the United States under the condition that they "were instructed,
in the name of [the] Savior, [the] Lord Jesus Christ" (Hanke 1937, 63) most
agree that the impact of the decisions taken by the Christian papacy decimated Native American freedom and belonging to their territories (Frichner 2010). Moreover, a series of papal bulls in the 1400s together forged the
"Doctrine of Discovery" that informed the European colonization of North
America, legitimizing the domination and destruction of non-Christian
people in territory seized by discovery and conquest (Miller et al. 2010).

The Doctrine of Discovery, alongside an overall legitimation of the conquest of the Americas under the pretense of spreading the word of God,
emboldened colonists to perform great injustices and crimes against Native
American populations (Stannard 1993). The children of Native Americans
were sent to residential missionary schools, and their culture and religion were
curtailed as "primitive" practices (Hanke 1937). Before European contact, and
before epidemics decimated Indigenous populations, North America's Indigenous population was estimated to be at "two to five million" (Borah and
Cook 1963). After European contact, Native Americans who had "swam out"
to welcome European settlers and shared their corn and agricultural knowledge with them at first (Stannard 1993, 52) suffered from a series of genocidal
campaigns in which colonizers would slaughter thousands at a time (70).
One Dominican friar recounted the brutality with which Native American
women and children were treated, saying that when "Christians encountered
an Indian woman who was carrying in her arms a child at suck . . . they tore the
child from the mother's arms and flung it still living to the dog who proceeded
to devour it before the mother's eyes" (Casas 2007, 16). Tales of the brutal
rape, murder, mutilation, enslavement, and torture of Native Americans litter

historical accounts of the early periods of American history, while noting that Native Americans extended hospitality to European soldiers shortly before these massacres occurred (Stannard 1993, 66). After the establishment of the republic, Native Americans continued to suffer from repeated campaigns of displacement, severing the relationship of Native Americans to their lands and stifling the cultural identity of Indigenous communities.

This treatment of Native Americans reveals the racist contradictions affecting American immigration hospitality from the outset, foreshadowing the contradictions of American hospitality to come. Because hospitality entails a relationship between a host community, which has established a belonging in a territory or home due to historical and ongoing inhabitation and cultivation of the land, and a guest, whose arrival and settlement is contingent on the hospitality of the host, the case of Native Americans upsets both sides of the relationship.

To this day, Indigenous peoples continue to identify one another by acknowledging a belonging to the territory that predates the arrival of European colonizers. In the view of Cree lawyer and Indigenous land rights activist Sharon Venne, Indigenous people "are the descendants of the peoples occupying a territory when the colonizers arrived" (1998, 88). This introduces a distinction between a nation that belongs to a land, whose language, legal system, and culture are indigenous to a territory, and a colonizer, whose language, culture, and legal system are being imported from the center of the colonizing empire, their nation of origin (Venne 2012). It also complicates the identity of the "guest" and "host" by suggesting that the risk to the host community within the context of settler-colonialism involves a different set of power dynamics than that generally assumed.

It is important to note that the territorial belonging of Indigenous peoples is recognized within the international legal system and human rights framework. For instance, in the midst of contentious debates regarding rights to natural resources and land in Canada, the Office of the High Commissioner for Human Rights acknowledged that "Indigenous or aboriginal peoples are so-called because they were living on their lands before settlers came from elsewhere . . . through conquest, occupation, settlement or other means" (UNHCR 1997). It is telling as well that the United Nations Declaration on the Rights of Indigenous Peoples (UNDRIP) was adopted by the United Nations General Assembly in 2007 with an overwhelming majority of 144 states in favor and only four votes against. The four countries that opposed the declaration were all settler-colonial states: Australia, Canada, New Zealand, and the United States (UNDRIP 2008).

The definition of Indigenous populations helps complicate productively the framework of hospitality I put forth. Indigenous communities are identified as "peoples and nations are those which, having a historical continuity with pre-invasion and pre-colonial societies that developed on their territories, consider themselves distinct from other sectors of the societies now prevailing in those territories or parts of them" (Martínez Cobo 1986).

This definition regards the position of Native Americans as Other and host at once, relegated by a particular form of colonizing migration to the position of the hostage within the host-guest relationship. Although the Native American population was not a "guest" population but rather the legitimate "host" community, its treatment by incoming settlers and its oppression by the nation-state that continues to rule over Indigenous descendants demonstrate the delicate balance struck in relationships of hospitality between the behavior of the host in acknowledging and welcoming the guest and the behavior of the guest in graciously accepting the welcome of the host and not imposing on his or her hospitality. Indeed, as in ancient Greek mythology, the tradition of *xenia* or hospitality may be infringed by either party, host or guest. Thus, in the context of settler-colonialism, the host-guest relationship transforms into one of guest-hostage, in which the host community is threatened and its freedom, security, and future are at risk because its belonging contests the efforts of the settler-colonist to colonize the territory.

The treatment of Native Americans thereby symbolizes a different relationship between a host and a guest community than a simple one of hospitality extended by the host. Here, the relationship between newcomers and the Indigenous populations represents one of conquest and colonization rather than assimilation or integration. This is due to the fact that, as a settler society, the United States perceived Native American belonging to the region as a threat to its assumed ownership of the continent. In response, colonizers implemented a process of "elimination" (Wolfe 2006, 387) because "indigenous people obstructed settlers' access to land" (368). Meanwhile, the United States actively sought to displace Native American populations and expropriate them of their land through treaties or in battle, a practice it deemed necessary to assert ownership over the territory that would allow the practice of hospitality toward newcomers.

Thus, as a settler-colonial model of immigration, the colonization of the United States represents a relationship of hospitality in which the guest encroaches on the host's hospitality, taking the host hostage and enslaving and killing the host community in order to displace it. Similar to accounts of abuses of hospitality in Greek mythology, such as Odysseus's murder of the Cyclops while he was a guest or Paris's abduction of the Helen of Sparta while he was Agamemnon's guest, these examples of the abuse of hospitality in literature all foreshadow a rupture of the ideals of hospitality, as limited to a host-guest connection.

How can a discourse of hospitality transform our understanding of immigration and the moral treatment of future waves of immigration? Indeed, the acknowledgment of Native Americans is central to establishing more inclusive policies of hospitality to all individuals living in a territory. In Canada, for example, a growing emphasis on First Nations peoples being recognized as the only native communities belonging to the land and the increasingly common use of the term *newcomers* to describe immigrants suggests one way in which a hospitality framework may revolutionize immigration policy and coverage. When speaking to the head of Mosaic immigration agency in Vancouver, British Columbia, he noted the importance of the term *newcomer* to draw attention toward First Nations history and away from assumptions of a White-European nation-state (personal communication 2016). Moreover, he emphasized the importance of land acknowledgments and First Nations involvement in welcoming newcomers to radically transforming the sense of belonging immigrants feel during their transition process. This primary retweaking of immigration hospitality places European settler-colonists and more recent waves of immigrants on equal footing as immigrants, illustrating how acknowledging Indigenous history presents new possibilities for immigration hospitality in the United States. It also raises fundamental ethical questions regarding the value of immigration hospitality when certain groups continue to be excluded from it and when it comes at the expense of the oppression of native populations.

The Host-Hostage Relationship:
The Slave Trade and American Immigration

> At the same time that millions of blacks were being transported across the Atlantic into slavery, millions of whites were migrating from Europe to America in search of greater independence in religion, work, and politics. The Atlantic frontier offered opportunity for whites only.
> —Rawley and Behrendt 2005

The paradox of the Native American population would be accompanied by a different contradiction in U.S. immigration hospitality: the slave trade. The early open-immigration policies of the United States, enjoyed exclusively by White immigrants, occurred against the background of enslaved African migrants being brought to the United States aboard ships during the transatlantic slave trade that lasted for approximately four centuries, from the 1480s until the 1800s (Deveau 1997, 49).

White immigrants, though some were fleeing persecution in their home countries, maintained a different degree of agency in their migration journeys to the "New World."[1] They were greeted with low barriers to arrival, a pathway to full citizenship, and equal treatment. In contrast, Africans were forcibly abducted and violently shipped across the Atlantic, representing the first foray of the young society in a "peculiar" form of international forced migration. While Native Americans represented the first domestic forced migrants, internally displaced within the United States, African Americans constituted their imported parallel. When viewed against the background of the nation's welcoming of White immigrants, the slave trade reveals the extreme outcome of the racialization that characterizes U.S. immigration policies. It highlights the degree to which the immigration hospitality exhibited by the nation's policies did not extend to non-White immigrants.

During the slave trade, immigration policy regulating the transfer of African slaves into the United States was mainly concerned with the registration of their numbers, physical features, and identifying characteristics for the purposes of recording their presence in the United States. All vessels were required to produce a record of all individuals aboard any ship upon arriving in the United States as part of the Passenger Act, which regulated immigration in general (Passenger Act 1847, 127).[2]

These records have since been used to produce systematic estimates of the slave trade by Curtin, Eltis, and others (Curtin 1969; Eltis and Richardson 2010), who estimate the Western Hemisphere's importation of enslaved Africans to be about 9.5 million, of which the United States is estimated to have received about 4 percent (Rawley and Behrendt 2005). Since the arrival of the first slave ship in 1619, hundreds of thousands of African slaves were brought

Estimates of the African Slave Trade in Mainland North America

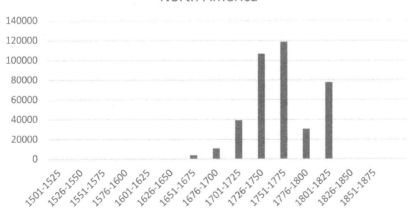

FIG. 2.3 Transatlantic Slave Trade Database estimated African slave trade figures. Created by the author.

to the United States. By 1775, "500,000 of the thirteen colonies' 2.5 million inhabitants were slaves" (Baptist 2014, 4).

The hundreds of thousands of African slaves brought to the United States were deprived of all rights extended to White immigrant arrivals. They were considered property that could be sold or transported according to a master's wishes (Morgan 1975). They could be whipped and coerced into labor, their children also considered slaves and sold into slavery. Women were often sexually assaulted or raped, while other slaves were helpless to protect them (Brown 1855, 17). They were often deprived of sleep in order to enhance their productivity, with slaveholders harnessing the potential of the newly discovered clock to that end (Smith 1997).

The forced migration of African slaves did not end with their arrival in the United States, for slaves were often transported like chattel or forced to march in shackles for hundreds of miles toward the south or west, exploited for their use in other pursuits. The tragic impact of these repeated forced migrations on African slaves' families can be observed in the diaries and accounts of slaves and then-recently free people. These accounts detail how slaves often begged to no avail to be sold with their husbands or parents and grandparents (Douglass 1854), while familial ties often served as a reason to exploit slaves further (Baptist 2014, 13). In fact, the separation of slaves from their brothers, sisters, parents, and spouses was a common strategy used by slaveholders in order to make them more "marketable" and productive (Mitchell 2008, 147).

The African arrivals in the United States represent a complicating lens through which to view hospitality. They were actively brought—against their will—to the continent. Indeed, African slaves did not encounter barriers to their entry into the United States, as they were forcibly transported to fuel the development of the nation. Their labor was actively pursued, and yet their humanity was not acknowledged and welcomed into the nation. The 1790 Naturalization Act explicitly precluded those of African origin from equal rights and citizenship, it denied them the possibility of integrating into the new nation.

Moreover, adding to the dehumanization of African forced migrants brought to America's shores during the slave trade, African slave numbers were collected and used to further the political and financial interests of slaveholders. The Three-Fifths Compromise agreed upon by Congress in the 1787 convention ensured that, although African slaves were deprived of their rights and were barred from voting, their numbers counted as three-fifths of the White population in slaveholder states, a political maneuver aimed at magnifying the political clout of slaveowners who hoped to sustain and expand the slave trade (Pope and Treier 2011, 293).

Thus, African forced migrants were precluded from the hospitality extended to "guests" in the theoretical framework of hospitality. Not only was the guest in this relationship brought against his or her will and denied the same access to food, shelter, and opportunity as his European counterpart, but this "guest" was also robbed of his or her freedom and denied his and her humanity, transforming the dynamic of the host-guest relationship to that of a host-hostage, in which the guest was being kept as security or a guarantee rather than being offered hospitality freely and without gain. Thus, much like that the position of Native Americans vis-à-vis European colonizers, African Americans were forcibly positioned as hostages rather than guests in the host-guest relationship of hospitality. This was accomplished in this case not by conquest, as with Native Americans, but by forced importation and enslavement.

Slaves were instrumental to maintaining the industrialization and development of the American economy. To that end, the one-drop rule would ensure that slave-hostages would multiply and that their children, borne of the colonizer or of other slaves, would continue to occupy an inferior position to Whites. Hospitality and hostage are distinct because while they both require welcoming a foreigner to the territory of the nation, they differ in the conditions of the movement and life of the foreigner once he or she arrives. In the case of the hostage, hospitality is not truly achieved because the foreigner is forced to abdicate his or her freedom. Meanwhile, the policies that allow the registration of slaves and their characteristics entail "keeping watch" on the body of the slave as security and guarantee of his or her fulfillment of the "work" as the condition of their existence on national territory.

While the slave trade and policies regarding native populations may seem to entail rupturing the record of immigration hospitality of early U.S. history, they instead point to previously overlooked factors motivating U.S. immigration hospitality, including the importance that race, space, and place played in the dynamics of American hospitality. They also illustrate how American hospitality often discriminated against non-European "Others" and placed them in hostage positions rather than as hosts or guests in the host-guest relationship.

Why Does This Matter?

Understanding of the dynamics of the forced internal displacement and international migration of Native Americans and African Americans is crucial to reconsidering not only the myth of the United States as a nation of immigrants but also the foundational relations buttressing American hospitality.

The relations of the host-hostage relationship between settlers and Indigenous nations in the United States and in North America as a whole provided what I call a poisoned beginning to American hospitality, naturalizing a racially exclusionary relationship from the outset that enables the displacement, oppression, and even the genocide of non-White peoples.

An important element of this violation of hospitality is the disproportionate role of settlers in establishing and enforcing a legal framework that defines and regulates regulatory hospitality. As Derrida observes in his reflection on *The Apology of Socrates*, the "foreigner" suffers a serious disadvantage in that he is unfamiliar with the language of the legal systems that determine his or her treatment, and this language barrier worsens the Other's lack of access to the legal and legislative rhetoric that determines his moral rights or belonging. As such, the Other remains "without defense before the law of the country that welcomes or expels him. . . . He has to ask for hospitality in a language which by definition is not his own, the one imposed on him by the master of the house, the host, the king, the lord, the authorities, the nation, the State, the father, etc. This personage imposes on him translation into their own language, and that's the first act of violence" (Derrida 2000, 15). Thus, in establishing a legal system based on English law during the colonial period, settlers had immediately displaced the Indigenous person to assume the position of the legal host who defines the parameters of hospitality in the United States.

Thus, in critically reexamining the genesis of American immigration hospitality, two things become clear: First, race from the beginning constituted a crucial determining factor for American immigration hospitality. Second, overlooking particular groups of migrants—Native Americans as internally displaced migrants, African slaves as forced migrants from abroad—has perpetuated a false image of the United States as a hospitable nation and allowed for the birth and sustenance of the image of the "immigrant nation."

Hospitality is to allow "passage to the other, the wholly other" (Derrida 1999, 80), an approach that does not reflect the exclusionary policies of U.S. immigration. To extend a welcome exclusively to European immigrants, particularly White Protestant Europeans, while displacing Indigenous people from their land or actively importing African slave labor as forced migrants represented an immigration regime that did not practice immigration hospitality toward the "Other."

The contrasting treatment of three different groups during the colonization of the territory of the United States—the high level of immigration hospitality shown toward White European settlers; the expropriation, displacement, and extermination of Native Americans; and the gross mistreatment of Africans transported to the United States during the African slave trade—demonstrates a more complex vision of U.S. immigration hospitality than has been assumed. It also suggests a variety of relationships by which to interrogate what hospitality has meant in the U.S. context over time. Because existing studies of immigration policy and discourse often contribute to the perpetuation of the myth of American hospitality by not including the widely divergent treatment of either Native Americans or African Americans, their inclusion provides a pertinent contextualization that illustrates the bifurcated and racialized nature of U.S. immigration hospitality, even if they are not the central focus of the case studies of this book. Their treatment sets the precedent for the enactment of discriminatory policies targeting other communities in later periods of history, and it confronts the long-held belief in the United States as a nation of immigrants and as a nation welcoming toward immigrants with the contradictions of American hospitality during its peaks and its nadirs. These forgotten histories have the capacity to inform more sensitive accounts of immigration that are particularly crucial to a discussion of hospitality as an ethical concept that may be practiced in the regulatory and media environments. If we are to examine the myth of the United States as a nation of immigrants, it is critical to build the foundations upon which this myth was anchored before analyzing how it was sustained and contradicted.

These considerations thereby drive the analysis of the three historical periods that are the focus of the following chapters of this book. It suggests a framework through which to understand how the United States has, from its earliest history, sustained a bifurcated environment for immigration hospitality that extended exclusively to White (predominantly Protestant), northern European immigrants while excluding ethnic, religious, and racial categories that were deemed "Other." This more complicated approach to immigration hospitality can help us understand how over time Chinese Americans, southern and eastern Europeans, and Muslim immigrants came to be excluded from the welcome of the "nation of immigrants."

I analyze regulatory hospitality by including all "acts, treaties and conventions that relate to the immigration, exclusion, or expulsion of aliens" (Johnson 1921). The analysis also considers executive actions signed by the administrative branch that affect the lives of immigrants arriving and living in the United States. It integrates these contemporary policies and decisions with constitutionally based rights inscribed in the foundational text of the nation and interpreted periodically by the judicial branch, particularly in Supreme Court decisions. Finally, it integrates the analysis of national regulations with international conventions such as the Geneva Convention and the Geneva Protocol that require member states to adhere to a level of immigration hospitality.

To provide an analysis of media hospitality, this project traces the dominant media narratives surrounding immigration during three periods of U.S. immigration that follow the widely celebrated open-immigration of the postindependence era: the exclusionist policies of the late nineteenth century, the nativist period of the early twentieth century, and the restrictive policies of the post-9/11 context. It examines this coverage in the main media organs of each period against the dominant media narrative of the United States as a "nation of immigrants." During each period of immigration restriction, immigrants, community organizations, and individual policymakers voiced opposition in the media throughout the policymaking process. As such, this book incorporates examples of alternative and immigrant press during each period to reflect upon the resistance to regulatory policies, the arguments resisters used, and the resonance/impact of their dissent.

Together, the applications of regulatory and media hospitality at the macrolevel of the public realm, rather than in individual interactions, are critical to the experience of immigrants as they integrate into an adopted home. As Derrida argued, and Silverstone agreed, there can be no hospitality without a home (Silverstone 2006, 142). In turn, I argue that extending hospitality in conditions of immigration may allow for the cultivation of a sense of being at home for immigrants, an ideal that allows a safer, more productive inclusion of the immigrant "other" into the self.

This analysis reflects on the actions of the executive, legislative, and judicial branches toward immigration and of the treatment of immigration in the media during three periods of U.S. national history, chosen for their ability to reflect different discriminatory contours that American immigration hospitality assumed in response to the increased arrival of certain immigrant groups over time. In chapter 3, I examine the passage of the Chinese Exclusion Act in 1882, designed to limit Asian immigration into the United States (1882). In chapter 4, I examine the 1920s passage of the national origins quotas, which regulated immigration according to country of origin and had a particular effect on immigrants of southern and eastern European origin (Johnson 1921). Chapter 5 analyzes policies toward immigrants from Muslim-majority countries post-9/11, with particular emphasis on the Patriot Act. In the conclusion, I reflect upon the contemporary context of the quasi closure of U.S. immigration policy (2000s–2010s) leading up to the Muslim travel ban of 2017 and 2018 and its public repudiation. In sum, I demonstrate how the myth of the "nation of immigrants" diverges from the history of the nation, yet it remains a promising avenue for inspiring future immigration reform.

3

The Move to Exclude:
Chinese Exclusion Act
(1880s)

• •

On December 31, 2019, the Wuhan Municipal Health Commission in the Hubei Province in China reported a cluster of pneumonia cases that were attributed to the emergence of a novel coronavirus (WHO 2020). Within a month of this announcement, the director-general of the World Health Organization (WHO), Tedros Adhanom, had declared the novel coronavirus a Public Health Emergency of International Concern (PHEIC), urging governments to begin taking mitigation measures to prevent the further spread of the virus.

Anticipating that racist sentiments may undermine global cooperation in public health, the World Health Organization immediately announced the name of the new virus as "2019-nCoV acute respiratory disease," explaining that "'n' is for novel and 'CoV' is for coronavirus," adding that this name "complies with the WHO Best Practices for Naming of New Human Infectious Diseases" (WHO 2020).

In spite of all the efforts to prevent racialized and xenophobic discourses surrounding the new pandemic, the COVID-19 crisis triggered a wave of anti-Asian sentiment throughout the United States and across the world. By April 2020, the Anti-Defamation League issued a report that documented seventy-five incidents of attacks against Asian Americans and Pacific Islanders in the United States. Asian Americans reported being harassed, attacked, and told to "go back to China" ("Reports of Anti-Asian Assaults" 2020). These hate crimes were encouraged by the inflammatory rhetoric used by several public officials, including then-president Donald Trump. At one of the coronavirus briefings, White House correspondent Yamiche Alcindor asked Donald Trump if he was concerned that some officials were using of the racist term "Kung Flu" to describe the disease, potentially putting Asian Americans at risk. Instead of exhibiting concern over the term, the president asked Alcindor to "say the term" again. He then dismissed her concerns, saying that he was "not at all" worried (Alcindor 2020).

As medical historians point out, the negative association of minorities and ethnic groups with disease, poor hygiene, and other practices detrimental to public health is not new. In fact, American immigration history has witnessed several moments where the association of immigrants with disease and poor hygiene impacted the hospitality shown toward immigrants in media coverage and policy. I argue that hospitality as a theoretical framework could radically transform immigration discourse by highlighting the historical continuities between old and new forms of discrimination. In the context of the anti-Asian backlash during the COVID-19 crisis, the anti-Asian media coverage and policies during the era of Chinese exclusion in the 1800s may help us to understand the legacy of medicalized racism and nativism in both media and policy circles. It also highlights how this legacy impacts American hospitality vis-à-vis Asian Americans and immigrants as a whole and the ways in which these communities have adapted to build a sense of home under the fraught conditions of exclusion.

In this chapter, I examine the immigration policy negotiated and legislated during the 1880s with the passage of the Chinese Exclusion Act, and thereafter in the decades of restrictive policy and the regular renewals of the Exclusion Act in the decades that followed. At the same time, I contrast the restrictive immigration policies with two trends in the American press of this period: the negative coverage of Chinese immigration and of Chinese people, as well as the overall consolidation of a myth of a nation of immigrants bolstered by the construction of the Statue of Liberty. Finally, I consider the ways in which Chinese immigrants cultivated a sense of feeling at home under the conditions of the Exclusion Act. Throughout this analysis, I demonstrate how the myth of welcome immigration persevered in the face of growing immigration restriction and how efforts to strengthen it in times of great injustice to immigrants succeeded at obscuring aspects of immigration restriction.

A Circular Turning Point

Shortly after the passage of the Thirteenth Amendment abolishing slavery in 1865, the United States began to experience a rise in immigration to replace slave labor, with the most noticeable wave of these migrations being that of

Chinese immigrants in the 1870s and 1880s (Guterl 2003, 309–310). Chinese immigrants arrived at a critical moment in American history, as the nation grappled with the reality of a postslavery society and economy and a reestablished racial hierarchy between White immigrants and freed slaves (Okihiro and Jung 2014, 34). Arriving to "serve the master-class" of White immigrants, Chinese and newly freed slaves shared a subordinate position vis-à-vis Whites, and thus "yellow [was] a shade of black, and black, a shade of yellow" (34). Chinese immigrants also entered the American public consciousness at a time when the nation was negotiating its identity following the abolishment of slavery (Miller 1969, 15), the conclusion of the Reconstruction period following the Civil War, and the redefinition of American citizenship necessitated by these changes. Shortly after abolition, industrialists and farmers turned to Chinese immigrants as a cheap labor source that would continue to sustain an economy modeled on the expropriation and land theft of Indigenous communities on the one hand (Acuña 2012) and the enslavement of African immigrants on the other (Genovese 1989, 180). These historical moments are essential to understanding the significance of the exclusion movement as part of a continuum within the political economy of U.S. immigration, with consequences for racial Others of Native American, African, Asian, and other non-White origins.

Sociologist Mary Roberts Coolidge's study of early Chinese immigration to the United States acknowledged that Chinese immigrants were welcomed at first (Coolidge 1909, 17). They were regarded as a useful and economical workforce to support the rapid industrialization and development of the nation, while simultaneously providing an alternative to slave labor following the Civil War. Moreover, the adaptability of Chinese workers to the shifting labor needs of the rapidly industrializing young nation placed "them among the most worthy groups of immigrants" to have come to the United States (Coolidge 1909, 15). As such, Chinese immigrants flocked toward each sector of the American economy that required labor at the time—from mining during the Gold Rush, to railroad construction and farming, and finally to the growing industries of shoes, cigars, and other consumer goods (Zinzius 2005, 11).

The early positive reception of Chinese immigrants quickly changed in character by the late 1870s and early 1880s, particularly on the Pacific coast. This was partially due to the fact that incoming Chinese immigrants were concentrated more densely in the Pacific states on the West Coast. Census data illustrates this pattern clearly, for while the Chinese represented a mere 0.002 percent of the population across the continental United States in 1880, they represented 10 percent of the population of California. This pattern was compounded by the concentration of Chinese immigrants across and within cities. In California, Chinese immigrants composed 35.7 percent of the San Franciscan population by 1890 (Zinzius 2005, 15), most of whom resided across a few blocks of San Francisco's Chinatown. Thus, as Chinese immigration grew, San Francisco's Chinatown expanded from housing 2,719 inhabitants in 1860 to 21,745 in 1880 and 72,472 by 1890, according to official records (U.S. Census Bureau 1880; Chou 2014; "Chinatown Area Plan" 1995).

The concentration of Chinese immigrants on the West Coast had serious consequences for their reception. In their study of Chinese migration to the West Coast, Fong and Markham observed that as minority populations began to represent a large proportion of a local population, they were more likely to be perceived as a threat by the residing ethnic majority. This is due to the increased visibility afforded by larger numbers as well as the perceived increased ability of the minority to organize for resources (Fong and Markham 1991, 472). Against the background of growing nativism and nativist labor mobilization, Western states became the fomenting ground of a significant anti-Chinese movement, articulated by policymakers and the press alike, which thereafter spread throughout the United States.

The rise of the labor movement in the West Coast had serious implications for the Chinese immigrants residing in the area. This was due to the competition between White and Chinese workers in the labor market (Fong and Markham 2002, 185). In response, White workers organized to combat Chinese labor competition, often driving Chinese minorities out of their jobs or homes (Minnick 1988). Gradually, the informal organization of White workers into "anti-coolie" clubs and bands offered opportunities for labor organizations to gather members by appealing to anti-Chinese sentiment. As such, trade unionism became the primary advocacy network of anti-Chinese sentiment within and beyond the West (Mink 2009, 150). Nativism became a defining characteristic of trade unionism, as labor unions devised labels to certify products produced by "native" labor (Baum and Harris 2009, 150).

Chinese immigrants were also impacted by the racial tensions that characterized the aftermath of abolition and the "great migration" northward of freed slaves fleeing persecution in the South. With the close of the Civil War, throughout the Reconstruction period that followed and for around a century thereafter, tensions between White and Black, free and formerly enslaved, continued to play out in society (Berlin 1998, 7). Particularly in the wake of the reorganization of industries and the mechanization of production during this period (Hitomi 1994, 122), White labor struggled to compete with the recently freed slave labor migrating from the South alongside incoming international immigration, a factor that would greatly influence the dynamics of the movement for Chinese immigration exclusion.

Additionally, the arrival of a new wave of immigration that included Russian Jews, Catholics, Italians, and to a lesser extent, Chinese, Portuguese, Polish, and other immigrants shifted the demographic, religious, and ethnic makeup of the country in unprecedented ways, threatening a resistance to change that would rear its head in discussions of the Chinese exclusion movement that ensued in the 1880s.

Regulatory Hospitality

Amid an environment of post–Civil War cultural shifts and labor mobilization, the House Committee on Education and Labor put forward a report issued on January 26, 1882, that addressed Chinese immigration to the United States. Noting that both political parties had passed resolutions condemning Chinese immigration but suggesting that further action be taken to restrict it, the report stressed that "the Chinese have no desire to assimilate with our people and have been and always will be a distinct race" ("Report Adverse to Chinese Immigration" 1882). Over the course of eight weeks, Congressmen and journalists debated, respectively, inside the nation's chambers and in the press on the constitutionality, feasibility, and morality of restrictions on Chinese immigration. During this time, the *New York Times* published the arguments made in defense of Chinese immigration as well as the drafts of legislation banning it. In this section, I consider both the congressional records of proceedings on the House and Senate floors and the political speeches published by the *New York Times* about the eight-week-long debates. Discussions surrounding immigration emblematized themes and ideological arguments that would continue to struggle for dominance in U.S. immigration policy and discourses of later periods.

At the center of the debates on Chinese immigration lay a proposal to exclude Chinese immigrants from arriving and settling in the United States. On one side of these debates was a diverse group of what came to be known as exclusionists who straddled both sides of the American political spectrum: Democrat and Republican. This heterogenous group included conservative Democrats who stressed that "Americans" were Caucasian with ancestors of European descent. The Democratic exclusionists instrumentalized the nation's Constitution and Declaration of Independence to justify the protection of the interests of White citizens. They wrote in the nation's newspapers that the Constitution was established by "white men" to secure the blessings of "liberty for posterity" ("Negro and Chinaman" 1882). They added that the Declaration of Independence "was made by a people for themselves and not for anybody else. It did not contemplate that all races should indiscriminately swarm into this country but rather the exercise of criticism as to the fitness of all immigrants to share this privilege" (Metrick-Chen 2012, 152). In publishing White supremacist arguments excluding Chinese citizens from the rights and liberties set forth in the nation's founding documents, media coverage exhibited hostility toward Chinese and other immigrant newcomers.

Arguments against Chinese immigration also connected the matter with that of African American enfranchisement. In fact, Democratic exclusionists who only reluctantly acknowledged African Americans as citizens (Metrick-Chen 2012, 157) justified Chinese exclusion by warning that Chinese immigrants may advocate for an eventual pathway to citizenship and enfranchisement just as African Americans had done before them. Democratic exclusionists accepted African American enfranchisement as an exceptional response to the extraordinary circumstances of slavery and the exploitation of African American immigrants (Metrick-Chen 2012, 157). Thus, the enfranchisement of African Americans only invigorated opposition to Chinese immigration.

Slavery and Chinese immigration would also come to be connected in the 1880s because emancipation necessitated a reconsideration of the 1790 Naturalization Act that reserved naturalization and citizenship for "free white persons" (Naturalization Act 1790). This stipulation that restricted slaves from being naturalized also rendered non-White immigrants ineligible for citizenship (Kerber 1997, 840). As such, emancipation simultaneously ended almost a century of uncontested White entitlement to citizenship, and in so doing, it paved the way for Chinese and other immigrants to become eligible for citizenship in time.

The utilization of emancipation as an example of the threats of incoming immigrants demanding citizenship was evident in the exclusion debates of the time. One debate among politicians, titled "Negro and the Chinaman," played out in the *New York Times* as a conversation about the "settled problem of negro citizenship and the unsettled problem of Chinese immigration" ("Negro and Chinaman" 1882). Democratic politicians remained concerned that Chinese immigrants would one day be at the center of a renewed debate surrounding citizenship and enfranchisement.

Ironically, the exclusionist movement also found resonance in the Republican party, which had only recently been instrumental in abolishing slavery. Antislavery Republican politicians argued for exclusion because they suggested that Chinese immigration constituted a novel means of importing slave labor under the "guise of immigration" (47th Cong., 13 Cong. Rec., 1st Sess. [1882]). The House Committee on Education and Labor held that Chinese immigrants "coming here was not voluntary and many are detained until their contract expires" ("Report Adverse to Chinese Immigration" 1882). In 1880, the Republican party platform considered Chinese immigration to be "a matter of grave concernment," promising to "limit and restrict that immigration by the enactment of such just, humane and reasonable laws and treaties" (UC Santa Barbara 1880). Four years later, the Republican party platform reinvoked this view, stating that "having its birth in a hatred of slave labor and a desire that all men may be truly free and equal, is unalterably opposed to placing our workingmen in competition with any form of servile labor, whether at home or abroad. In this spirit, we denounce the importation of contract labor, whether from Europe or Asia, as an offense against the spirit of American institutions; and we pledge ourselves to sustain the present law restricting Chinese immigration, and to provide such further legislation as is necessary to carry out its purposes" (UC Santa Barbara 1884).

Abolitionist Republicans' fears were not entirely unfounded. Chinese immigration had already been instrumentalized by Southerners to counter the effects of emancipation, as Southerners encouraged immigration to potentially offset Black suffrage (Jung 2005, 215) and preserve White supremacy (173). These strategies helped bolster the position of exclusion as an antislavery, proimmigrant legal solution (6), whereby denying naturalization and immigration rights to Chinese immigrants invigorated the national and racial celebration of the "land of immigrants" and valorized White immigrants at the expense of all other arrivals.

The convergence of abolitionist-exclusionist stances resonated with members of the American labor movement, which called for the exclusion of Chinese immigrants to protect workers' rights (Coolidge 1909; Saxton 1975; Ngai 2014). The Workingmen's Party in California adopted the slogan "the Chinese must go" (Lee 2003, 26). Throughout the country, unions devised union-approved labels certifying products produced without Chinese labor (26). Labor leaders warned politicians that "no man who is in favor of coolie immigration to the degradation of free labor can expect to receive a workingman's vote" ("Re-action" 1882). In turn, these warnings were heeded by politicians as indicators of public opinion in the 1880 election, when both parties competed over who could "out-Chinese the other" (Gyory 1998, 187), using racial appeals and rhetoric to win over voters in the East and West, North and South.

Boycotts such as the one advertised in figure 3.1 illustrate the language used by organized labor to discourage the employment of Chinese labor. In the flier, the Butte Tailors Union called for a boycott of "scab" tailor houses that had hired Chinese laborers, encouraging citizens to "patronize home industry" that hired White laborers to work in "fair and sanitary conditions." Of course, the flier listed "all Chinese tailor shops" among the "scab" tailor shops. Ironically, labor organizations did not recognize the paternalistic and racist position they adopted toward Chinese workers, who were assumed to lack agency to manage their own work conditions. These calls also perpetuated harmful stereotypes of "dirty" and unsanitary immigrants, which would be replicated in media coverage of Chinese immigration that can be seen later in this chapter.

The American Federation of Labor (AFL) argued that Chinese immigrants degraded American labor by accepting wages and living conditions that no

FIG. 3.1 Tailor Union boycott fliers and label (1884). National Archives and Records Administration, Records of the U.S. Circuit Courts, Record Group 21.

White worker would or should tolerate (Lee 2003, 26). The AFL president Samuel Gompers wrote an essay titled "Meat vs. Rice: American Manhood against Asiatic Coolieism. Which Shall Survive?" (Gompers 1901). His essay presented Chinese immigration as an existential threat to White workers that must be combatted to ensure the survival of American labor, institutions, and values. Gompers framed Chinese immigration as a threat to American manhood, as it jeopardized the livelihoods of America's male-dominant bread-winners. Throughout this period, Chinese immigrants argued that racism fueled the discriminatory resistance toward Chinese labor. As the Chinese Six Companies pointed out, "Up to 800,000 Europeans enter the United States per year, yet the labor unions hardly cared" (Takaki 1994, 86).

Under these circumstances, Congressmen in both chambers debated the suitability of Chinese immigrants for American integration, often comparing assessments of their potential for assimilating to that of African Americans. Some argued that the Chinese, unlike African Americans who had lived in the United States for many years, were not "here to stay" and thus did not intend to assimilate into the United States ("Negro and Chinaman" 1882). Senator George Edmunds (R-Vt.) voiced these views in his comments on Chinese immigration, stating that there was no common ground for assimilation with the Chinese immigrants. Some congressmen dehumanized Chinese immigrants by denying them free will, arguing that Chinese immigrants were "being imported as slaves" even as they arrived of their own volition (Cong. Globe, 41st Cong., 3d Sess. 5124 [1875]). Congressmen did not limit themselves to attacking the ability of Chinese immigrants to freely migrate but went further, attacking the humanity of Chinese immigrants. Republican George Hazelton claimed that the Chinese immigrant is a "loathsome revolting monstrosity who lives in herds and sleeps like packs of dogs in kennels" (Cong. Rec. 2210 [1882]). In his descriptions of Chinese immigrants, Hazelton never addressed them as sentient, conscious beings, preferring instead to use the pronoun "it" (Cong. Rec. 2210 [1882]). Other congressmen went further, comparing Chinese immigrants to rats, insects, mildew, rot, and cancer (Gyory 1998, 4). In these instances, media and regulatory hostility worked in tandem to dehumanize, infantilize, and denigrate Chinese immigrants with consequences for their ability to safely live and work in the United States.

Nonetheless, there remained a strong movement against exclusionary policy, with its most notable moment and powerful expression in the speech given by Senators Platt and Hoar on the Congress floor on March 8, 1882. Senator Hoar argued that the true interpretations of the Declaration of Independence and the Constitution prohibited the "exclusion of any race from this country" ("Vote Not Yet Reached on the Anti-Chinese Bill" 1882). Hoar challenged arguments to limit Chinese immigration based on the assumed irredeemable and unassimilable character of the Chinese immigrant by alluding to the fact that these arguments had been exchanged and refuted regarding African Americans (13 Cong. Rec. 1710 [1882]). A longtime advocate of Native American and African American rights, he argued that the Exclusion Act was yet another attempt to legalize racial discrimination in U.S. policy (Daniels 2011, 54).

The antiexclusionist camp could not fight the growing strategic importance that Chinese exclusion represented in the political arena. By 1879, the makeup of Congress had shifted with the end of the Reconstruction period following the Civil War. With Republicans holding a narrow majority in the Senate and Democrats commanding a strong twenty-one-member majority in the House of Representatives, both parties were eager to "pander to any strong groups that might influence the election of 1880" (Gold 2012, 202). This would include anti-Chinese groups and labor unions opposed to Chinese immigration on the West Coast. Moreover, witnessing the significance of the anti-Chinese issue in previous California elections (Mink 2009, 150) and eager to win the votes of Californians in presidential elections, Republican and Democratic politicians alike turned to anti-Chinese sentiment to appeal to voters. Opposition to the exclusion of Chinese immigrants grounded in industry and fiscal arguments dampened in the 1880s, as the improving economic conditions at the time somewhat decreased the importance of Chinese immigrants as taxpayers (Kanazawa 2005, 786–787).

Even though employers who were eager to sustain access to affordable labor had lobbied against the Exclusion Act in previous decades, they nonetheless bowed under the pressure of the boycotts, attacks, and strikes of White workers' organizations. For example, unions would regularly condemn employers who hired Chinese workers, instructing members to "guide themselves accordingly" (fig. 3.2).

Putting aside the political expediency of anti-Chinese rhetoric, several cultural crises contributed to limiting immigration hospitality during this period. Understanding the impact of such variables may further elucidate the dynamics of immigration hospitality during the exclusion period and beyond, with significant insights for the future of U.S. immigration hospitality. First of all, religion in the United States was undergoing radical change. The incoming immigration of Catholics, Jews, and those of other religious denominations during the 1800s was transforming the religious makeup of the nation and diminishing the preexisting Protestant majority (Higham 1988, 28). This in turn influenced congressional debates surrounding color-blind naturalization and citizenship that led up to the Exclusion Act, particularly raising concerns that color-blind naturalization would give "heathens and pagans power to control our institutions" (Cong. Globe, 41st Cong., 2d Sess. 5171–5172 [1870]), as Senator Williams from Oregon warned.

As evidenced in Congressman Williams's statement to Congress, race morphed into an indicator of religion, and religion transformed into an indicator of race—namely, non-Whiteness—as incoming waves of migrants increasingly originated from non-Anglo-Saxon and non-Protestant countries. Thus, racism became one of the main motivators of arguments against color-blind naturalization. Policymakers and politicians maintained that the

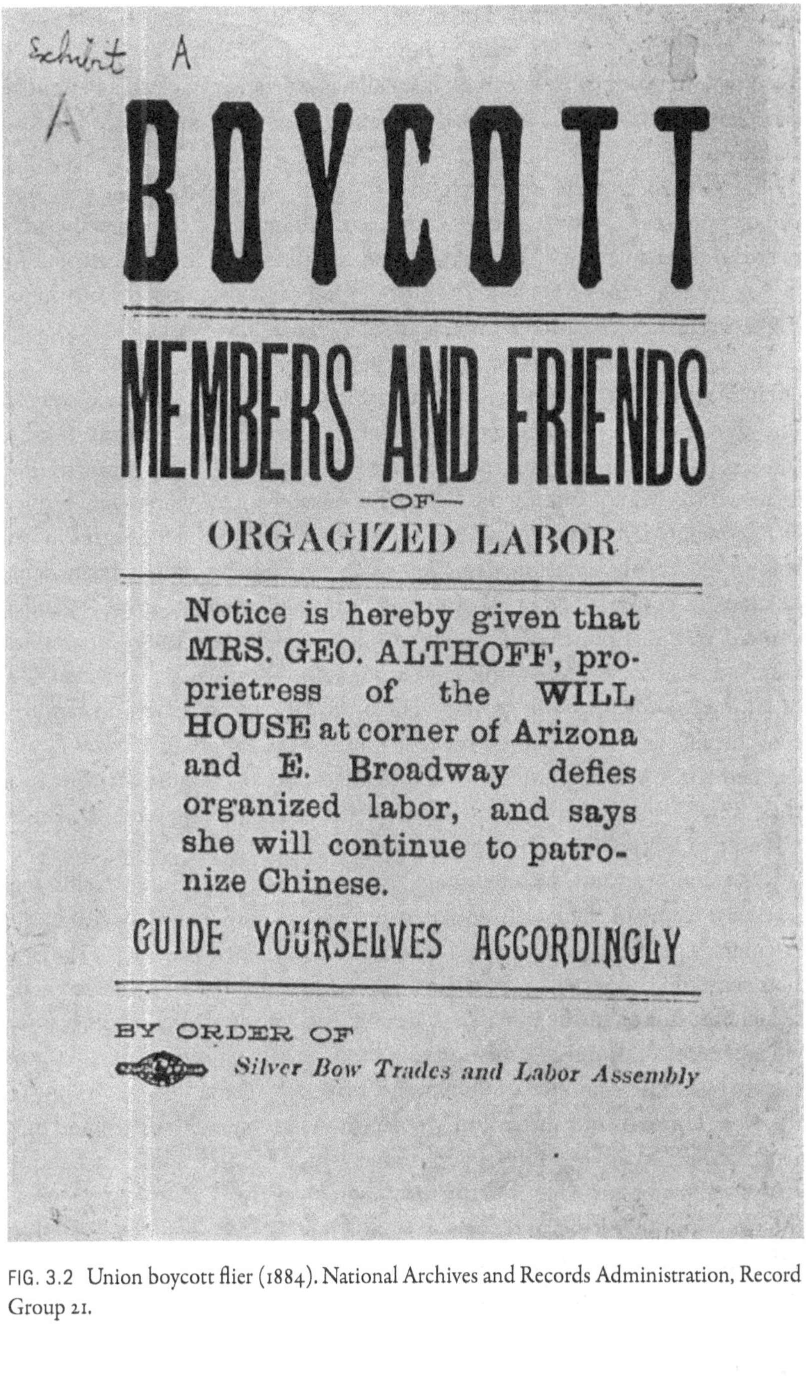

Schint A

/A

BOYCOTT

MEMBERS AND FRIENDS

—OF—

ORGAGIZED LABOR

Notice is hereby given that
MRS. GEO. ALTHOFF, pro-
prietress of the WILL
HOUSE at corner of Arizona
and E. Broadway defies
organized labor, and says
she will continue to patronize Chinese.

GUIDE YOURSELVES ACCORDINGLY

BY ORDER OF

 Silver Bow Trades and Labor Assembly

FIG. 3.2   Union boycott flier (1884). National Archives and Records Administration, Record Group 21.

United States should remain a predominantly White country (Daniels 2004, 17). Unsurprisingly, when Senator Sumner suggested in the Forty-First Congress that the word *white* be struck from all naturalization laws so as to remove racial discrimination, the proposed amendment was overwhelmingly rejected (Gold 2012, 31).

Racial tensions were intricately tied to the sexual anxieties of the White population. Arguments against Chinese immigration cited the disparity between male and female immigrants and the threat of Chinese men taking White wives (Jorae 2009, 93). They capitalized on racist concerns surrounding racial mixing. As Marchetti explained, "One of the most potent aspects of [the] Yellow Peril discourse is the sexual danger of contact between races" (Marchetti 1993, 3). At the same time, racial and sexual tensions converged into discourses on immigration that hinged on the presumed threat of Chinese sexuality. On the one hand, arguments against Chinese immigration raised concerns surrounding the "lascivious Asian women" who would seduce White men (Marchetti 1993, 3). Moreover, as Catherine Lee illustrates in her study of Chinese exclusion, arguments against Chinese immigration demonstrated a convergence of race making, ethnic differentiation, and gender construction that presented Chinese women as a threat to American families and American society as a whole (Lee 2010, 248). The discursive construction of Chinese women as a singular threat to the sanctity of American families rose to the level of the highest office in the land, as President Ulysses Grant deemed them a "worse evil" than the immigration of Chinese men because they were allegedly brought to the United States for "shameful" purposes ("President Ulysses Grant" 1874).

On the other hand, arguments against Chinese immigration recycled earlier racist tropes of the racialized sexual predator to conjure the specter of the Asian male predator who exploits innocent White women (Marchetti 1993, 3). Hoppenstand connects the anxieties surrounding the threat of the Asian male sexual predator to the Yellow Peril narrative, illustrating that the former individualizes cultural anxieties surrounding the Mongolian invasion of American society by Chinese and Asian immigrants by personalizing the issue as one of the violation of White American women by Asian men (Hoppenstand and Doctors 1983, 174). The Yellow Peril frame, which I will detail further in the analysis of media coverage of Chinese immigrants in the 1920s, resonated with the American public because it drew from a repository of fear that had been cultivated among Western civilizations since medieval times. These Yellow Peril narratives drew from the fear of Genghis Khan and Mongolian invasions of Europe in earlier eras. They connected those historical fears with the then-contemporary fear of Asians in the United States, articulated in the 1880s as a threat of cheap labor flooding American markets and threatening the livelihoods of White European immigrants (Marchetti 1993, 2). In this fashion, the historically grounded Yellow Peril frame provided new prejudices a wealth of material to support racial discrimination—from historical battles to art, poetry, and literary works created in light of those ancient anxieties. Moreover, Yellow Peril narratives had been used in previous eras to justify imperialism and colonial domination because a powerful Asia was a threat to Christian civilization (Marchetti 1993, 2). As a result, the morphing of the Yellow Peril narrative in the 1880s as a dominant framework through which immigration could be viewed rationalized restrictive and unjust policies against Chinese immigrants as necessary measures to ensure the safety of the American public.

The demographic patterns of Chinese immigrants exacerbated these sexual anxieties. Men outnumbered women at a rate of about twenty-to-one (Daniels 2004, 16). However, although the disproportionate numbers of men among Chinese immigrants conformed to Ravenstein's laws of immigration and thus resembled the demographic patterns of European immigrants that had come before them, the predominance of males among Chinese immigrants in the United States was perceived as a threat to the ethnic White population (Ravenstein 1876; Grigg 1977). Even before the passage of the Exclusion Act and the emergence of discriminatory policies against Chinese immigrants in the 1870s and '80s, Chinese immigrants complained that "it is impossible to get a Chinese woman out here unless one goes to China and marries her there, and then he must collect affidavits to prove that she is really his wife" (Takaki 1994, 107). Of course, such procedures were prohibitively expensive to Chinese laborers who had immigrated to the United States, and they were reserved for wealthy merchants with the means to secure passage to the homeland and back. As such, the male-dominant Chinese immigrant population was portrayed as a threat to the domestic well-being of American families.

Fear of radical ideology provided yet another push toward exclusionary rhetoric and policy. As John Higham explains, Anglo-Saxon nativism was tied to antiradical and anticommunist nativism, inspired by the view that anarchy and radicalism was a "blood disease" with which the English were not afflicted (Higham 1988, 138). This problem emerged, according to this narrative, with the arrival of new immigrants and particularly Chinese immigrants. It followed that legislation was needed to limit the immigration of subversives, hostile immigrants, and disrupters (Johnson 1997, 843).

White workers also came face-to-face with additional pressures during this period. Many suffered from the discrimination being leveled against them (Takaki 1994). Non-English-speaking White immigrants to America—Poles, Italians, Greeks, and Slavs, arriving to replace Black slave labor after the abolition of slavery (Fogleman 1998, 43)—were seen as foreign competition to the White Anglo-Saxon American working class (Olzak 1989, 133). Among these "not-yet-white ethnics" (Goldberg 1992) were the Irish, who were perceived as threatening to the emerging "national culture" and accused of being "wicked, naturally given to idleness, barbarous and papists" (Canny 1973, 585), as well as lacking real Christian faith or good manners (Takaki 1994, 29). Ethnic discrimination against Irish immigrants was often connected to racial discrimination against African Americans, as Irishmen were often compared to Negroes and described as "negroes turned inside out" and "Negroes as smoked Irish" (Ignatiev 1995, 34). Disdain for Irish immigrants may indeed have had roots in the British colonial period (Takaki 1994, 29), when Irish immigrants could not own land, carry weapons, bear witness, or hold office (Quinn 2007, 76). However, it escalated noticeably in the years following the Potato Famine (1845–1850) and thus was well-poised to play a role in motivating Irish workers to oppose Chinese immigration in the 1870s and 1880s (Daniels 2002, 126).

Similarly, Italian immigrants were perceived as dangerous criminals and described as "blacker than the blackest Negroes in existence" (Barrett and Roediger 1997, 38). In fact, immigration historian Barry Goldberg argued that the "not-yet-white ethnics" of the late nineteenth and early twentieth century experienced a hostility that approached, although to a lesser extent, the hostility shown to African Americans (Goldberg 1992, 201). The irony of White supremacy's fascination by Hellenic thought in spite of its intimidation of Greek immigrants is also characteristic of the contradictions that riddle the history of White-ethnics in America. It is most poignantly illustrated in the Ku Klux Klan name, derived from the Greek word *Kyklos*, an organization that drove Greek immigrants out of towns and forced them to anglicize their names and adopt Anglo-Saxon cultural mannerisms to avoid intimidation (Odzak 2011).

The dual effect of facing racial discrimination by Anglo-Saxon Whites and the increased competition and political valorization of Blacks played an immense role in motivating racial tensions between White workers and African American internal migrants as well as Chinese immigrants. White workers saw exclusion as a means to valorize White ethnic identity vis-à-vis an "inferior" category of labor (Roediger 1994, 186). In turn, anti-Chinese sentiment amid the tensions of the 1880s enabled White ethnics to coalesce around protecting White entitlement to resources, particularly in the West (Ngai 2014, 109). In essence, the construction of the Chinese immigrant as the racial Other provided a foil against which White identity could be reshaped to encompass White non-Anglo-Saxon ethnics. As scholars continue to debate the mechanism through which "not-yet-white ethnics" became White (Yang and Koshy 2016), most scholars agree on two main avenues behind the assimilation of White ethnics into "Whiteness." Communities firstly achieved Whiteness by acquiring social status (Ignatiev 1995; Jacobson 1998; Roediger 1999), a goal evident in labor's arguments for Chinese exclusion because Chinese immigrants depressed wages and threatened native labor. Secondly, White ethnics achieved Whiteness via changes in racial classification (Arnesen 2001a), exemplified by the circumstance of the Chinese exclusion movement. In this case, the ability of White workers of all ethnic groups to collectively mobilize around Chinese exclusion positioned Whites in a singular racial category in the midst of a fight over resources with more distinct racial communities: Chinese and Black.

Ultimately, the Chinese Exclusion Act passed with overwhelming bipartisan support on May 9, 1882. Originally envisioned as a twenty-year-long restriction of Chinese immigration, the act initiated a thirty-nine-year period of racialized exclusionary immigration policy against the Chinese (Daniels 2004, 3). The language of the act reinforced the image of Chinese immigration as an invasion or a threat, stating that "in the opinion of the Government of the United States the coming of Chinese laborers to this country endangers the good order of certain localities within the territory thereof" (Exclusion Act 1882).

Even though the Exclusion Act was originally intended as a provisional measure, the years that followed witnessed the renewal of Chinese exclusion measures as well as further legislation intended to discriminate against Chinese immigrants already in the United States. This included the 1888 Scott Act, which barred Chinese residents from reentering the country unless they had family or property in the United States, a condition that the vast majority of Chinese immigrants could not satisfy. Implemented haphazardly, the measure ensured that legal Chinese immigrants who were abroad at the time of its passage would no longer be permitted reentry to the United States. A series of measures at the local level that are often referred to as the Alien Land Acts thus prevented Chinese immigrants from owning land or property, closing the opportunity associated with landownership and homeownership to Chinese immigrants.

In 1892, Congress passed yet another immigration policy that further limited immigration hospitality toward the Chinese, placing burdensome requirements on Chinese immigrants' movement and residence in the United States. The Geary Act required that all Chinese immigrants "legally present in the United States" carry a certificate of legal residence (Geary Act 1892). This requirement was intended to cut down on illicit border crossings, authorizing the deportation of illegal immigrants. In addition, the Geary Act extended the exclusion period set up by the Exclusion Act another ten years. Most importantly, the implementation of the act reinforced the importance of racial origin in the interpretation of the law. In 1883, when a Chinese man born in Hong Kong and thereby a British citizen claimed that he could be excluded by the Exclusion Act as a British subject, the associate justice of the Supreme Court of the United States ruled that the subject was "Chinese by race, language and color" and possessed "all the peculiarities of the subjects of China" ("Chinese from Hong Kong" 1883). Finally, in the wake of emancipation, White Americans sought to enforce segregation in schools, housing, transportation, and services, driving Chinese immigrants to raise such issues in the highest courts of the nation. Neither Black nor White, Chinese existence in the post–Civil War era entered into the existing debates on the "separate, but equal" White and Black components of American society. In fact, the first family to contest Jim Crow laws, long before the *Brown v. Board of Education* ruling, was a Chinese family whose daughters were expelled because they were "colored" and were not admissible in a Whites-only school in Mississippi (Cohen 1984).[1]

The passage of the Chinese Exclusion Act and the immigration hostility that defined the period had devastating consequences for Chinese immigrants to the United States. The legislation inspired an "abatement" campaign throughout the United States aimed at violently driving Chinese immigrants out of their homes and workplaces. During this time, Chinese immigrants were harassed and expelled from thirty-four communities in California, nine in Washington, three in Oregon, and four in Nevada, while millions of dollars of Chinese immigrants' property was destroyed (Miščević and Kwong 2000, 99). The deadliest of these attacks occurred in California in the towns of Eureka (1885), Redlands (1893) and Chico (1894), and in Juneau, Alaska (1886). These "outrages," as they were called in the news, became increasingly common as White laborers organized against Chinese men. The most referenced example of anti-Chinese riots was the Rock Springs massacre of 1885, when a mob of 150 armed White miners attacked Chinese miners in the town of Rock Springs, Wyoming. The labor riot resulted in the deaths of twenty-eight Chinese miners and $150,000 in property damage to Chinese workers. Yet coverage of the massacre in the *New York Times* articulated many of the anti-immigrant sentiments of the period. An opinion-piece titled "The Wyoming Troubles" (1885) reported "the massacre of heathen Chinese by so-called Christians in Wyoming." Meanwhile, *New York Times* journalists observed that the local newspapers of Rock Springs "recounted the atrocities with cynical and ghastly joy" ("Mob Law in Wyoming" 1885).

In response to anti-Chinese mob violence in 1885, Chinese immigrants sought safety in numbers in major cities such as New York, Philadelphia, Boston, Cleveland, and Chicago (Miščević and Kwong 2000, 102). In those cities, Chinese immigrants often lived concentrated in a few overcrowded blocks. Shut out from many state services, Chinese individuals established their own community organizations, such as the Six Companies and Chinese Consolidated Benevolent Association (Miščević and Kwong 2000, 104). These organizations provided important services and protected their interests because of the neglect by government agencies of the needs and rights of the Chinese immigrant population (Hom 1987, 13).

The inability to bring families and children to the United States contributed to a widespread feeling of loneliness and boredom among Chinese immigrants. "On Sundays," noted Takaki, "Chinese men had no families to take on outings" (1994, 111). Instead, festivities and holidays, a source of joy for many communities, exacerbated the loneliness of Chinese immigrants, as one wrote in a poem, "Each festival arouses my feelings of home" (Hom 1987, 172). At the same time, the estrangement of Chinese men from their spouses and children fractured family life. In a chapter titled "Lamentations of Estranged Wives," Hom collected poems of lonely Chinese wives left behind as their husbands sought wealth and prosperity out west. It included numerous songs of Mandarin ducks, separated and longing to be reunited.[2]

Fear of attacks by White workers also prevented Chinese immigrants from bringing their wives and families to the United States (Takaki 1994, 88). In turn, this exacerbated the large imbalance between men and women among Chinese immigrants (Daniels 2004, 16) and contributed to the emergence of a prostitution trade to alleviate the loneliness of the "bachelor societies" in the Chinatowns of the country (Jorae 2009, 76). Thus, according to the 1870 census, 61 percent of the 3,536 Chinese women living in California were sex workers, eventually dropping to 24 percent of 3,171 in the 1880 census, as Chinese men were briefly able to bring wives before the Exclusion Act came into force (Takaki 1994, 102–104). The combined impact of familial estrangement and the threat of racial violence limited the ability of many Chinese immigrants to cultivate a sense of home in their new surroundings.

In sum, the time of the Chinese Exclusion Act is an era in American history that reveals the racial, gendered, religious, and linguistic boundaries constricting American immigration hospitality. It also provides a case study of the influence of the exploitative organization of the American economy and thus the labor market competition that affected the reception of immigrants in the public sphere. Returning to the ethical concept of hospitality as one that extends welcome to the Other while also asserting the authority and ownership of the native population over the national sphere, these circumstances demonstrated the conditions under which hospitality could be restricted in the name of protecting the perceived rights, economic well-being, and sovereignty of the native population.

Media Hospitality

Reflecting on media coverage of Chinese immigration, Stuart Miller noted that "the Chinese arrived in the middle of the slavery controversy, when modern racist theory was being developed and when Americans were becoming more conscious of antisepsis and germs . . . this stimulated editorial fear of coolieism, of alien genes and germs" (1969, 15). Miller's writing points to some of the media biases that dominated American discourse on Chinese immigration at the time.

In my exploration of media hostility during the Chinese exclusion era, I will draw attention to the dominant representational tropes in media coverage of the time, with an eye toward the lasting impact of these stereotypes for media hospitality.[3]

Dominant Media Tropes

Media coverage of the issue of Chinese immigration was dominated by four tropes: The Yellow Peril or Mongolian Invasion trope characterized the representation of Chinese immigration as a threatening invasion of an alien other that undermined the racial, linguistic, and cultural makeup of the United States. The "servile coolie" presented Chinese immigrants who arrived voluntarily in the United States as "coolies," belonging to a hybrid form of slave labor. The trickster trope emphasized the deviousness, unreliability, and ungovernability of Chinese immigrants. And finally, the inferior being trope emphasized the racial inferiority of Chinese immigrants, likening them to animals, vermin, and other creatures. This section outlines these tropes in detail.

Yellow Peril

One trope that dominated coverage of Chinese immigration was a textual and visual comparison between Chinese immigration and settler-colonialism, a form of colonialism in which colonization takes place through the mass immigration of people into a country (Veracini 2014, 615). According to this portrayal, Chinese immigrants were compared to White settlers who had arrived in the early periods of American history and eliminated the native population before them. Settler-colonialism, as Patrick Wolfe put it in his highly influential essay on colonialism, "is inherently eliminatory" (Wolfe 2006, 287), threatening the genocide of the native population (287–288). As such, media coverage that employed the settler colonialist lens to explain Chinese immigration often implied that Chinese immigrants would exterminate, enslave, or displace White Americans, as European immigrants had done to Native Americans. It portrayed Asian civilization as a threat to American culture. As the *Record-Union* said of the Chinese in 1882, "We believe that their exclusion is necessary to the settlement of California and the Pacific Coast with Americans and maintenance of the Anglo-Saxon civilization" ("Watch the Rascals" 1882).

News coverage drew on the language of the Exclusion Act to bolster the view of Chinese immigration as a form of invasion. Thus, the media both encouraged the passage of the Exclusion Act prior to its passing and used the legislation's language afterward as an indication of the validity of the claims of exclusionists, a circular logic that silenced critique and contributed to the continued exclusion of Chinese immigrants. One article in the *New York Times* argued that if Congress believed "the coming of [Chinese laborers] to the United States or their residence affects our interests and endangers order," then it was important to "accept the views of Congress" ("Watch the Rascals" 1882). Moreover, the words used to describe the wave of Chinese immigrants also reinforced prejudice: Chinese immigration was likened to a "horde" ("Of One Mind" 1882), a Mongolian invasion, or a slave trade ("Watch the Rascals" 1882).

Visual representations complemented the verbal portrayal of Chinese immigration as an invasion, depicting the Chinese immigrant as a plotting colonizer, whose hypothesized domination of White Americans was seen to avenge previously oppressed races, such as Native Americans and African Americans. In "Every Dog (No Distinction of Color) Has His Day," a political cartoon by Thomas Nast (fig. 3.3), a Native American whispered in the ear of a Chinese man, "'fraid you['ll] crowd [them] out, as he did me." The Chinese man was shown to be looking thoughtfully at anti-Chinese slogans and newspaper headlines plastered on a wall. In the background, a Black man was portrayed napping with the words "my day is coming" in his head, a depiction that perpetuated racist stereotypes of Black workers as lazy and reaffirmed the position of Blacks as a lingering latent threat to White society. The cartoon combines racial anxieties of White Americans with the fear of Chinese immigration. It depicts the latter as an invasion akin to European settler-colonialism. In turn, this depiction exemplified the linkages between Chinese immigration, Native American expropriation, and African American enslavement. At the same time, the cartoon misrecognizes Chinese immigration as settler-colonialism, ignoring the barriers to citizenship preventing Chinese immigrants from settling at all, let alone displacing White citizens.

Servile Coolie

The "Mongolian invasion" or "Yellow Peril" narrative worked in conjunction with the "coolie" theme connecting Chinese immigrants with anxieties surrounding slavery following the conclusion of the Civil War (Miller 1969, 190). On the one hand, those opposed to the "experiment" of the enfranchisement of African Americans feared that Americans would one day consider the "Chinese question," as they had the "Negro question" before ("Negro and China-man" 1882). On the other hand, concerned politicians on the East Coast worried that the new immigrants were not "voluntary immigrants but absolute slaves" (Miller 1969, 192). Indeed, many Chinese immigrants could not afford the price of passage, and as a result, Chinese immigrants entered into contracts that allowed them to repay the price of passage over several years. This credit-ticket system allowed Chinese merchants to pay for workers' passage to the United States, binding the latter to work for a determined period. However, as Zinzius pointed out, the arrangement did not make them "unfree as coolies were" (2005, 12). More importantly, this system did not substantially

FIG. 3.3 "Every Dog (No Distinction of Color) Has His Day." Thomas Nast, *Harper's Weekly*, 1879. Library of Congress.

differ from the choices other groups of immigrants had made during the seventeenth, eighteenth, and early nineteenth centuries. Long before the arrival of the Chinese, immigrants had traveled to the New World as indentured servants, agreeing to work for an employer for a limited amount of time in exchange for passage, food, and shelter (Wolfe 2015). The historian Edmund Morgan argues that for much of the seventeenth century, indentured servants were White English men and women—with a smattering of Africans, Indians, and Irish (Morgan 2003).

The origins of the term *coolie* are further evidence of the racialized discourses about Chinese immigrants. First used to describe Chinese indentured or contract laborers sent primarily to Cuba, Peru, and the colonies of the West Indies, the term reappeared in the United States in the 1870s and 1880s to describe Chinese immigrants who arrived voluntarily in order to associate Chinese workers with the much-loathed slave trade. Indeed, the "coolie trade" and the slave trade were connected, as Chinese labor arrived in many countries just as slavery was being abolished as a replacement for slave labor. For instance, some 125,000 Chinese laborers were "imported" into the island nation of Cuba from 1847 to 1874, just as slavery was being abolished. Similarly, when Peru abolished the African slave trade, 95,000 individuals were imported from China to work in plantations (Hu-Dehart 1993). The transplantation of the term *coolie* from its original context to the American one distilled the problem of slavery to one of the immigration of Chinese people. Further, it demonized Chinese people for bringing back slavery to the United States without placing any blame on exploitative plantation owners and capitalists who continuously sought cheap labor.

By the 1880s, "a rhetorical shift" had occurred, "magnifying the image of the coolie as the new slave" and allowing workers with antislavery positions to proclaim immigration exclusion as a justified stance (Metrick-Chen 2012, 152). As labor organizations struggled to compete with incoming immigrant workers, "the trade union response to this pressure was to mobilize, and then to lobby, for immigration restriction" (Miller 1969). In turn, "virtually every labor newspaper and organization opposed Chinese immigration after 1870" (Miller 1969, 140). The workers' stance against Chinese immigration was echoed in mainstream newspapers as well.

A call-to-action titled "Of One Mind," published in the *San Francisco Chronicle* (1882), echoed these views (fig. 3.4). The call to action suggested that people were mobilizing across the country for restrictive legislation to stop the "evils" of "the non-assimilable horde" of Chinese immigration. Announcements like this one in the nation's newspapers warned of "monster mass meetings" ("Of One Mind" 1882).

Alongside portrayals of slave labor as devoid of political opinions or free will, several other related themes dominated coverage of the Chinese

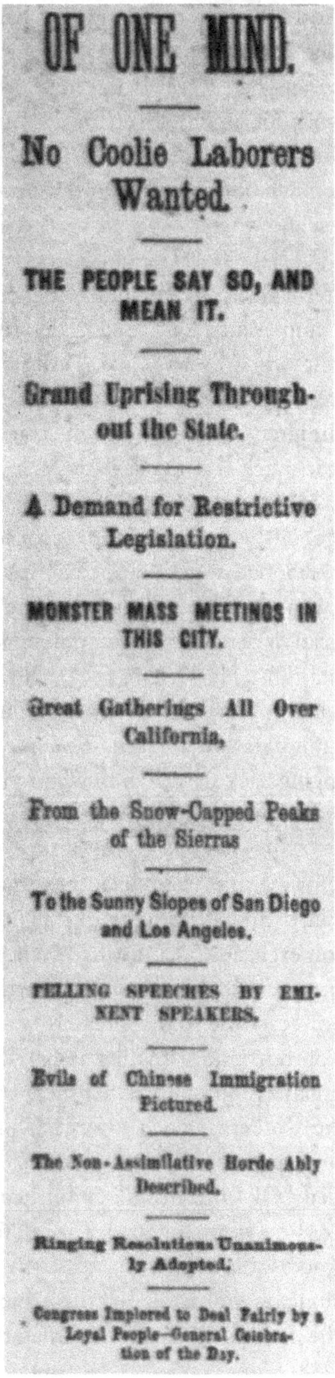

OF ONE MIND.

No Coolie Laborers Wanted.

THE PEOPLE SAY SO, AND MEAN IT.

Grand Uprising Throughout the State.

A Demand for Restrictive Legislation.

MONSTER MASS MEETINGS IN THIS CITY.

Great Gatherings All Over California,

From the Snow-Capped Peaks of the Sierras

To the Sunny Slopes of San Diego and Los Angeles.

TELLING SPEECHES BY EMINENT SPEAKERS.

Evils of Chinese Immigration Pictured.

The Non-Assimilative Horde Ably Described.

Ringing Resolutions Unanimously Adopted;

Congress Implored to Deal Fairly by a Loyal People—General Celebration of the Day.

FIG. 3.4 "Of One Mind." NewsBank/ Readex, *San Francisco Chronicle*.

immigrant as coolie. First, the transformation of the term *coolie* from a signi-
fier of class to one of race accompanied a gradual transformation of the term
from an identifier of workers to a term describing cargo and objects, devoid of
humanity. Thus, the first article on the Exclusion Act in the *New York Times*
argued that Chinese immigration is "too much like an importation to be welcomed without restriction, too much like an invasion to be looked upon without solicitude" ("Report Adverse to Chinese Immigration" 1882). As such,
Chinese immigrants were being compared to objects, cargo imported in trade
between countries. The *West-Coast Record-Union* echoed this view, discussing
"the coming coolie cargoes" aboard the steamers due to arrive at California's
ports. Noting that "the Oceanic should leave Hong Kong coolie laden," it suggested offloading coolies in British Columbia if the shipment did not arrive in
time ("Coming Coolie Cargo" 1882). Some publications dehumanized Chinese
laborers by treating them as either catalysts or impediments to economic expansion, a variable whose exclusion could form part of an economic experiment in
the United States. In an article appearing in March 1882, the *New York Times*
noted that the twenty-year exclusion then being debated in Congress would
allow time to test the "experiment of excluding the Chinese." With time, it
argued, "the statistics of labor and commerce would shed new light on the problem" ("China in the Senate" 1882). Such treatments of Chinese migrant labor
that depicted immigrants as shipments to be loaded, unloaded, or imported,
as they framed discussions surrounding immigration restriction as policy
experiments, obscured and deliberately ignored the impact of such hostile
policies on the daily lives of Chinese immigrants living in the United States.
    The use of the term *coolie* for Chinese immigrants, which increasingly per-
vaded news coverage across the country, also allowed the press to describe
people of Chinese descent without addressing them by name or acknowledging their humanity. As *coolie* morphed from an indicator of class to a derogatory racial term for Chinese immigrants, its use became widespread in the
media. A search for the term *coolie* in newspaper archives from 1882 to 1920
returned 74,287 results, distributed unevenly across the territory of the United
States. As evidenced by the results of a search of the term *coolie* in all American
press during the 1920s (fig. 3.5), the use of *coolie* as a term to discuss Chinese
immigrants corresponded in large part to the states with the highest numbers
of Chinese workers. The term was most widely used in mining and labor-
intensive states such as California, Pennsylvania, and Kansas, while its use in
those regions influenced the use of *coolie* in media coverage in political and
cultural centers of the nation such as New York or Washington, D.C. In spite
of the lack of significant Chinese immigrant populations in those cities, this
may be due to the prominence of several national newspapers.
    Perhaps the most important aspect of the widespread acceptance of the
term *coolie* to describe Chinese immigrants rested in the racial tensions it

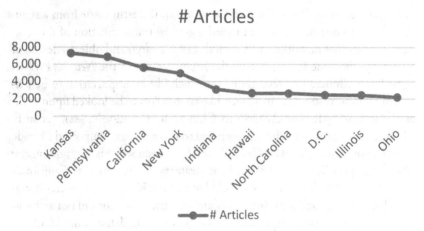

FIG. 3.5 The ten states with the highest occurrence of the term *coolie* in the press. Created by the author based on Newspapers.com digital archive materials.

revealed. Tellingly, Chinese immigrants did not fit the coolie classification simply because they voluntarily accepted contract work in return for passage to the United States. Nor did the terms of their passage differ greatly from those of poor Irish immigrants or other ethnic groups who had signed similar contracts of labor in return for passage during their migration to the United States. Despite the similarity of the arrival of many English and Irish immigrants as indentured servants, White immigrants were not classified as coolies or slave labor as Chinese immigrants had been. The targeting of Chinese and Asian immigrants as coolies is evidence of the racial rather than ethnic prejudices inherent in media discourses of immigration. While White immigrants could be "immigrants," Chinese immigrants were designated as "coolies" even when they arrived of their own will. In turn, as outlined by Moon-Hu Jung in her extensive study of the use of "coolies" in the sugar plantations of Louisiana, the term *coolie* did not reflect a legal category but rather an amalgamation of racial imaginings (2005, 8). In a nation that was struggling to redefine the value of Whiteness and racial difference in the wake of emancipation and reconstruction, the emergence of the coolie as an alternative racial category sustained the racial hierarchies of the era. Thus, commending the coolie's efficiency allowed White employers to criticize the indolence of Black workers. Meanwhile, criticizing their (often assumed or coerced) servitude and docility ensured their racial inferiority vis-à-vis White Americans, immigrants, and natives.

Trickster Chinee

Another common trope in the coverage of the Chinese immigrant was the promotion of narratives about Chinese cunning and trickery, promoting distrust while legitimizing discriminatory policy as necessary for dealing with supposedly troublesome individuals. One newspaper article in the *Marshall County News* in Kansas recounted the experience of a botanist who had been robbed by Chinese people while on a botanical expedition in Solio Falls. Using the coolie trope discussed earlier, the article emphasized the trickery and untrustworthiness of Chinese people. The Chinese companion identified merely as a "coolie" became indistinguishable from the "coolie" thieves who approached the group. Mistrust of the Chinese was further emphasized when the botanist commended another companion's command of the Chinese language that had enabled negotiation with the attackers ("Entertaining Loh Fau Brigands" 1917). The botanist's retelling of his experience accused the Chinese companion of collusion with the Chinese robbers and celebrated the expedition's seeming neutralization of his role by relying on a White traveler to translate. The article points to two trends that recur in U.S. media coverage of immigration. First, it exemplifies the tendency to blur distinctions between individuals and groups, making each immigrant responsible for any infraction committed by a member of their community. Second, it reflects the tendency to regard immigrants with suspicion.

Alongside these depictions of untrustworthiness, Chinese immigrants' deviousness was often connected to a parallel trope of the ungovernability of Chinese residents. Thus, news of the tensions arising from governing and living with Chinese immigrants filled newspapers on the West Coast. One article written by Leonidas Pratt, the district attorney of San Francisco in 1882, recounted the case of a crime in the city's Chinatown where the accused was assumed to have paid witnesses—all Chinese—to testify that he wasn't at the site of the crime. The Chinese were, in his eyes, "a set of murderous, irresponsible heathen[s]" whom one could not "put too much cursedness" in describing ("Chinese Criminals" 1882). More importantly, these testimonies continued to emphasize the inability to govern or control Chinese communities living in the United States, portraying Chinese immigrants as a threat to the rule of law.

The inability to govern Chinese immigrants who often subverted the law and moral codes was frequently connected to the religion of Chinese immigrants in press coverage. Thus, tales by Pacific Coast officials stressed the difficulty of dealing with Chinese immigrants, arguing that such efforts required adopting tricks "darker than a heathen's." For example, the county assessor in San Francisco described in the *Oakland Tribune* a novel method he had devised to collect taxes from "the heathen Chinee." His method consisted of driving an express wagon to a location and waiting for "the Mongolians [to] swarm up the wagon like a flock of turkeys in a stubble field." Paradoxically portraying both the supposed cunning and the animalistic naïveté of Chinese immigrants, the tax collector rejoiced that he had found a method that is "darker than a heathen's" ("Assessor's Strategy" 1882). A similar theme appeared in articles suggesting that the "cunning coolie" would find ways to subvert the exclusion measure by collecting papers of returning Chinese workers and smuggling illegal immigrants to replace them. Yet another article traced the ungovernable character of Chinese immigrants to their being "irresponsible, murderous heathen[s]" ("Chinese Criminals" 1882). Together, these painted a picture of Chinese immigrants as being incomprehensible creatures who defied the moral, religious, and legal codes that bound the native population of the United States.

Inferior Beings

When not referred to as heathens or coolies, Chinese immigrants were likened to animals, vermin, or inanimate objects. Inspired by the eugenic movement's conviction that the Chinese represented an inferior race, cartoonists, editorialists, and journalists often portrayed Chinese immigrants as subhuman, using dogs or pigs to illustrate their inferiority. One political cartoon titled "Darwin's Theory Illustrated" (fig. 3.6) depicted a Chinese man as a primitive lifeform, less evolved than the pig he evolves into at a later stage of the cartoon, as the visual turns the man's pig tail into a literal one.

The depiction of Chinese immigrants as animals associated with unhygienic habits and pigs most specifically stems from deep misunderstandings of Chinese immigrants' culture in the United States. Alongside the rise in the number of Chinese Americans on the West Coast, several traditions within Chinese society were misunderstood, fueling the racism toward Chinese immigrants of the time ("Chinese Question" 1885). In spite of the copious coverage of the conditions of Chinese immigrants' housing, the reasons motivating Chinese immigrants' choice to live in crowded quarters were poorly communicated. Decades later, Takaki demonstrated that immigrants made housing choices in response to violence in non-Chinese neighborhoods (1994, 16). During the 1870s and 1880s, 153 riots occurred in the West, during which Chinese workers were attacked and killed and their property burned and damaged. Thus, as Takaki argued, Chinese immigrants sought safety in numbers within Chinatowns on the West Coast (Takaki 1994).

In addition, individualism as understood by non-Chinese immigrants in the United States was not viewed the same way among Chinese immigrants. Instead, all Chinese workers with the same family name considered themselves relatives (Zinzius 2005, 17). Accordingly, members of the same family clan willingly organized shared housing with one another. Describing their living arrangements, Chiu wrote, "Most of the men lived in boarding houses, crowded small rooms with other members of their family or village. To save space, beds were sometimes nailed to the walls, two or three above each other. In some crowded rooms, the men slept in shifts. At the end of the year, expenses were divided among members. These fongs, or rooms,

FIG. 3.6 "Darwin's Theory Illustrated—the Creation of Chinaman and Pig," *The Wasp*, January 6, 1877, 217.

were the basic living arrangements in Chinatowns across the country" (Chiu 1960, 50–51).

Thus, the intricacies of the Chinese family clan system were poorly understood in the press, and these unfavorable depictions of Chinese immigrants on the West Coast influenced the coverage of national newspapers, particularly ones in areas where Chinese immigrant populations were negligible. For instance, a *New York Times* article in 1885, publishing from a city that lacked a significant Chinese population, argued that Chinese immigrants accepted unhygienic and crowded living conditions because they were "filthy" by nature ("Chinese Question" 1885).

The four overwhelmingly negative tropes that dominated coverage of Chinese immigration and Chinese immigrants in the American press thus emphasized the existential threat that Chinese immigration represented to the local population ("Yellow Peril"). They stoked existing tensions surrounding labor competition by emphasizing the servile "slave-like" nature of Chinese immigrants ("servile coolie"). They also justified discriminatory policy such as the Exclusion Act by drawing on government spokespersons as experts and by

emphasizing the ungovernability of Chinese immigrants that thereby necessitated exceptional restrictiveness ("trickster Chinee"). In sum, the vilification
and at times utter dehumanization of Chinese immigrants ("inferior being")
minimized public opposition to Chinese exclusion.

Compassionate illustrations of Chinese immigrants in the media were lacking, in particular due to the lack of Chinese voices in the American press. As
the prominent Chinese American radio personality Betty Lee Sung told the
historian Ellen Wu, she was "appalled at the image" that the American public had of Chinese Americans as "coolie labor, highbinders, hatchetmen," and
other negative stereotypes, and she strove throughout her career in the 1940s
to rectify the negative image of Chinese immigrants in the American media
(Wu 2008, 398). Yet until the Cold War began to motivate editorialists to
recruit Chinese American journalists as a display of inclusion in American
society, the voices of Chinese people would continue to be stifled, which in
turn allowed misunderstandings and stereotypes of Chinese immigrants to
thrive in the 1880s.

Home-Building Efforts of Immigrants

One of the most important and neglected consequences of the Exclusion
Act was its impact on the ability of Chinese immigrants to achieve a sense
of "feeling at home" in the United States. Indeed, many Chinese immigrants
do not speak of that dark chapter of history. Professor Erika Lee described
the difficulty of conducting ethnographic research on the period; she wrote
that Chinese grandmothers refused to speak of the "old days," because they
were "times that were full of pain and wounds that never healed" (Lee 2003, 6).
She spoke of one grandmother who reluctantly recounted her memories
of the Exclusion period, saying that "when I could coax her into talking
about her past, I had to take surreptitious notes under the dining room
table" (Lee 2003, 6).

During this time, many Chinese immigrants could only aspire to be part of
"split-families," with relatives residing back home as they worked in the United
States (Jorae 2009, 11; Peffer 1986). Thus, Chinese families took to a primitive
form of photoshopping to create an illusion of family intimacy. Often, they
would cut and paste absent family members into photos, making their absence
almost unnoticeable, at least in image. One 2015 exhibit displayed these photographs of visually reunited families, demonstrating how family photographs
offset the consequences of the Exclusion Act on Chinese immigrant families
(Yelsey 2015).

The images of multiple generations of Chinese families reunited in photographs present haunting evidence of the unfair impact of the act on the domestic life of Chinese immigrants. Particularly captivating was the bridal couple

FIG. 3.7 Low family portrait, circa 1940. Museum of Chinese in America Collection.

at the center of the photograph (fig. 3.7), turned toward each other though thousands of miles apart, revealing in the intimacy of their portrait the unjust consequences of exclusion and the harsh reality of estrangement. These mechanisms of coping were a testament not only to the lack of hospitality by the American community as a host to Chinese immigrants but also to migrants' creativity in finding avenues to simulate feeling at home and build resilience in the face of a hostile host environment.

Due to the lack of welcome Chinese immigrants experienced in both media coverage and immigration policy, time and again, Chinese immigrants distinguished between their current residence and the place of their belonging. As one self-described wanderer lamented his estrangement from the land of his ancestors, he wondered, "Who is taking care of the ancestors' graves?" The temporary position of the United States was then reiterated as he asked, "How can I be with my family again? I wish to set sail for home, but my fortune is not yet made" (anonymous poet cited in Hom 1987, 173). Another Chinese poet hoped to "leave this barbaric land on the earliest possible day. It can't be compared to the warmth of home" (Hom 1987, 169). Another wrote, "I look around north, south, east, west, I don't know which direction is home" (Hom 1987, 163).

Yet Chinese immigrants succeeded in building a sense of home through multiple strategies of cultural, linguistic, and legal mobilization toward cultivating the identity of the Chinese American immigrant. One such avenue toward home-building was through food. Sustaining the culinary taste of home presented one avenue to home-building for Chinese immigrants who responded to the sense of feeling displaced by bringing native cooking traditions to their new environment. Thus, immigrants expressed their attachment to their *guxiang*, or native place, through consumption of food in particular, as Chinese immigrants imported tea, opium, shark fins, preserves, bamboo, seaweed, mushrooms, and duck, along with "well-polished chopsticks" with which to eat (Qin 2016, 110).

Political mobilization to advocate for more hospitable immigration policies represented yet another component of Chinese immigrants' home-building strategies. In 1892, Chinese immigrants in the United States mounted a resistance movement challenging the constitutionality of the Chinese Exclusion Act. The former commissioner of education Yung Wung declared that the Chinese community hired two leading constitutional lawyers, Joseph H. Coate and Charles H. Seward. The Oriental Club of New York also announced that it would convene meetings to arouse sympathy for this effort among Chinese immigrants, declaring that it would be levying a head tax of one dollar for all Chinese immigrants in the United States to defray the legal costs of the case ("Resistance by the Chinese" 1892). The resulting Supreme Court case, *Fong Yue-Ting v. United States* (1893), resulted in a six-to-three decision for the United States, with the majority opinion reaffirming the constitutionally grounded authority of the U.S. government to regulate immigration as it saw fit (149 U.S. 698, 1893). This decision to affirm the constitutional rights of the government to regulate immigration while denying the right of Chinese immigrants to habeas corpus was criticized by Justice Melville Fuller, who wrote in his dissent that the decision had "the germs of the assertion of an unlimited and arbitrary power, in general, incompatible with the immutable principles of justice, inconsistent with the nature of our Government, and in conflict with the written Constitution by which that Government was created and those principles secured" (149 U.S. 698, 1893). While the Chinese immigrants did not receive the decision they had hoped for, the Supreme Court case nevertheless exemplifies a successful effort by Chinese immigrants to mobilize legal and financial resources toward bettering their position.

At the same time, Chinese immigrants responded to the discrimination they encountered by advocating for their worthiness in the media. Chinese foreign minister Wu Tingfang, for example, wrote in the *North American Review* that justice demanded the equal treatment of Chinese and other immigrants (reprinted in Wong and Chan 1998, 12). Similarly, Chinese writers protested the labels used to attack Chinese immigrants, such as an essay by Wong Chin Goo in *North American Review* that demonstrated pride in his identity as a "heathen," a position he took to be morally and logically superior to the teachings of Christian missionaries, intent on stamping out one's godless nature. In a humorous tone, the author described how when he got to the new dispensation and the promise of sin forgiveness that was granted by the crucifixion of Christ, he "figuratively went to pieces on Christianity" (*North American Review*, August 1887, republished in Yung, Chang, and Lai 2006, 70).

Above all, the passage of the act and the discourses around it highlighted one important reality to Chinese immigrants of the time: that "immigrants with white skins did not remain strangers in America the way Asians did" (Takaki 1994, 87). The recognition by Chinese immigrants of their perceived racial inferiority and Otherness hindered their ability to feel at home in their new environment as publications ridiculed their appearance, mocking their long hair, clothing, and cultural practices and decrying their traditional gambling games and opium smoking. The trauma of being refused belonging in the nation was palpable in the response of Amy Chin, a Chinese American curator who noted that "the trauma of feeling unwanted is still present" (Yelsey 2015).

Race and ethnicity scholars of the twenty-first century continue to stress the lesson that Chinese grandparents learned in exclusion-era America: visible cultural indicators of difference exclude non-White immigrants from national belonging (Lim 2006, 9). Yet the contemporary echoes of these discourses on immigrants' lives offer a moment of opportunity as they show the impact of immigration exclusion more openly than in past periods in our history. By examining the history of a period of strong bipartisan support for immigrant exclusion and discrimination, a history that is often overlooked in narratives of American immigration history as a whole, this project hopes to reveal a few of the limitations of the "nation of immigrants" narrative, as illustrated in times of intense restriction. As Chin says of her curatorial efforts to display Chinese immigrants' lives, "I'm putting something out there that had been kept secret . . . : our immigration history" (Yelsey 2015).

It is this realization that forms the core of the contradictions of American hospitality that I wish to highlight in this project. In line with the views espoused by Professor Amy Wax on immigration in the United States, American immigration historically has extended greater welcome to European White immigrants than non-White immigrants bearing visible markers of difference from Caucasian settlers. These immigrants, over time, would be told to go back to their countries of origin, even as they were born, raised, and elected to public service positions in the United States. All the while, this discrimination against immigrants of non-White origins did not undermine the identity of the United States as a nation of immigrants because of its presumed continued welcome extended to immigrants of European origin.

Nevertheless, reckoning with the factors that influenced immigration and media hostility as well as recognizing the tropes used in media coverage can serve to enhance immigration hospitality in the future. One path toward enhancing media hospitality lies in identifying and avoiding previous stereotypical and racist coverage. Another important intervention lies in rectifying the misunderstanding and harm that had been done by these tropes over time. For instance, some media coverage during the COVID-19 crisis consciously averted the tropes of the unhygienic and diseased Other by clarifying what wet markets were to the public (Mara and Phoenix 2020) and highlighting the rise of xenophobic attacks on Asian immigrants and Asian Americans (Chin 2021).

Anchoring a Myth against the Tides

It has been argued that Americans possess a "variability, if not schizophrenia" in their thoughts on immigration (Feagin 1997, 14). This is due at least in part to the fact that popular culture and the media selectively draw from an early history of hospitality, painting it as a period of "open-gates" immigration policy without paying heed to the reasons behind hospitality's decline and without reckoning with the racially determined periods of exception such as the Exclusion Act. This section reflects on the demographic factors that bolstered the image of the United States as a nation of immigrants, particularly the numbers of immigrants of European origin that arrived during this period and helped bolster the image of the "immigrant nation." Moreover, it explores the role that the monument dedicated to immigrants par excellence played in supporting this myth.

The 1880s witnessed several demographic shifts that bolstered the myth of the United States as a nation of immigrants. Moreover, this era began to witness the arrival of new groups of immigrants such as the Irish, Russians, Jews, and others, alongside changes in U.S. Census data that captured these new ethnicities as they arrived. These conditions allowed the census to paint the image of the United States as a nation that was attracting immigrants with its policies and welcoming immigrants en masse. Immigration numbers continued to rise, portraying the United States as a hospitable nation. In fact, the 1880s began a period in which the United States would gain a reputation as an industrial powerhouse fueled by its open immigration policy (Khan 2015, 7).

One anchoring element of this reputation was the idea of the Statue of Liberty greeting immigrants at the nation's gates. Initially intended by legal scholar Édouard-René Lefebvre de Laboulaye to celebrate the United States as an example of liberty and representative government throughout the world (Khan 2015, 5), the statue was to be erected on the centennial of the Declaration of Independence. Announced in a ceremony with the music of La Marseillaise and Hail Columbia, when copies of the Constitution and the Declaration of Independence were placed in its cornerstone ("Liberty's Place of Rest" 1884), the statue symbolized a feat of modern architecture. When artist Frédéric

Auguste Bartholdi had unveiled the project in Paris in 1882, hosting a dinner party atop a scaffolding at the statue's knee, he had imagined a monument that would rival the great wonders of the world ("Beacon of Liberty" 1882). Indeed, by the time the project was completed, it was hailed as the eighth wonder of the world, as well as its first modern wonder (Khan 2015, 4).

Inadvertently, however, and in a twist of fate and a flourish of Emma Lazarus's pen, Bartholdi's lady liberty, enlightening the world would come to take on a meaning far more resonant and captivating than even the loftiest aspirations of its male architects. At the time, fundraising efforts to build a pedestal to support the statue were struggling. As a result, the American fundraising effort reached out to Jewish poet Emma Lazarus in 1883, asking her to dedicate a poem to the new monument.

History owes a large part of the shift in the meaning of the Statue of Liberty to Lazarus. Working with Jewish refugees during that time, the poet was inspired by the plight of European Jewish forced migrants arriving in the United States as she was writing her tribute to the new colossus. The 1882 work shifted her focus to the themes of forced migration and persecution and to the role of the United States as a place of refuge. This inspired her to rename the statue "The Mother of Exiles" and to convey in her sonnet "The New Colossus" a strong sentiment of welcome to newcomers (Lazarus 1882). Her poem brought Lady Liberty to life, transforming Lady Liberty into a welcoming figure who greeted the world's most vulnerable immigrants at the gates of the nation. Send me the world's "homeless," Lazarus wrote, assuming the voice of the new colossus, as she reinterpreted the statue's stance as an effort to welcome the nationless forced migrants of the earth by raising a lamp to guide them "beside the golden door."

Lazarus's poem had resonance in U.S. governmental circles. Speaking in his official capacity as U.S. president during the unveiling ceremony of the statue on October 28, 1886, President Grover Cleveland dedicated the statue in the following manner: "We joyously contemplate . . . our own deity keeping watch and ward before the open gates of America, and greater than all that have been celebrated in ancient song. Instead of grasping in her hand thunderbolts of terror and of death, she holds aloft the light which illumines the way to man's enfranchisement" (Cleveland 2013).

Cleveland's words illustrated how Emma Lazarus's verses fundamentally transformed the fate of Lady Liberty from one denoting transatlantic cooperation and the promise of participatory democracy to that of a central figure grounding the identity of the nation as a welcoming refuge to the immigrants and forced migrants of the world.

Lazarus's poem emblazoned on the statue in 1903 further echoed these sentiments: "Give me your tired, your poor, your huddled masses yearning to breathe free, the wretched refuse of your teeming shore, send these, the homeless, tempest-tossed, to me: I lift my lamp beside the golden door" ("Unveiling of the Statue" 1886).

Thus, after worrying in *Songs of a Semite* whether Jewish refugees arriving in the 1880s and beyond would ever find a "fire-cored cloud" and "divine guide" to illuminate their journey from persecution (Lazarus 1882, 9), Lazarus emblazoned her answer on the pedestal of the deity standing at the nation's most prominent gate.

Both the statue and the words it carried would come to represent the central symbol anchoring the myth of the United States as a "nation of immigrants" and as a country welcoming of immigrants and refugees. The National Park Service affirms the enduring impact of Lazarus's reframing of Lady Liberty, calling it the "immigrant's statue" and noting that it "has come to symbolize the statue's universal message of hope and freedom for immigrants coming to America and people seeking freedom around the world" ("Immigrant's Statue" 2015).

Given its location at the gates of New York and the role of the statue as a lighthouse in its early history, Bartholdi's statue thus inadvertently turned into an image of harbor, safety, and refuge that would become the core image of the United States as a hospitable nation. It endures to this day as a central figure, anchoring the myth of the United States as a welcoming nation. Significantly, the symbolism attached to the statue endures even though it belies the reality of U.S. immigration policy at the time that it was erected. The narratives surrounding the "open-immigration policy" of this period referenced the high regulatory hospitality that is often nostalgically evoked in narratives of a "nation of immigrants." They also, however, corresponded to a period in American history where incoming migration was strategically inclusive. Almost exclusively White, it left out all those who did not fit its aspired immigrant population.

Hospitality is always a fraught concept that acknowledges the powerlessness of the arriving guest. In this case, the hospitality of Lady Liberty obscured the injustice inflicted on Chinese immigrants, even as a narrative of open gates and hospitality was being cultivated. Reflecting on the meaning of the Statue of Liberty, Yasmin Khan wrote in 2015, "How we interpret the statue's meanings depends on our own personal history, along with the mood of the country at any given moment" (Khan 2015, 3). In the 1870s and 1880s, the nation's reputation was blossoming into one of vitality derived from its unique blend of people and its "open gates," in the words of President Cleveland at the unveiling ceremony. Thus, coupled with net population figures that obscured the racial divides plaguing the national public, the construction of a "colossus" at the gates of the nation's largest port of entry cultivated an image of the United States as a welcoming nation of immigrants and refugees despite the political realities of the time.

Ironically, as Lazarus's poem and the image of the female deity embodied the myth of the nation of immigrants, they both contained within them a critique of U.S. immigration restrictiveness and a vision of a potentially more inclusive immigration policy. History owes a large part of this critique to Lazarus, who gave Bartholdi's "lady liberty, enlightening the world" a radical position that she would occupy again and again.

Lazarus, who had until then "laid aside her diffidence as a Jewess" because of the "narrow spirit of hostility which still pervades Christian communities" ("Emma Lazarus" 1887), returned to her Jewish roots as inspiration for her poem dedicated to the statue. Lady Liberty suggested a figure who resisted efforts at transforming her into a mechanism to obscure injustice. For some, she emblematized a critical view of U.S. immigration policy restrictiveness. Consider for instance this cartoon from the exclusion era (fig. 3.8).

Illustrated by Thomas Nast in *Harper's Weekly* in 1871, "Columbia" (Lady Liberty) was shown protecting a desolate Chinese immigrant from an angry mob of armed protestors. In one view, the Nast illustration sympathized with the Chinese immigrant, shielding him from the Irish (center) and German (right) men depicted (Kennedy n.d.). Columbia, the "feminine symbol of the United States, was positioned in the foreground with a Chinese immigrant before a wall plastered with all of the negative descriptors used for Chinese immigrants in the press" (2018). Despite these negative stereotypes, Columbia was shown recognizing the Chinese man's true human nature and vulnerability as she laid one hand on the migrant's head in reassurance and had the other fisted as she glared at the advancing angry crowds. This image presented Columbia as a symbol of empathetic welcome and a reassurance of justice to which many continue to turn, using her as a tool of subversive critique of American immigration policy restriction.

The image of the Statue of Liberty resisted the various attempts by her engineers, funders, and builders to establish a monopoly over her hermeneutic meaning. Rather, her interpretation and reinterpretation allow the democratic creation of new narratives of not only herself but the ideals of the American nation, what America can and should stand for vis-à-vis its immigrant guests.

Conclusion

The 1882 Exclusion Act is argued by historians to have marked a turning point in U.S. immigration history, signaling the first time an "immigration law ever passed by the United States barring one specific group of people because of their race or nationality" (Gyory 1998, 4). Since the passage of the Exclusion Act, the law continues to appear in immigration policy history as a singular moment of racially based immigration exclusion. Indeed, no law ever passed before had ever barred entry to a group because of their race.

FIG. 3.8 "The Chinese Question—Hand's Off Gentlemen!" Thomas Nast, *Harper's Weekly*, February 18, 1871. Library of Congress.

Its historical treatment, however, belies two important populations that this analysis points toward. Exclusionary immigration policy, as I show in my discussion of hospitality, is not restricted to limits on entry into the United States. Rather, it extends to the equal treatment, legal ability to work, pathway to citizenship, and acknowledgment of legal rights of immigrants arriving in the nation. In this regard, the simplistic interpretation of the Chinese Exclusion Act in U.S. immigration history as a singular moment of racial discrimination in immigration policy neglects the exclusion of both Native Americans and African forced migrants from the immigration system entirely and the historicization of its realities.

The implications of this neglect should be clear. For many immigration historians, Daniels noticed, "the words European and immigrant were interchangeable" (2002, 238), while Chinese immigrants, African immigrants, Native Americans were instead designated as coolies, slaves, or inconvenient premodern tribes. In turn, that has permitted immigration history to continually paint injustices toward either Native Americans or African American immigrants as symptoms of indigeneity or slavery without reckoning with the racially discriminatory character of U.S. immigration hospitality. In addition, these distinctions have continued to deprive non-White immigrants of many of the rights and privileges granted to White immigrants, such as access to land and property, freedom, citizenship, and enfranchisement.

The Chinese Exclusion Act is often deemed an interruption, a brief intermission in American immigration history. This treatment has facilitated the compartmentalized approach that many Americans have toward immigration, which champions the large numbers of immigrants who were allowed to arrive and settle in the United States while treating excluded groups as exceptions at the peripheries of American immigration history. This approach has thus far obstructed a complete appraisal of how periods of intense restriction, such as the Chinese Exclusion Act, may illustrate important dynamics at play in American immigration hospitality and of how important factors that impact Americans' readiness to extend hospitality may be being obscured.

Most importantly, the Chinese Exclusion Act (and the media surrounding its legislation and maintenance) reveals how indigeneity, slavery, and Chinese immigration restriction can all be seen as responses to the racial limitations of American hospitality, which in the 1800s was unconditionally extended only to White, predominantly Protestant, European immigrants. The period also reveals the structural violence perpetrated by the American political economic system, which relied on an exploitative production process. As long as the dependence of American agriculture, industry, and manufacturing on cheap labor continues unabated, the consequences of these pressures on the labor market continue to influence anti-immigrant sentiment.

In later periods, historians of slavery tried, and failed, to bring a critical political economic lens to bear on the matter of slavery. For instance, *The Political Economy of Slavery* (Genovese 1989) was thoroughly disparaged in scholarly reviews at the time. In the *Journal of American History*, Joe G. Taylor found the work "disappointing" (1966, 120). In the *American Historical Review*, the reviewer Carl Degler disagreed with Genovese's political economic arguments and countered that these dynamics could be more readily explained by considering White solidarity (1966, 305). This rejection of a critical political economic perspective on the connections between slavery and immigration from a labor market perspective illustrated the debilitating limitations immigration scholars had set on the definition of the immigrant.

The siloed nature of debates about indigeneity, slavery, and immigration has also precluded scholarly comparisons between the African American and Native American slave trade, which in turn could potentially bring forth multiple critiques surrounding the dependence of American development on slave and cheap labor from its earliest history during the colonial era, as well as the need for European colonization to enslave and displace non-European communities. Indeed, slavery featured prominently in the colonial project that became the United States, as Christopher Columbus kidnapped and enslaved thousands of Native Americans to bring back to Europe and sell to European nobles and to entice the latter to migrate to the New World (Stannard 1993, 66–67). Such connections were made by Columbus himself when he wrote in his diaries that he applied lessons he learned abducting and transporting African slaves to his endeavors in the New World (Morison 1963, 93).

Media of the time in part reflected upon the connections between the Exclusion Act and the historical mistreatment of Africans who had been brought to the United States "against their will and domesticated during many years of residence" ("Negro and Chinaman" 1882). But even their uneven mention revealed the degree to which the issues of Chinese immigration and African American oppression are interconnected. Moreover, the discrimination against Chinese immigrants as "new slaves" and "coolies" and the other negative portrayals of low-income workers disguised racial oppression by blaming the victim rather than addressing the rapid industrialization and economic development in the country that not only increased the demand for labor but also artificially depressed wages by importing labor either through slavery or through the immigration of low-income workers from other countries.

In sum, the American economic system has been constructed over centuries with a dependence on cheap labor, whose needs economists eagerly announce can be satisfied via immigration. As a result, native labor has continued to articulate anti-immigrant stances in response to increased labor pressures brought about by immigration without acknowledging that the political economy of the United States continuously works to depress wages by immigration or any other means necessary. Revisiting Genovese in a 1995 review, historian James Oberly opined that "historians today may not accept Genovese's argument . . . , but they are far more likely [to] than they were in 1964" (Oberly 1995, 5). Indeed, elevating the economic imperatives and racial politics of labor markets back to the forefront of the discussion could pave the way for greater immigration hospitality vis-à-vis migrant workers.

The contradictions of the 1880s—a period when the American myth of a nation of immigrants was materially and symbolically cemented against a simultaneous period of unjust exclusion toward Chinese immigrants— address the reality of what Feagin regards as American immigration schizo- phrenia (Feagin 1997, 14). This chapter demonstrates how this myth prevailed in the face of media coverage of immigration policy closure and the passage of the racially discriminatory Chinese Exclusion Act. It testifies to the myth's moral force in American politics and media. From Emma Lazarus's words to Lady Liberty's light, this chapter illustrates the birth of a distinct image of the United States as a welcoming nation, one that embraced the world's poor exiles into its bosom, even as it categorically excluded the Chinese from its embrace.

4

The Rise of Nativism: National Origins Act (1920s)

• •

During my graduate studies at the University of Pennsylvania, I lamented the temporary closure of a famous Prohibition-themed bar—Hop Sing Laundromat. The hip bar's lavish interiors hid behind the facade of a faux-Chinese laundry. Discretely hidden inside was a speakeasy that nostalgically transported patrons to the golden age of flappers and moonshine, serving libations in a Prohibition-era-inspired venue. I regretted that the bar had closed its doors to patrons before I had had the chance to visit it, unaware as a recent immigrant at the time of the significance that a Prohibition-era bar posing as a Chinese laundry establishment would come to have for my future research on immigration. In fact, the bar successfully repackages the injustice toward Chinese immigrants in the exclusion era (symbolized by the Chinese Laundromat exterior) with that inflicted on southern and eastern European immigrants in the Prohibition era. The lavish Prohibition-era furnishings bypassed the restrictiveness into a commercial outlet enjoyed by tourists and immigrants in the 2000s.

Such anecdotes illustrate the continuities that define the history of American immigration hospitality. They also point to the outsized international impact connected to nostalgic reimaginations of a hedonistic 1920s in film and literature (Biesen 2016, 160), belying the immigration hostility that characterized this period. The international allure of the 1920s continues to attract global tourists almost a century later. The Lonely Planet tourism guide promises tourists that "they can live like it's the roaring twenties" to promote a self-guided tour of "Gatsby's best places" in New York (Collier 2021). Visitors and new immigrants in the United States are eager to attend Gatsby-inspired soirees upon arriving in the country, fueling a cottage industry of twenties-themed tourist festivals and New Year's Eve–themed galas.

The popularity of 1920s-themed cultural products to the global imaginary of the era does not surprise scholars; the decade was a period of artistic creation that provided seductive symbols of economic attainment associated with the "American Dream" (Pearson 1970). However, mediated reimaginations of the era are often written from the perspective of affluent citizen-protagonists, failing to capture the experience of non-English-speaking "new immigrants" of Italian, Polish, Greek, Russian, and other backgrounds during this period.

The realities of the 1920s leave little for immigrants to aspire to. For southern and eastern European immigrants to the United States, the 1920s represented an era of intense discrimination, where inhospitable policies and media rhetoric targeted the "new immigrant stock" arrivals to the United States (Rawlings 2016, 112). Consonant with the immigration policy and discourse of the previous period, a schizophrenic character pervaded American immigration: the 1920s was an era rife with the emergence and resurgence of violent anti-immigrant groups that particularly targeted eastern and southern European "new immigrants." These groups included the KKK, the American Eugenics Society, and the Immigration Restriction League.

This chapter focuses primarily on the history of restrictiveness and discrimination of the period, particularly as it confronted the influx of "new immigrant stock" from eastern and southern Europe. It foregrounds its analysis of the period by establishing the political, cultural, and social context of the time, paying particular attention to the emergence of eugenic and racial thought as well as the resurrection of the Ku Klux Klan, both of which would come to affect the environment for immigration discourse in media and policy circles. The chapter then turns to policies that encompassed immigration policy, the Prohibition movement, and other regulatory decisions during the 1920s that impacted the hospitality shown toward immigrant communities. Finally, the chapter considers the print media of the time, focusing on the three largest newspapers of the period: the *New York Times*, *Wall Street Journal*, and *Washington Post*. In so doing, it offers a narrative that exemplifies what Ronald Allen Goldberg called "the dark side of the twenties" (Goldberg 2003).

1920s in Context

Cultural and Demographic Tensions

By 1915, the United States was coming to terms with the World War I armistice and the transition to a peacetime economy following the war (Goldberg

2003, 1). During this time, the release of about two million servicemen from duty and the subsequent termination of several government war contracts resulted in a dramatic economic collapse in the spring of 1920 (Goldberg 2003, 3–4). By the late nineteenth century, immigrants represented less than 1 percent of the annual expansion of the national population (Zolberg 2006, 4), and the country had not only formulated a distinct "Anglo-American" culture, but it had developed a nativist movement led by earlier immigrants and aimed at combatting the arrival of new categories of immigrants into the United States (Higham 1988).

In the meantime, global immigration patterns were shifting, with non-Anglo-Saxon and non-English-speaking immigrants representing a growing share of immigration flows into the United States (Zolberg 2006, 4). As a result, much of American society became increasingly gripped by a nativist movement that classified immigrants as "new immigrant stock" and distinguished them from the primarily White, Protestant, English-speaking population resulting from prewar immigration. According to this narrative, old immigrants who came from the British Isles and northwestern Europe resembled the existing population of the American colonies and were thus relatively easy to assimilate. In contrast, the "new immigrants" of the 1880s onward were ethnically distinct, "spoke strange languages and worshipped strange gods," and were thereby less suitable for assimilating into the United States (Daniels 2002, 121). This movement portrayed new immigrants as threats to American democracy and its political institutions, justifying strong denunciations of unfettered immigration (Higham 1988).

Moreover, the 1920s witnessed a backlash against the restructuring of "whiteness" that had begun during the era of Chinese exclusion. If debates surrounding Chinese exclusion offered up Chinese immigrants as a foil against which Whiteness could be expansively reimagined, then the exclusion of Chinese immigrants created the conditions of retrenchment that culminated in an anti-immigrant movement targeting Irish, Italian, German, Polish and other ethnic white immigrants.

The author Henry James reflected this sentiment when he described Ellis Island in *The American Scene* (1907). James commended the liberal hospitality of the Ellis Island commissioner who helped introduce the author to the island but warned that immigration "is a drama that goes on, without a pause, day by day and year by year." He likened the scene he witnessed to that of a grotesque, "visible . . . ingurgitation on the part of our body politic and social, . . . beyond that of any sword-swallowing or fire-swallowing of the circus" (James 1907, 85).

Alongside immigration at the nation's seaports, the agricultural transformation of the greater southwest region attracted a significant rise in Mexican immigration on the country's southern border. Incoming immigration from the South was met with warnings from congressmen, university professors, and small farmers of the dangers of incoming Mexican immigrants. In the annals of the American Academy, Congressman James Slayden blamed large planters and industrialists for being too preoccupied with their cotton crops or railroads to consider the social costs of welcoming Mexican immigrants (1921, 121). Moreover, as Montejano observed, the Midwest and Rocky Mountain states were gripped with a form of "statistical terrorism," whereby Mexicans were argued to be genetically inferior to the Nordic race but also more sexually "fecund," as policymakers provided fabricated statistics of Mexican birth rates to substantiate claims of demographic takeover (Montejano 1999, 172). Thus, employers who encouraged incoming immigration in order to supply their economic activities with cheap labor were accused of corrupting the racial superiority and stability of the country by employing new immigrants. The arguments for curbing immigration because of the "social costs" of inferior and "sexually fecund" migrants call to mind the case Amy Wax makes in a later era for "low and slow" immigration because incoming immigrants lacked the work ethic and family planning to successfully contribute to the country (Hermann 2019).

The largest influx of immigrants of the time came primarily from a European wave of forced migration following World War I. In 1919, 430,000 refugees from Europe landed in the United States, and the number doubled in 1920 (Stephenson 1926, 178). This encouraged Congress to search for more methods to curb immigration into the country, positing that "the literacy test alone was not enough to prevent most potential immigrants from entering" ("Immigration Act of 1924" 2016). This restrictive push continued in spite of reports that refugees denied entry were repatriated to their countries and often to their deaths, a reality that could have been avoided had the United States welcomed those seeking refuge.

At the time, the United States had yet to stretch the administrative borders of immigration policy abroad, prompting countries to process and review immigrants in their countries of origin before arriving in the United States. However, the repatriation of immigrant arrivals regardless of their potential safety stifled the humanitarian potential of the American immigration processing system. The harsh fate of repatriated forced migrants was discussed in Congress, albeit rarely, and reported unevenly by the press. In figure 4.1, for example, the *New York Times* reported in 1921 that Armenians in search of refuge from genocide, starvation, and disease were being deported to their deaths, a reality that was relayed to Congress and publicized in the press by the Welfare Council, which advocated extensively in favor of foreign aid and the refugee resettlement of Armenians affected by forcible deportation, genocide, and oppression in the 1910s and 1920s (Watenpaugh 2010). This reality however did not sway government officials'

DEPORTED ARMENIANS SLAIN

Welfare Counsel Tells House Committee of Immigrants' Fate.

FIG. 4.1 *New York Times* headline, December 19, 1921.

intransigent stance against refugees, as they hoped that setting a precedent of deporting immigrants regardless of their potential safety in their countries of origin would deter future asylum seekers.

As immigration flows were shifting, the 1920s also brought about noticeable changes in immigration policy and administration. A historic rise in immigrant arrivals to 14.5 million immigrants between 1900 and 1920 motivated the creation of two immigration administrative bodies that would oversee the processing of new immigrants and collect information on immigrant arrivals, naturalization, and countries of origin: the Bureau of Immigration and the Bureau of Naturalization ("Records of the Immigration and Naturalization Service," 1995). The creation of these bodies enabled greater oversight over the number of immigrant arrivals and the conditions of their settlement in the United States.

Moreover, changes in patterns of immigration prompted a shift in the survey of immigration numbers by census officials. As a result, when immigration began to rise from its World War I stagnation in May 1920, reaching five thousand daily immigrant arrivals at Ellis Island (Higham 1988, 267), population statisticians were prepared for the influx. They had developed measures to capture a picture of the immigrant arrivals as well as document their native languages, ethnicities, and racial backgrounds. In this way, U.S. population statisticians were able to capture the rise in the foreign-born share of the population from 10 million in 1900 to 13.9 million in 1920. At the same time, they were also able to compare the changing geographical origins and ethnic makeups of these immigrants with the first available records of countries of origin. These measurements revealed a great transformation taking place in American immigration: new immigrant aliens were not Englishmen and Dutchmen but Italians, Poles, Russians, and Greeks; they were Catholics and Jews, and they were arriving in large numbers. Among the fourteen million immigrants arriving in the United States between 1901 and 1920, statisticians counted more than five million newly arrived Italian Catholics and Russian Jews (Tucker 1990, 7).

The shift in incoming immigration patterns in the United States mirrored the changes in global immigration patterns, suggesting a long-term and global move toward non-European and southern European immigrants representing a growing share of global immigration flows from the 1900s onward. European migrants, who had represented 85 percent of global migrant flows from the 1880s to 1920s (Castles 2000, 271), no longer represented the majority of global international migrants from the 1920s onward (Castles 2000, 271; Koser 2007).

The most striking shift in immigration in the United States was the shift within European immigration, as southern and eastern Europeans outnumbered western European immigrant arrivals. According to the statistics provided by the U.S. Census Bureau, the number of immigrants from northern and western Europe in the United States dropped from 7.2 million in 1900 to 6.2 million in 1920. Meanwhile, the number of immigrants from southern Europe more than doubled over the same time period, rising from just over 500,000 in the 1900 census to 1.9 million in 1920 (National Archives 2002).

The observation of these shifts was also accompanied by a rise in public suspicion and distrust of Eastern European political ideologies, notably communism and anarchism. As Goldberg observed, the 1920s saw a nation gripped by an unprecedented anti-Hun, anti-Bolshevik, anticommunist hysteria that became known as the "Red Scare" (Goldberg 2003, 9). The literature on the Red Scare illustrates how unsuspecting migrant workers organizing for workers' rights in an atmosphere of growing unemployment and job precarity after the war found themselves detained and deported under charges of being members in the Union of Russian Workers or similar political organizations (Murray 1955, 176). The Red Scare motivated fear of immigrants, particularly those of southern European and eastern European backgrounds, because they were perceived as sympathetic to communist and anarchist ideologies. Alongside the demographic shifts in immigration to the United States in the 1920s, the Red Scare and other concerns helped create an environment that was particularly hostile toward the immigrants arriving during the 1920s.

Eugenics and Racial Thought

One particular movement of the time—eugenics—fueled anti-immigrant sentiment. The shift in immigration demographics toward southern European and non-European immigrants, as well as the enhanced ability of census statisticians to capture changes in immigrants' countries of origin, revivified interest in eugenics and racial theory in the postwar era. Madison Grant's *The Passing of the Great Race*, published in 1916, scarcely received any attention upon its publication. Yet it "enjoyed a substantial vogue in the 1920s" (Higham 1988, 271), motivating its republication in 1918, 1920, and 1921.

Grant's pseudoscientific racial theories received marked interest abroad, influencing the emergence of National Socialist ideology in Germany and providing Nazi leaders with the first notion of blond, blue-eyed people as a *Herrenvolk*, or the master race (Grant 1916, 12). To that effect, Madison Grant received a letter in the early 1930s from Adolf Hitler thanking him for his book, which he considered his "bible" (Spiro 2009, xi). At the close of World War II, Dr. Karl Brandt cited the German translation of *The Passing of the Great Race* in his trial for crimes against humanity at Nuremburg. Ironically, the defense in *United States of America v. Karl Brandt et al.* forced the Nuremberg judges "to come to terms with the discomfiting irony that the Nazi doctor was tracing the roots of the Third Reich's eugenics program to a best-selling book by a recognized American scholar" (Spiro 2009, xi).

Indeed, the prevailing approach to "scientific" racism to this day is that eugenics and racial thought are distinctly un-American and inconsistent with American ideals. They are more readily associated with German National Socialism, a consensus that has perhaps hindered a reckoning with the roots of eugenics in the United States. And yet, Grant's work, which predates National Socialist ideology by nearly a decade, was published amid a rise in American White nationalism and met with approval in the United States of the 1920s (Higham 1988, 270). It was also published amid a furor of anti-German propaganda during the World War I effort (Spiro 2009, 161).

Instrumental in defining American racist thought (as well as responses to incoming migration flows) in the 1920s, Grant identified race, language, and nationality as three distinct categories. This logic would come to motivate a change in annual census instructions in later years, distinguishing between foreign-born citizens' reported place of birth and their "real" origin as per their spoken language and ethnic identity (National Archives 2002). It also drew greater attention to the origins of southern European and non-European immigrants arriving from northern European countries or their colonies. Grant was also credited with teaching "American people to recognize within the white race a three-tiered hierarchy of Mediterraneans, Alpines, and Nordics" (Higham 1988, 272). He emphasized that the pure White races displayed measurable physical characteristics, such as the size of their skull, hair color, eye color, and height, and that the intermixing of races produced "disharmonic combinations" such as tall brunettes or blond, brown-eyed people (Grant 1916, 12). Grant's ideology was accompanied by a strong antidemocratic and antiegalitarian rationale, positing instead that democracy was intended as a system of governance among Western races. If applied to a mixed-race society, it would lead to the rule of the lower races of immigrants. Grant also contended that slaves were necessary for the advancement of racial elites (Grant 1916, 5).

Grant's ideas afforded the author considerable professional success throughout the 1920s. In his biography of Madison Grant's life, historian Jonathan Spiro counted as many as thirty-five organizations where Grant had served as a board member, founder, or cofounder. Among them were the American

Eugenics Society, the New York Zoological Society, the American Geographical Society, and the American Museum of Natural History (Spiro 2009, 391). At the same time, his book received praise from prominent American political figures, including this response by Theodore Roosevelt in *Scribner's Magazine* (fig. 4.2), which says that the book demonstrated a "fearlessness in assailing

The Origin and Evolution of Life

By

Henry Fairfield Osborn

President of the American Museum of Natural History

From the latest discoveries Professor Osborn pictures the lifeless earth and presents a new conception of the origin and early evolution of living forms in terms of energy.

The wonderful and beautiful succession of life from its dawn to the time of the appearance of man is richly illustrated and philosophically interpreted.

"Rich in scholarship, discreet in argument, and engaging in manner. . . . A volume creditable in the highest degree to American scholarship."

—*New York Tribune.*

Illustrated. $3.00 net

Men of the Old Stone Age

THEIR ENVIRONMENT, LIFE, AND ART

By Henry Fairfield Osborn

The first full and authoritative presentation of what has been actually discovered up to the present time in regard to human prehistory.

". . . In this volume Professor Osborn has done a splendid service both for his chosen science and for the reading public. His work is at once a creative summary of the latest discoveries and a surprisingly human introduction to paleolithic man in his home."—*New York Times.*

Illustrated. Fifth printing. $5.00 net

The Passing of the Great Race

OR THE RACIAL BASIS OF EUROPEAN HISTORY

By Madison Grant

Chairman, New York Zoological Society

With a Foreword by HENRY FAIRFIELD OSBORN

The vast subject of the origin, relationship, evolution, migration, and expansion of European man is here considered in connection with the phenomena of the civilization of to-day.

"The book is a capital book; in purpose, in vision, in grasp of the facts our people most need to realize. It shows an extraordinary range of reading and a wide scholarship. It shows a habit of singular serious thought on the subject of most commanding importance. It shows a fine fearlessness in assailing the popular and mischievous sentimentalities and attractive and corroding falsehoods which few men dare assail. It is the work of an American scholar and gentleman; and all Americans should be sincerely grateful to you for writing it."

—THEODORE ROOSEVELT.

$2.00 net

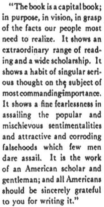

HENRY FAIRFIELD OSBORN

Mankind

RACIAL VALUES AND THE RACIAL PROSPECT

By Seth K. Humphrey

An untechnical view of racial influences in their broad social aspect, showing the fundamental part played in human affairs by inborn racial quality. Many diverse subjects, such as marriage, social work, immigration, and race mixtures, are discussed from the unusual viewpoint of race conservation. Chapters are devoted to the racial values in the nations at war and to the probability of English or German racial dominance after the war.

$1.50 net

CHARLES SCRIBNER'S SONS   FIFTH AVENUE, NEW YORK

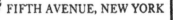

FIG. 4.2 Theodore Roosevelt's review of *The Passing of the Great Race*, *Scribner's Magazine*, 1917.

popular and mischievous sentimentalities" regarding evolution and migration. To that, he added that every American "should be sincerely grateful" for Grant's book (Roosevelt 1917).

From his various affiliations, Grant was well positioned to inspire a younger generation of historians, journalists, politicians, economists, and academics to publish similar racial thoughts. In 1920, Grant's disciple Lothrop Stoddard published *The Rising Tide of Color*, warning that the war between the primary races of mankind, which he called the "conflict of color," would become the greatest problem of the twentieth century and beyond (Stoddard 1920, 16). In a fiery introduction to Stoddard's book, Grant warned of nothing less than the end of civilization if "the great Nordic race" dwindled, stating that democracy was only acceptable among a homogenous population of Nordic blood. It was a different entity, he argued, for "the white man to share his blood with, or entrust his ideals to, brown, yellow, black or red men" (1920, xxxii).

The mushrooming of scholarly publications on eugenics did not take long to convert American universities to their cause. Whereas only 9 percent of American colleges and universities offered eugenics courses before *The Passing of the Great Race* was published, by the late 1920s, eugenics was being taught at 75 percent of American institutions, including Harvard, Columbia, Brown, Cornell, Northwestern, and the University of California (Spiro 2009, 168). A series of eugenics textbooks would bolster this trend, publishing readings that catered to these courses. One was *Applied Eugenics* (Popenoe and Johnson 1918), coauthored by a professor of eugenics at the University of Pittsburgh, whose professional title alone was a testament to the growing acceptance of eugenics as a legitimate research area.

Popular culture complemented the sweeping tide of eugenics and racial thought emerging in the nation's university halls, literature, films, and other artistic creations, impacting the conversation on immigration. This is due to the fact that cultural production in the United States was intricately tied to the creation and resurrection of civil society groups that would actively mobilize toward limiting immigration. Key here was the decision of Kentucky-born D. W. Griffith, the son of a Confederate soldier shot in the Civil War, to commit Thomas Dixon's novel *The Clansman* to the big screen in 1915, the fiftieth anniversary of the end of the Civil War. Seeing an opportunity to visualize the Civil War from the perspective of the antebellum South, Griffith's blockbuster production *Birth of a Nation* met widespread success, and it was broadly distributed, showing in working-class neighborhoods (Rogin 1985, 155), upscale theaters (Lenning 2004, 119), and even the White House before an audience of Supreme Court justices, congressmen, and senators. In fact, *Birth* captured so much public attention that the U.S. president requested a private White House viewing, which helped endow the film with "a political seal of approval" (Rogin 1985, 154).

Reflecting on the themes of the film, Eisenstein wrote that Griffith captured the "second side of America—America the traditional, the patriarchal, the provincial" (Eisenstein 1949, 147). However, most strikingly, the film portrayed cloaked Klansmen as "avenging spectral crusaders" riding in as heroic characters (Rogin 1985). In fact, White aggression was defanged because the director chose to overlook the violent ideology of the Klan and focus on the Herculean efforts the depiction of the Klan movement on-screen required. Rather than discuss the movement's ideals, Griffith bragged of the twenty-five thousand yards of white cloth stitched into uniforms for the production of the movie (Turner Classic Movies n.d.). Such statements transformed the KKK uniform, a symbol of White aggression and racial violence in the United States, into a harmless and even impressive feature of the film. At the same time, the creation of a Black antagonist named Silas Lynch was a deeply symbolic choice that transformed the act of lynching from a symbol of White aggression against Blacks to an indicator of a Black aggressor. In turn, this furthered Griffith's general portrayal of the submission of the White South under Black domination (Rogin 1985, 166).

The Ku Klux Klan and Other Majority Groups

Exploiting the release of this racist celluloid blockbuster and riding on a national wave of racism following the blockbuster's success (Gitlin 2009, 12), the once-defunct secret society of the Ku Klux Klan capitalized on the new-found popularity of racial thought, garnering new supporters (Streissguth 2009, 65). The Klan of the 1920s emerged as a formalized fraternal order that had to some extent abandoned the more violent tendencies of its roots. It was also more widely geographically distributed than its ancestor had been, attracting supporters in the North because of Northern resentment toward Black migration after emancipation (Gitlin 2009, 14).

By 1920, the organization had already amassed several thousand members (Streissguth 2009, 65). By 1923, this number rose to an estimated four million members nationwide as a result of the Klan's embrace of a savvy mass communications strategy and multipronged approach to publishing, marketing, and having interviews in major outlets (Gitlin 2009, 76). Scholars credit this media savvy with fueling the popularity of the group and particularly the role played by two media strategy experts: Edward Clarke and Elizabeth Tyler, founders of the Southern Publicity Association. The Southern Publicity Association had previously helped the Red Cross and Anti-Saloon League raise funds and was subsequently contracted to help promote the Klan (Gitlin 2009, 13). Media coverage, intended to warn the public of the dangers of the organization's rise to prominence, served the unintended purpose of boosting the group's popularity. Notably, the *New York World*'s ambitious two-week investigative exposé of the organization in September 1921—which uncovered 152 crimes, four murders, and forty-seven tar-and-featherings—inadvertently led to an increase in the KKK's ranks, as some readers saw the negative portrayal of the exposé as a prime example of big-city arrogance and condescension, as well as urban liberal bias against "ordinary people" (Gitlin 2009, 15).

The Klan's core tenets required members to accept the immigration restriction of "new immigrant stock" as an important goal for the organization and its members (Rawlings 2016, 112). This was reflected in an informal survey conducted by *Outlook* in 1924, which provided a rudimentary portrait of the agreement of members of the organization on immigration policy change. The survey found that more than 90 percent of Klansmen households responded that foreign immigration should be further restricted (Rawlings 2016, 214). The KKK dedicated many of its resources to this end, using the financial contributions of its swelling member base to position itself as a main donor and supporter of political candidates. The strategy paid off: in the 1922 off-year elections, seventy-five members of Congress owed the success of their campaigns to Klan support ("Hylan Asks Harding to Stop Klan Paper" 1922). Moreover, the Klan enhanced its influence by sending threatening letters to candidates that were unfavorable to the group as they ran for office in local elections or to judges and jurors in court cases against the organization ("Klan Letters Sent to Grand Jurors" 1922). In Oregon, the Klan was also instrumental in enforcing compulsory public education to prevent immigrants, Catholics, and other groups from seeking private schools that reflected their religious views or language differences ("What the Klan Did in the Oregon Elections" 1922). In conjunction with their role in supporting candidates, Klan leaders conducted regular visits to Washington to secure the interests of their organization among policymakers with meetings and lobbying efforts. Finally, the group emphasized its aims to pursue its agenda democratically through political lobbying and voting. At the same time, the matter-of-fact media coverage of the Klan's involvement and influence in local and national elections shrouded these activities in a veil of transparency and legitimacy.

The growing influence of the Ku Klux Klan, at a scale far beyond its progenitor, was accompanied by the establishment of several majority-group organizations that gradually shifted their focus from spreading racial theories to lobbying for discriminatory policy toward immigrant minorities. First, there were Grantian-inspired organizations that maintained that "the new immigration . . . contained a large and increasing number of the weak, the broken and the mentally crippled of all races drawn from the lowest stratum of the Mediterranean basin and the Balkans, together with the hordes of the wretched, submerged populations of the Polish ghettos" (Grant 1916, 88). Among these majority-group organizations were the American Eugenics Society and the Immigration Restriction League (IRL), which also counted Grant among its members. The Immigration Restriction League was

II.

OBJECTS.

The objects of this League shall be to advocate and work for the further judicious restriction or stricter regulation of immigration, to issue documents and circulars, solicit facts and information on that subject, hold public meetings, and to arouse public opinion to the necessity of a further exclusion of elements undesirable for citizenship or injurious to our national character. It is not an object of this League to advocate the exclusion of laborers or other immigrants of such character and standards as fit them to become citizens.

FIG. 4.3 The purpose of the Immigration Restriction League as stated in its constitution. Harvard University Archives.

established on May 31, 1894, by three Harvard graduates—geographer and climatologist Robert DeCourcy Ward and lawyers Charles Warren and Prescott Hall—in response to the "invasion" of the United States by "undesirable immigrants." The IRL was created with the purpose of advocating for "restriction and regulation of immigration" (fig. 4.3) by issuing documents and publishing advocacy research to "arouse public opinion to the necessity of further exclusion" (Immigration Restriction League 1893?).

To that end, the league would embrace the efforts of journalists, politicians, and philanthropists to further the exclusion cause. In a letter penned by the league's secretary Prescott Hall, interpersonal communication was intermingled with written correspondence to disseminate arguments, encouraging one philanthropist to support anti-immigrant legislation in Congress and discuss these matters with friends and any charitable or other organizations of which he was a member (Hall 1898). The arguments set forth in many of the circulars produced by the Immigration Restriction League echo the arguments previously made against Chinese immigration, which lead to the Chinese Exclusion Act in 1882.

Consider, for example, this statement from a circular delivered to citizens of New York in 1905: "The rushing into New York city of a foreign population that is fitted only for push cart and sweat shop work and garment making is creating alarm and making the situation intolerable" (Immigration Restriction League 1905, 2). This statement also recalled similar themes to those evoked by Samuel Gompers's famous essay "Meat vs. Rice: American Manhood against Asiatic Coolieism. Which Shall Survive?" (Gompers 1901), which presented Chinese immigration in the 1880s as an existential threat to White workers and White manhood because of the relative lower skill and pay of Chinese workers that endangered American labor and workers' rights.

The combined effect of the racial trends in popular culture and civil society on the horizons of the immigration debate was noticeable in Thomas Bailey Aldrich's poem "The Unguarded Gates," which vocalized the fears of many middle and lower middle-class Americans that the incoming immigration of inferior peoples was threatening the national demographic makeup. Describing immigration at the gates of the country, he wrote,

> Wide Open and unguarded stand our gates
> And through them passes a wild motley throng
> Men from the Volga and Tartar steppes
> Featureless figures from the Hoang-Ho
> Malayan, Scythian, Teuton, Kelt and Slav
> Flying the Old World's poverty and scorn
> These bringing with them unknown gods and rites
> Those tiger passions here to stretch their claws
> In street and alley what strange tongues are these
> Accents of menace in our ear
> Voices that once the Tower of Babel knew.
>
> —Aldrich 1982

Highly influential, this poem was discussed and shared by policymakers and influential public figures as a critique of the United States' immigration policy to that date. The poem represented the image of "open-gate" immigration[1] as a threateningly unguarded gate, soliciting the transgressions of immigrants from around the world. Moreover, the image of the guarded gate painted the immigrant as a criminal trespasser, even as he or she arrived within the framework of existing immigration regulations. Finally, the latter section of the poem presents the diversity of immigrant origins as a "wild motley throng," like a wildfire threatening to overwhelm the American national identity with "strange tongues" and "unknown gods." The menace of immigration, as shown by the poem, spelled the destruction of the United States, forebodingly likening the unfamiliar languages of immigrants to "voices the Tower of Babel knew."

These cultural and demographic tensions created a context that helped foster anti-immigrant sentiment directed at the "new immigrant stock" of southern and eastern European origin. Together and alone, they created fruitful conditions for the conversations that would take place on the floors of the House and Senate and in the leading newspapers of the country.

Regulatory Hospitality

The sentiments that arose from the cultural and demographic tensions of the 1920s were influential in informing the immigration policy debates from the 1920s onward. These debates drew heavily from the idea that "new immigrant stock" differed greatly from the "old immigrant stock" in character, cultural proximity to the "native" population, and assimilability. Thus, amid the convergence of nativist anti-immigrant sentiment across popular culture, academia, journalism, and several other spheres, immigration policy in the 1920s approached incoming immigrant arrivals as an alarming development that needed to be swiftly and decisively dealt with. Responding to reports that eight hundred thousand immigrants had entered the country in twelve months ("805,228 Immigrants" 1921), Congress was eager to discourage "undesirable" southern and eastern European immigrants.

Deportations, Raids, and Rights

One important factor influencing the legal context of the interwar period was the dramatic rise in deportations, as well as changes in U.S. policy that crafted extrajudicial hearings to assess deportation cases. Against the background of economic depression and the increased mechanization and unemployment that came with the close of World War I, deportations and raids became less objectionable as the nation became gripped by an unprecedented anti-Hun, anti-Bolshevik, anticommunist hysteria commonly known as the "Red Scare" (Goldberg 2003, 9). The anticommunist movement of the 1920s replicated several characteristics of the antianarchist movement of the early 1900s. When the self-proclaimed anarchist Leon Czolgosz fatally shot President William McKinley in 1901, his actions set in motion a wave of antianarchist sentiment and inspired the Immigration Act of 1903, which excluded "anarchists, or persons who believe in or advocate the overthrow by force or violence of the Government of the United States or of all government or of all forms of law, or the assassination of public officials" from immigration to the United States ("Act to Regulate the Immigration of Aliens" 1903). This Red Scare disproportionately affected southern and eastern European immigrants, or "new immigrant stock," because they were perceived to possess a greater affinity to Bolshevik and communist political thought (Kraut 2020, 38). At the time, a judge insisted that anarchists did not deserve constitutional protection, declaring, "It was said by a distinguished English judge, in the celebrated Somerset slave case, that 'No slave can breathe the free air of England.' It would be well if the laws of this country were such that it could be said truthfully that no anarchist can breathe the free air of America" (Kraut 2012, 176).

The Red Scare of the 1920s was equally fueled by several violent attacks occurring between 1918 and 1920, many of them associated with individuals of southern or eastern European lineage. The mail bomb attacks in the spring of 1919 were central, when thirty-six packages containing crude bombs were stamped as having come from the Gimbel Brothers department store and addressed to prominent businessmen, senators, and cabinet members (Ferrell

2006, 141). The bombing of the private home of Attorney General Mitchell Palmer on June 2, 1919, instigated the highly controversial Palmer deportations in 1920. Although the bomber in the latter case was found dead and dismembered as a result of the explosion, the incident led to four thousand arrests without cause of suspected anarchists and radical leftists across twenty-three states, many of them from eastern and southern Europe, as well as the deportation of 529 immigrants (Wilson 2012, 455). Then-assistant secretary of labor Louis Freeland Post later described the Palmer deportations as "a delirium" (Post 1923), stressing the negative consequences of suspicion toward immigrants on civil rights. Indeed, the Palmer deportations revealed the risk to which America's immigrant aliens were exposed, because immigrants were arrested and not given trials due to the lack of protection of non-citizens' rights under the Constitution.

It is worthy of note that the wave of deportations disproportionately affected immigrants from the "new stock" who were perceived to possess an affinity for communist thought. As Panunzio observed, of a sample of two hundred cases he could examine, 74 percent of the defendants were Russians, followed by Poles, Lithuanians, Austrians, and Croatians as well as a smattering of Italians, Yugoslavians, Bulgarians, and other eastern and southern European immigrants (1921, 17).

In this respect, the deportations of the 1920s realized the aspirations put forth by the judge in 1903 who had said that anarchists do not deserve constitutional protection (Kraut 2012, 176). The Immigration Act of October 18, 1918, amended the Immigration Act of 1903 by bolstering the ability to deport anarchists and communists as well as excluding them from immigration to the United States (Immigration Act 1918, Sections 1 and 2). The Act notably did not distinguish between members of anarchist organizations and the broader platforms of such organizations. Also, it placed the enforcement of such rules "upon the warrant of the Secretary of Labor" (Anarchistic Aliens Exclusion Act 1918, Section 2).

Moreover, being an administrative rather than criminal matter, the cases of immigrants would be heard by immigration officers who possessed neither knowledge of residents' rights by law nor experience dealing with groups of immigrants (Panunzio 1921, 15). As a result, in cases where a charge could not be substantiated, officers could simply create new charges under which they could deport immigrants, notably using the charge that immigrants were liable to "become public charges" upon their entry to the United States as grounds for deportation. As a result, many immigrants decided to leave the United States voluntarily after being questioned and held on high bail (Panunzio 1921, 45).

Attorney General A. Mitchell Palmer had been appointed by President Woodrow Wilson in 1917 as the alien property custodian, a position that entailed seizing the assets of suspected disloyal immigrants during the wartime mobilization of World War I. As such, Palmer's career had long represented the violation of immigrant rights that had preceded the Palmer raids. In spite of his advocacy on multiple civil rights issues, including women's suffrage and children's rights, Palmer exhibited the same disregard toward immigrant's rights in the 1920s that he had in 1917, as he rounded up and deported suspected anarchists. Defending the raids, Palmer wrote in *The Forum* in 1920, "Like a prairie-fire, the blaze of revolution was sweeping over every American institution of law and order a year ago. It was eating its way into the homes of the American workmen, its sharp tongues of revolutionary heat were licking the altars of the churches, leaping into the belfry of the school bell, crawling into the sacred corners of American homes, seeking to replace marriage vows with libertine laws, burning up the foundations of society" (Palmer 1920).

The essay, titled "The Case against the 'Reds,'" described individuals of immigrant background using dehumanizing terms denoting danger and disease. Its use of verbs and adjectives elicited connections with subhuman objects—including descriptions of anarchists "crawling" like insects or likening them to vermin and associating them with disease. Yet again, this pattern of medicalized nativism and hygiene-related Othering of immigrants recalls similar tropes that were used against Chinese immigrants in the 1800s.

The most extensive study at the time of the legal consequences of these deportations on immigrants was that of Panunzio, who conducted interviews with 168 alien prisoners held in three prisons across the country and followed their case proceedings with the permission of the Department of Labor (Panunzio 1921). His study concluded that several immigration policy decisions had created severely unjust circumstances for foreign-born residents in the United States. Firstly, the 1918 Immigration Act stipulated that "anarchists" as well as any aliens teaching or advocating for the overthrow of the United States government could not only be excluded from entry, as earlier immigration policy had ordered, but they could also be deported if already residing in the United States. The acts went further, placing the enforcement of decisions under the purview of the Department of Labor, making deportations an administrative matter that did not require criminal court hearings (Panunzio 1921, 13). Meanwhile, the role of the Department of Justice was restricted to gathering evidence that supported the charges of espionage or communism filed against the immigrant being reviewed. A century after Panunzio's study, Julia Rose Kraut reaffirmed the historical importance of deportation within U.S. immigration policy. She traced the roots of ideological exclusion and deportation in the United States from the Alien Friends Act of 1798 to the extreme vetting of the Trump administration, arguing that the history of U.S. immigration reveals a national identity shaped by the fear of dissent (2020, 9–11).

The Palmer deportations were just one example of the numerous deportations of immigrants that took place in the 1920s under the pretense of combatting anarchism, radicalism, communism, and other "isms" perceived to be political vices. In fact, suspicion toward immigrants reached such heights that journalist A. J. Liebling exclaimed that if an alien dropped a penny in the hat passed around by an unemployment council speaker or bought the *Daily Worker*, he would find himself deported (cited in Moloney 2012, 165). Distrust toward immigrants motivated new criteria for immigration processing, including a test of loyalty, character assessments, and statements of nonaffiliation in left-wing parties for eligibility of immigrants (Streissguth 2009, 69).

Prohibition

The Prohibition movement marked a policy change that transformed the social and political environment in ways that directly targeted immigrants. On January 16, 1919, the Constitution was modified to include the Eighteenth Amendment, which prohibited the manufacture and distribution of alcohol, a shift that would mark the beginning of the Prohibition era in the United States. The Prohibition movement represented a period of great injustice to immigrants, as it was coupled with a distinct anti-immigrant mobilization that connected the prohibition of alcohol to the restriction of immigrants and their way of life (Caves 2012). According to Higham, the constitutional amendment initiated a crusade by "drys" against foreigners who were associated with lawlessness, inebriation, and foreign interventionism (Higham 1988, 267). Concurrently, the prohibitionists associated immigration with moral corruption in the nation's largest cities, criticizing them as dens of vice and harbors of Catholic and Jewish immigrants while warning of the threat of spillover because of mass communication and transportation (Streissguth 2009 28).

The problem of alcoholism was often connected to the question of immigration in the 1910s, and prohibitionists saw their campaign as a solution to the "tide of problems brought ashore by immigrants from strange lands" (Streissguth 2009, 28). As Gusfield observed, the Prohibition movement represented a symbolic struggle between old immigrants and new immigrant arrivals from southern and eastern Europe (1962), who were perceived to be a demographic obstacle to a dry nation (Moore 2014, 525). It was no coincidence that most alcohol breweries were German-owned and operated. Drinking in the social contexts of saloons, taverns, and beer gardens was an integral part of the common immigrant experience of the time (Wasserman 1989, 886), and immigration laws during the Prohibition era reflected the suspicion that immigrants were often drunkards and alcoholics. For instance, the Immigration Act of 1917 introduced alcoholism into the list of characteristics that disqualified immigrants from being able to settle in the United States. The result was immigration policy that approached the immigrant as a suspected alcoholic and a risk to society, creating a connection between immigration and alcoholism that persisted beyond the retraction of the Eighteenth Amendment. Thus, the Prohibition era had a lasting effect on immigration policy, introducing drunkenness and alcoholism as disqualifying factors for immigration to the United States while cultivating a lasting connection between the issue of immigration with that of alcoholism and drug addiction by constructing the figure of the immigrant as that of a suspected alcoholic. Alcoholism would reappear in the 1952 Immigration Act, which banned naturalization to any "habitual drunkard" (Immigration Act 1952).

Moreover, Prohibition era politicians exhibited a contradictory relationship with mass communication. This contradictory relationship was exemplified in the position of Roy Haynes, who was appointed by President Warren Harding as commissioner of the Treasury Department's Prohibition Bureau. A former newspaperman, Haynes acknowledged the need to maintain positive relationships with journalists to create positive publicity about the Prohibition administration (Lee 2008, 276). Yet the former newspaperman saw the press as an instrument in the "carefully planned propaganda" by "wets" against Prohibition ("Denies Dry Law Failed" 1922). He also argued that a major impediment to Prohibition enforcement was apathetic citizens ("Denies Dry" 1922), who often jeered and booed as officials raided establishments where liquor was sold ("Sees Rum Raiders Gaining Sympathy" 1922).

Media and mass communication were also instrumental in constructing the imaginary geography of the "inner city" vis-à-vis neighboring towns and even rural areas. As such, the media contributed to the cultivation of an image of the inner city as "a grey, shabby, derelict, poverty-ridden fairytale land" (Burgess 1985). It validated views that the inner city was a morally corrupt place where criminality, drunkenness, and other vices threatened to infiltrate the stability of American society. Ironically, mass communication was viewed as the vehicle (along with transportation) through which the moral corruption of the inner city threatened to reach into the American home.[2] As John Durham Peters reflected in his essay "Satan and Savior," mass communication was treated during the 1900s as a vehicle that could "reconstruct, or further ruin, community life" by exposing it to the vastness of a larger society whose sheer scale and geographical spread precluded firsthand acquaintance of its dispersed members (Peters 1989, 250).

The arguments for Prohibition and immigration restriction often echoed one another. They borrowed from the lamentations of Madison Grant and the Immigration Restriction League regarding the concentration of immigrants in city "slums" in New York, Boston, and Philadelphia. Thus, the morning Prohibition went into force, famous evangelist Billy Sunday held a mock funeral over the body of John Barleycorn and declared, "The reign of tears is over. The slums will soon be only a memory. We will turn our prisons into factories and our jails into storehouses and corncribs. Men will walk upright now, women will smile, and the children will laugh. Hell will be forever for rent" ("Billy Sunday" 1920; "Thousands Hear" 1920). Sunday's declaration connected immigrants to criminality, immigrant slums, alcoholism, and all social ills.

In sum, Prohibition policies reflected a culmination of social anxieties regarding the rupture of community life in the face of mass communication, transportation, and the increasing urbanization of the United States. Together, these anxieties were applied toward enacting policies that shrunk immigration hospitality in the United States by attacking immigrants' livelihoods and lifestyles.

A Duo of Immigration Acts

The influence of these anti-immigrant cultural movements and the burgeoning role of majority-group organizations would reach its apex in the fall of 1920, when Senator Albert Johnson (R-Wash.), the chairman of the House Committee on Immigration and Naturalization with whom eugenicist Madison Grant had been cultivating a friendship for several years, invited Grant to the nation's capital to draft emergency legislation limiting immigration arrivals. The result was a bill that "loudly proclaimed to the world [U.S.] determination to cease being a nation of immigrants" (Zolberg 2006, 243).

The Emergency Immigration Act (officially referred to as the Act to Limit the Immigration of Aliens) of 1921 put in place a quota system that would temporarily limit the number of immigrants from any European country to 3 percent of the total number of immigrants from that country according to the 1910 census. This promised to reduce immigrant arrivals to 355,000 as well as dramatically reduce the share of immigrants coming from eastern and southern Europe (Johnson 1921). To limit immigration from Africa and Asia, Congress excluded African Americans, who composed 9 percent of the American population at the time, from the quotas as well as Asian immigrants, since they were "ineligible for citizenship" (Ngai 1999, 72). Moreover, the act considered nation of origin to be place of birth, while excluding any colonies or territories of a country, in order to yet again limit the immigration of Asian or African immigrants. In excluding these two groups, the resulting calculus gave 85 percent of the annual quota to northern and western European immigrants (67). Grant rejoiced after the passage of the bill, stating that it would favor Nordic immigrants over "Jewish tailors and Greek banana vendors" (Grant 2016).

The debates in the chambers of Congress revealed many of the tensions at the heart of U.S. immigration policy hospitality. On the one hand, Meyer London, a Socialist congressman from New York who had become famous for being the only vote against the Espionage Act of 1918 that made it illegal to criticize the president, stated on the floor of the House of Representatives that "to prevent immigration means to cripple the United States" because the "most developed industrial States are those which have the largest immigration." To emphasize this link further, he added, "The extraordinary and unprecedented growth of the United States is as much a cause as the effect of immigration" (66th Cong., 59 Cong. Rec., 2d Sess. [1918]).

The most poignant criticism that London leveled at proponents of immigration restriction addressed the fallacy of "old" and "new" immigrants at the heart of the debate. He stated, "Defenders of this bill thoughtlessly repeat the exploded theory that there have been two periods of immigration, the good period, which the chairman of the committee fixes up to the year 1900, and the bad period since. The strange thing about it is that at no time in history has any country made such rapid progress in industry, in science, and in the sphere of local legislation as this country has shown since 1900. The new immigration is neither different nor worse, and besides that, identically the same arguments were used against the old immigration" (66th Cong., 59 Cong. Rec., 2d Sess. [1918]).

Similarly, Frederick Rowe from New York stressed that "we need laboring men and women of certain-classes . . . not because we have not plenty of men in this country." Instead, he argued, "people of the second generation in this country will not carry a hod or dig a trench" (66th Cong., 59 Cong. Rec., 2d Sess. [1918]).

However, proponents of the immigration restriction bill continued to stress that although the "time once was when [the U.S.] welcomed the oppressed and down-trodden people from all the world . . . that time has passed" because we "must protect ourselves from the poisonous influences that are threatening the very foundation of Europe" (66th Cong., 59 Cong. Rec., 2d Sess. [1918]). The debate surrounding immigration reform in Congress entertained arguments for and against immigration from both political parties, albeit immigration restriction received widespread approval in both houses, passing by a majority and receiving only one dissenting vote in the Senate in 1921 (Stephenson 1926, 180). Lucien Walton, a Democrat representative, instead demanded that "we . . . stop immigration entirely until such a time as we can amend our immigration laws and so write them that hereafter no one shall be admitted except he be in full sympathy with our Constitution and laws, willing to declare himself obedient to our flag, and willing to release himself from any obligations he may owe to the flag of the country from which he came" (66th Cong., 59 Cong. Rec., 2d Sess. [1918]).

It is important at this juncture to take pause and note the continuities in American immigration hostility from one period to the next, and thereby acknowledge the lasting threats to immigration hospitality. Lucien Walton's call to suspend all immigration until the political positions of incomers could be vetted foreshadows President Donald Trump's rationale for creating the Muslim travel ban as "a total and complete shutdown of Muslims entering the United States until our country's representatives can figure out what is going on" (Taylor 2015).

Ultimately, the 1921 Emergency Immigration Act enforced quotas that succeeded at limiting eastern and southern European immigrant numbers: Italian immigration fell to 7 percent of its prequota level. Similarly, the number of Polish immigrants, who were often Jewish, fell from 21,076 to 5,156 (Kohler 1924a). In conjunction with the quota system, the Department of State took charge of the enforcement of immigration regulations, putting in place a remote-control system that allowed immigrants to be processed before they arrived in the United States. The new system thus transferred processing that once took place at ports of entry to processing centers in countries of origin, and it discouraged immigration by placing accompanying restrictions on arrival, including a number of highly selective eligibility criteria, and placing the burden of proof on immigrants (Zolberg 2006, 244).

By 1924, several senators had put forth plans to make the Emergency Immigration Act permanent, restricting immigration by country of origin further and introducing new requirements to the process. Representative Albert Johnson, chairman of the House Committee on Immigration, proposed a bill that would make the provisional effect of the Emergency Immigration Act permanent. The Johnson Bill cemented immigration quotas by country of origin, and it would become known afterward as the 1924 Immigration Act.

Superficially, the 1924 Immigration Act was intended to limit immigration in general. However, the policy represented a form of discrimination because it mandated skewed quotas, favoring immigrants from northern European countries who were present in high numbers prior to 1890, and thus would receive higher annual quotas for new arrivals. The 1924 Immigration Act also restricted the naturalization of Chinese, Japanese, and other Asian immigrants as well as Hindus. Even as the Exclusion Act remained in place and a gentleman's agreement with Japan limited Japanese immigration, the addition of Asian countries of origin to this bill consolidated other restrictive measures into the United States' universal policy governing all immigration. In addition, the act restricted immigration to any category that was ineligible for citizenship, as the 1921 Emergency Act had done. As a result, immigration from Asia was entirely halted.

The Immigration Act of 1924 regulated all immigrant arrivals, limiting them to 2 percent of the total number of immigrants from that country according to the 1910 census. The act also included a provision excluding unmarried children or wives of citizens of the United States from the national origins quotas (Immigration Act 1924). In 1925, Albert Johnson introduced an amendment to the bill removing the exception placed on "wives and minor children of citizens" if the citizen did not reside in the United States ("Bill to

Amend the Immigration Act of 1924" 1925). Since the 1924 Immigration Act remained in place for three decades, this move would extend and formalize racially motivated immigration restriction for several decades.

The 1924 act was also accompanied by a general agreement among politicians and academics regarding the superiority and thus higher desirability of northern European immigrants. In a report issued by the Committee on Selective Immigration by the Eugenics Committee of the United States, it was argued that "there were fewer Southeastern Europeans in 1890 than in 1910," thus using the figures of the 1890s census that would most effectively curb the wave of new immigration ("1890 Census Urged as Immigrant Base" 1924). If the conclusions of the Eugenics Committee seemed tangential to the passage of the law, it is worthy to note that Albert Johnson, also chairman of the House Committee on Immigration and the drafter of the 1924 Immigration Act, was also a member of the Eugenics Committee (Kohler 1924b).

In sum, the Immigration Act of 1924 enforced quotas on the number of immigrants allowed from each country with the aim of restricting immigration from southern and eastern Europe. At the same time, the measure excluded countries in the Western hemisphere, such as Canada and Mexico.[3] In parallel, it provided higher immigration quotas to immigrants from northern European backgrounds, who benefited from high immigration quotas because of the high numbers of their compatriots in the United States prior to 1890.

It is worth noting that many individuals protested the policy as discriminatory. Former district attorney Max Kohler pointed out in the *New York Times* that the policy discriminated against incoming immigrants who were not part of the old immigrant stock, arguing that it targeted "chiefly Catholics and Jews" (Kohler 1924a). In fact, after leaving the New York district attorney position to become a partner in the law firm Lewinson, Kohler, and Schattman, Kohler continued to take pro bono immigration cases for twenty-five years, helping immigrants of various ethnicities and supporting the work of the Hebrew Immigrant Aid Society (HIAS). As memorialized in the Center for Jewish History's Max Kohler papers, "Kohler's conviction that the United States was founded as a 'haven of refuge' for the oppressed of all countries" motivated his activism against alien registration and deportation, immigration restriction, and religious discrimination in immigrant admissions ("Max James Kohler Papers" 1888–1935). Similarly, rabbis protested the act's discriminatory nature, particularly as Palestine's annual quota was limited to one immigrant. This sentiment was echoed in contemporary reflections on the impact of the act on Jewish demographics in the United States, as Rabbi Waxman stated in 2016 that the 1924 act eliminated "America as a refuge for Europe's Jews" (Young 2017). Similarly, the Black press criticized the immigration restriction of the 1920s, noting that arguments for immigration restriction "also came from enemies of the race" who were preoccupied with limiting the immigration of Eastern European Jews to the United States ("Italy Feels Hard Hit by Immigration Bill" 1924, 116). Representatives of foreign countries also added to the debate. The Italian foreign minister argued in the press that the restriction of the Italian immigrant quota to eight thousand annually represented a dramatic decrease from the forty-two thousand Italian immigrant arrivals in the United States the year before, arguing that the policy amounted to "discrimination against Italians" ("Italy Feels Hard Hit by Immigration Bill" 1924). Likewise, the Japanese ambassador Hanihara wrote in the *New York Times* that the passage of the 1924 act would be a violation of the gentleman's agreement between Japan and the United States. In the aftermath of the quotas enforcement, the annual limits to immigration were often rapidly exhausted by June ("Japanese Protest the Immigration Bill" 1924). Moreover, the universal maximum of 339,381 total immigrants was filled before the end of the year ("Immigration Today" 1924).

However, the critiques of 1920s immigration policies were ineffective because they emanated from the exact immigrant groups that were deemed "undesirable" by policymakers—largely those from eastern and central Europe. These critiques failed to resonate with most White, Protestant Americans from earlier generations of immigrants, who had firmly fallen into the grip of nativist and anti-immigrant sentiments. The inefficacy of the critiques put forth by foreign dignitaries highlights the inadequacy of current regimes of immigration that place immigrants and some allies at the forefront of the struggle for equal recognition and rights, as the response to Max Kohler's writing demonstrates. These critiques also reveal the importance of hospitality as a framework and the moral responsibility of the host population to contest anti-immigrant policy and extend welcome to newcomers.

The 1921 and 1924 acts are significant to the study of U.S. immigration policy for two reasons. Firstly, the 1924 act identifies the first instance of American restrictionism that was tied to countries of origin. The 1924 Immigration Act equally denied entry to "any alien who by virtue of race or nationality was ineligible for citizenship" (Office of the Historian 2017). As such, it represented the first implementation of a quota system to limit immigration according to country of origin that contained a number of "undesirable" countries in its scope. While the 1921 Emergency Immigration Act was intended as a temporary measure for one year, it remained in place until 1924, when it was made permanent.

However, as this discussion illustrates, immigration policy during the 1920s did not represent the only means by which a lack of regulatory hospitality manifested during this era. When one considers the growing political influence and lobbying power of majority-group organizations, such as the

Immigration Restriction League or the KKK, it is clear that the growing power of these groups represented a regulatory system that was hostile toward immigrants from "new immigrant stock," particularly those of eastern or southern European origin. The connections between the eugenics and anti-immigrant movement and the inhospitable immigration policies drafted in this era are particularly evident given the intersection between these groups' members and the selected politicians and members of the public who were invited to draft immigration laws proposed in Congress. Additionally, the passage of Prohibition policies during this same period demonstrates an example of regulatory hospitality that targeted immigrant lifestyles and livelihoods rather than simply immigration policies.

Media Hospitality

Media coverage of immigration in the 1920s echoed the restrictive climate set up in the regulatory, cultural, and demographic spheres of public life, with public opinion on incoming immigration so negative in the 1920s that George Stephenson characterized it as "hysterical" (Stephenson 1926, 172). It is perhaps no surprise that it was sensationalist in nature. Editorialists pointed to the high incidence of criminality among the immigrant population and warned readers of the radical political leanings of newcomers (172). Moreover, the coverage of immigrant arrivals from eastern and southern European countries in 1921 often focused on the diseases and alcoholic tendencies that "new immigrants" were introducing into the American body politic.

The news coverage of the 1920s reinforced anxieties in public opinion about outsiders and connected them directly to the question of immigration. In attributing the ills of society to immigration, press coverage emphasized a connection between immigrants and criminality, inebriation, disease, radical political ideology, and threats to national political, social and institutional stability. Through these themes, media coverage reinforced and justified legal discrimination against immigrants, particularly those from eastern and southern European countries.

Dominant Media Tropes

Media coverage of immigration in the 1920s was dominated by four tropes: The immigrant "wets" trope characterized immigrants as predisposed to drunkenness and violence. Medicalized nativism presented eastern and southern European immigrants as vectors of deadly diseases. Other articles emphasized the genetic inferiority of eastern and southern European immigrants vis-à-vis "old immigrant stock" of Anglo-Saxon heritage. And finally, the trope of the security threat emphasized that immigrants were predisposed to radical ideologies that threatened the security of the nation.

This section illustrates these dominant themes of media coverage across the largest publications in the nation—the *New York Times*, *Wall Street Journal*, and *Washington Post*. The section also addresses their expression of media hospitality, or inhospitality, toward immigrant arrivals.

Inebriation and Immigrant "Wets"

A common theme in 1920s media coverage of immigration linked inebriation, alcoholism, and criminality with immigrants. An article by the Board of Temperance Prohibition and Morals of the Methodist Church published in the *New York Times* argued in 1924 that foreigners were bootleggers who "should be sent where they belong" ("Ask Drastic Change" 1924, 2). Such statements did not simply attach the crimes of selling alcohol to foreigners; they also called into question the belonging of immigrants to the United States by stating that they should be sent elsewhere.

Waves of new immigrants from southern and eastern Europe, particularly Catholics and Jews, were considered a threat to the "Protestant way of life" in the public consciousness because of their propensity to drink alcohol (Rathod 2013, 803). For example, German immigrants were vilified for their consumption and production of beer (Welskopp 2013, 32). Prominent figures in the temperance movement mobilized against Catholic Irish immigrants and warned against racial mixing, for fear of introducing their "hard drinking and immoral ways" into the American body politic (Rathod 2013, 804). Meanwhile, Italian immigrants were stereotyped as criminals and distrusted because of their expertise in winemaking (Baughman 2006, 385). These perceptions were reinforced by the fact that most saloons were immigrant-owned and frequented by immigrant patrons (Behr 2006, 50).

Coverage focused on the illicit materials and stowaways hidden in the luggage of immigrants arriving in the United States as well as the vessels carrying them. On October 15, 1921, customs inspectors reported finding fifteen Chinese immigrants hidden in various spots across a vessel arriving in Brooklyn, New York City ("Seek Drugs and Find Chinese Stowaways" 1921). The connection between these border crossings and alcoholism was made explicit in a *Washington Post* article, which stated that the "border 'bootlegging' of aliens is highly organized," thereby associating the process of producing and smuggling alcohol (an illegal substance during Prohibition) with the transportation of immigrants ("Immigration Today" 1924). Other articles connected the legal border crossings of immigrants to the threat of dangerous ideals or substances being brought to the United States. For example, though the immigration of citizens from the contiguous countries of Canada and Mexico was considered legal, it was nevertheless characterized as highly dangerous because the crossings were being used as the "bases of operation" for smuggling illegal aliens, narcotics, and illicit alcohol ("Problems of Immigration" 1924).

The discursive connection between a proclivity to drinking among immigrants and the threat they posed to society had a number of effects. First, the proclivity of immigrants to drinking was framed as a factor in the inevitable criminality of immigrants, as they were portrayed as culturally inclined to producing and consuming illicit substances. Second, portrayals of immigrant drinking often connected these stereotypes with those of the relatively inferior intelligence of "new immigrant stock," suggesting that the addition of alcohol exacerbates already-existent biological limitations on immigrants' cognitive abilities.

Medicalized Nativism

Media coverage of the 1920s also exhibited what Young has called "medicalized nativism," which justified a fear of immigrants bringing disease and degenerate genetic material into the American body politic. This provided the impetus for immigration restriction due to various illnesses brought ashore by immigrant arrivals (Young 2017, 223). In line with the medicalized nativism that characterized critiques of Chinese immigration, coverage focused on the threat of encroaching disease arriving with incoming immigrants, suggesting that new arrivals would reverse decades of work by the health department to eradicate disease. The *New York Times* warned elsewhere that authorities were struggling to contain the typhus, lice, vermin, and other ills brought with incoming immigrants at ports of entry ("141 Infested Aliens" 1921).

Newspapers also regularly reported updates on the number of cases of ill immigrants ("Cabin Passenger Brings Typhus to the City" 1921), warning that immigrants allow "disease against which the health authorities have set up many barriers" to "invade the city" (1921). Much coverage of the time reinforced fear of disease, arguing that isolated incidents reported by the media only represented a small minority of existing cases of diseased immigrants, since many "diseased immigrant arrivals" were assumed to pass undetected and unquarantined at the border. An opinion piece published in 1921 considered the ramifications of immigrant arrivals, asking "how many have slipped through who are in the early stages of typhus and bring with them the carrier louse can only be conjectured" ("Typhus Menace" 1921). On those grounds, another article published on February 1921 suggested that 9,799 of the 10,002 immigrants admitted over the span of six months in 1920 should not have been admitted because they suffered from contagious diseases, citing the testimony of Surgeon General Cumming before the House Immigration Committee in Congress ("Charges" 1921).

Recognizing that reports of immigrants being barred from entry were bad for the morale of public health officials and Ellis Island employees ("Charges" 1921), Ellis Island officials released the following statement in the *New York Times*, blaming migrants for their own troubles: "It is not Uncle Sam that is separating families, but the families that are separating themselves." This was due to the fact that, according to these officials, "in the majority of cases in which one member of the family is refused admittance the conditions that cause of the refusal are . . . evident . . . before [immigrants] sailed from the other side." This suggested that immigrants took the risk of travel in the hope that "they might affect the entrance of the person likely to be barred" ("Blame Migrants for Own Hardships" 1923).

The connection between immigration and illness was further supported by testimonies from health officials advocating for a complete ban on immigration until a number of diseases could be eradicated at countries of origin ("39 Typhus Cases" 1921). This included a statement by the Health Commissioner that "drastic measures [must] be inaugurated at once to prevent the plague from getting a foothold" (1921). The following month, the *New York Times* quoted the health commissioner, saying that "it is neither safe nor decent to permit filthy newcomers to get within the city lines" ("New Plea to Wilson" 1921). Finally, the threat of disease became connected to a portrayal of immigrants as threats that drained the federal budget. One public official demanded seventeen million dollars to cover the unpaid medical expenses of infected immigrants then being treated in U.S. hospitals ("Smith Seeks" 1924).

Disease was also linked with Bolshevism, echoing the "Red Scare" of the time. When the *New York Times* warned of twenty thousand Bolshevist propagandists trying to enter the United States, it connected their efforts to avoid visa restrictions with "efforts to avoid the quarantine restrictions against typhus, smallpox, and cholera" ("Seek to Keep Out Reds and Disease" 1920). The inference was clear: Bolshevism, like all other global epidemics, would come to the United States via immigrants. Thus, the dominant tropes in media coverage that provided a negative portrayal of immigrants reified one another by connecting immigrants to concerns regarding inebriation, lowered intelligence, communism, and many other societal problems, broadening public fear.

Inferior Genes

Media coverage also pondered the effect of the "wholesale importation of a low-grade people" leading to a drop in the country's intelligence ("Congress to Tighten Immigration Curb" 1924). Coverage underscored the "need to select immigrants" due to the inferior intelligence of the new immigrant stock, often bolstered by a proclivity to alcoholism (Hoffman 1924). Projection of this racial and classicist animus toward the mental capacity of immigrants, calling both control over mental faculties and capacity for learning into question, rested on an argument about biologically and genetically determined limitations to immigrants' mental capacity. By doubting their ability to learn the languages and skills needed to integrate into American society, these discussions contributed to the nature versus nurture debate at the core of U.S. immigration policy.

A stream of articles emphasized the disease-like invasion of inferior genetics into American society, threatening the existing genetic makeup of the American public. The *New York Times* relied on the "expert opinions" of eugenicists in an article titled "Eugenists Dread Tainted Aliens." The article advocated reform in immigration policy with the inflammatory statement, "Severe restriction of immigration is essential to prevent the deterioration of American civilization." It then proceeded to conduct interviews with prominent eugenicists who argued that "the melting pot is a fallacy" because it convinced Americans that a "poor stock" of immigrants could overcome its biologically determined inferiority with the help of improved education and health care in the United States ("Eugenists Dread Tainted Aliens" 1921).

Contributing again to the nature versus nurture debates at the center of American immigration hospitality, immigration was seen as favorable so long as immigrants could integrate into society. The diminished ability of immigrants to integrate for biological reasons was therefore instrumental to steering public opinion against immigration. Such articles thus argued that racial mixing and immigration were deteriorating the quality of the "good stock" of Americans of Nordic descent ("Eugenists Dread Tainted Aliens" 1921). This focus resulted in expressions of public concern over the racial mixing of English and "Nordic" immigrants, who had arrived in earlier waves of immigration, with the southern and eastern European immigrants, who arrived in the early twentieth century (Rathod 2013, 508).

Indeed, the early twentieth century witnessed discrimination against new immigrants who were perceived to be racially inferior and less White than their Anglo-Saxon counterparts (Barrett and Roediger 1997, 37). New immigrants who arrived to provide cheap labor were described with an array of slurs that often were used interchangeably for African Americans—including guineas, hunkys, and negroes—reflecting inferior positions in the American racial hierarchy. As the Irish American immigration historian Quinn told *Time* in an interview, "when people talked about intermarriage [. . .], they weren't talking about black-white, they were talking about Irish-Italian," Catholic-Protestant, and Anglo-Saxon-Celtic marriages (Quinn as quoted in Begley 2015), echoing Grant's argument that they contributed to the "racial mongrelization" of the "Nordic race" (1916).

The centrality of inferior genes to coverage of the racial logic of the 1924 immigration policy can be summarized in an article titled "Like-Minded or Well-Born?" published in the *New York Times* in 1924. Reflecting on the veracity of the "science and art" of eugenics underlying the Immigration Act, the article remarked on eugenics' belief in the birth of superior and inferior races and men, which had led the Eugenics Committee of the United States to endorse the 1924 bill. In its reporting, the article reified the legitimacy of eugenicists arguments that immigrants and particularly visible minorities possess inferior biologically defined mental, physical, and moral capacities ("Like-Minded" 1924).

Security Threat

A fourth strain of media coverage of immigration was the specter of the security threat presented by immigrants, a threat seen as undermining the stability of the United States' political institutions and social fabric. In November 1920, the *Wall Street Journal* reported a speech by the chairman of the House Committee on Immigration, Albert Johnson, in which he stated that the "United States cannot become an asylum for the broken nations of the world. Europe is bending every effort to pour her restless hordes within our borders by hundreds of thousands." Johnson's solution was to "either suspend immigration or quadruple the inspection service" ("America No Asylum" 1920).

The tone of Johnson's speech permeated coverage of immigration over the years that followed, as newspapers presented the issue of immigration as a threat to the security of the United States and its population. Immigration officials were invited by the press to discuss the pernicious effects of immigrants. One article penned by the commissioner of immigration at Ellis Island in the *New York Times* warned that the country was "dangerously near being discordant, disunited and divided against itself," because the United States had too many "foreign colonies, foreign loves and foreign points of view" as a result of its open-gate policy over the past several decades ("Curb Immigration to Save the Nation" 1924).[4] Thus, the diversity of thought, ethnic origin, religion, and language brought about by immigration was argued to threaten national cohesion and democracy in the country.

Media coverage appeared to converge toward one conclusion: open immigration was an ideal that threatened the health, security, cultural and political cohesion and democracy of the United States. By that logic, immigration restriction was necessary, it argued, to limit the threats it posed to society. This view was emblematized in a *New York Times* article from 1921 that quoted a scholar who said, "Either we can never become a homogenous American people, either unassimilated masses of European nationalities must share our domain with us, or we must set limits to the tide of immigration so that a unified national life and consciousness shall remain possible" ("Melting Pot Fails" 1921). Similarly, the *Wall Street Journal* conceded that immigration restriction was necessary, drawing on the opinions of policymakers and experts. It quoted members of the Chamber of Commerce reaffirming the need for selective immigration to address the immigration problem ("Chamber of Commerce Meeting" 1922). Because the 1921 Emergency Immigration Act was due to lapse on June 30, 1924, with no permanent immigration restriction policy in place, newspaper coverage emphasized the importance of reinstating existing immigration restriction. In that vein, the *Washington Post* expressed an urgency in advocating for immigration restriction: "Has Congress failed to realize the momentous importance of the immigration problem? Having eyes, does it not see the looming specter of an unrestricted immigrant horde that is hungrily looking in across the expiring date of the present law? Does it ignore the insistent demands of the nation's best interest for the placement of barriers against the ever-pressing flood of aliens to take the place of those that will automatically collapse on June 30?" ("Speed Immigration Legislation" 1924). Other coverage similarly urged Congress to enact new legislation, such as a *Washington Post* article in April 1924 that stated, "The country does not deserve to suffer from the procrastination of Congress in the matter of suitable immigration legislation" ("Problems of Immigration" 1924).

By 1924, the commissioner on immigration announced in the *New York Times* that "the day of open door for all oppressed peoples is past" ("Expects Our Curb on Aliens to Stay" 1924). His statement concluded the debate over immigration policy in favor of restriction. All of this coverage urging Congress to act on the issue of immigration relied on the logic that immigration posed a legitimate and substantial threat to political institutions, democratic governance, and social cohesion in the country, and it threated to topple the delicate political balance if left unchecked.

Once the 1924 Immigration Act was passed, limiting immigration from 1924 onward, coverage turned to government officials who were supportive of the act as expert sources. The editorial choices of the *New York Times* and *Washington Post* privileged the perspectives of experts and spokespersons whose positions and titles predisposed them to favorable views of the law. One article published on January 13, 1924, in the *New York Times* stated that the commissioner general of immigration met applause as he declared the era of the immigrant over and the era of "America First" begun ("Expects Our Curb on Aliens to Stay" 1924).

In this article (fig. 4.4), the commissioner general of immigration declared that the future of American immigration policy would no longer be designed to benefit the immigrant but to put "America First." Moreover, the article suggested a widespread acceptance and popularity of immigration restriction policies ("Expects Our Curb on Aliens to Stay" 1924).

It is worth noting that the *Wall Street Journal* advocated for and cited employer interests, even as it accepted the need for immigration limitation ("House Passes Immigration Bill" 1921; "Proposes Suspension of Immigration" 1921). Covering immigration restriction from an industry perspective, it discussed the impact of immigration restriction on labor shortages in the mining, steel and metal, agriculture, and automobile industries ("Labor Shortage Found to Be Increasing" 1922; "Wages Continue to Move to

EXPECTS OUR CURB ON ALIENS TO STAY

Day of "Open Door" for All Oppressed Peoples Past,
Says W. W. Husband.

SPEAKS AT LAWYERS CLUB

Chief Difficulty Now Is to Know
Whom to Keep Out, De-
clares Commissioner.

Commissioner General of Immigration
W. W. Husband was applauded yesterday afternoon when he declared at a
luncheon at the Lawyers' Club that immigration no longer were to be designed
for the benefit of the immigrant, but
that in their making the thought would
be "America first." He touched on

FIG. 4.4 The commissioner general of immigration
declared the era of the immigrant over and the era
of "America First" begun. *New York Times*, January
13, 1924.

Higher Levels" 1922). Yet it conceded that immigration restriction remained
necessary to address the problems it created. The paper acknowledged the
pleas by industry leaders and the secretary of the Treasury to limit immigration restriction while admitting that the policy had passed in Congress
nevertheless ("Seeks Further Immigration Restriction" 1922). The *Wall
Street Journal* even expressed concerns about how immigration restriction
was impeding the arrival of seemingly desirable wealthy immigrants, pointing out that several first-class passengers were detained upon arrival because
the quota for their country of origin had already been reached ("First-Class
Passengers Detained" 1921).

These editorial choices made by the *Wall Street Journal* reflected a slightly
more critical approach to the policies, unlike those taken by the *New York
Times* and *Washington Post* that adopted a more neutral tone in reporting any
opposition to the policies. For instance, articles in the *New York Times* and

Washington Post plainly stated that the provision to ban Asians had passed in Congress, without indicating the problematic nature of the provision for treaties the United States had signed with countries of origin affected by the bill. This general lack of critical treatment reflected a tacit acceptance of discriminatory immigration policy. Further, given the choice to feature experts who had helped draft the policy in newspaper coverage, it is surprising that the papers showed a cursory, if any, consideration of opposing views.

The *New York Times*'s tacit acceptance of discriminatory policy can also be gleaned in the foreign-language opinions gathered to reflect on immigration policies of the 1920s. One article about foreign-language coverage of immigration restriction selected only the positive reviews from all foreign-language news sources in the United States, particularly northern European newspapers that supported the relative advantages the quotas gave their community. Based on this evidence, the article concluded that not all foreign-language newspapers were opposed to selective immigration in light of the different contributions of "different races" (Lewis 1924). Other articles focused on relaying the opinions of northern European immigrant groups who had been favored by the Immigration Act. William Redfield, executive vice president of the Netherland-America Foundation, wrote in support of greater immigration restrictions by advocating for improved "quality" rather than quantity restrictions. He argued that such "percentages shall exclude men not alien to our people and ideals" whose relations had resided in the United States for centuries ("Wants Scientific Immigration Laws" 1924). Thus, even critical views of the policy published in the newspaper reflected suggestions to change selection criteria rather than demands for open immigration. As such, using seemingly balanced coverage, newspapers published contestations of the policy that went no further than suggesting adjustments in the administration of the law. For example, an article titled "Calls Quota Law Cruel" criticized then-current policy on the grounds that it admitted fewer worthy immigrants rather than considering the "physical, mental and moral fitness" of incoming immigrants (1924).

The most prominent dissenting voice in the *New York Times* and other newspapers was that of Max Kohler, who published numerous opinion pieces in 1924 advocating for the repeal of the act (Kohler, January 7, 9, and 25, 1924). His contributions did not go unrecognized, however. Numerous letters to the editor disparaged his population statistics and arguments. Some conceded that the comparison of "race value" felt morally objectionable, but they retorted that "immigration policy was less concerned with feelings" than it was with facts. As such, it is "plain [that] the new immigrants average considerably below Americans in intellectual capacity" (Hoffman 1924). The attacks on the logic of Kohler's argument were also an implicit attack on Kohler's own intellectual capacity and worthiness given his own "new immigrant stock" lineage, coming from a Jewish family that had immigrated from Leipzig. As the articles subtly disparaged his intelligence and proclivity to sentimentality, they also critiqued his belonging to the exact groups that were deemed undesirable by the policy. In sum, the ineffective results of Kohler's twenty-five years of legal and media advocacy, alongside the critiques of his advocacy in opinion pieces during that period, points to one important limitation of discussions of immigration hospitality and the myth of the "nation of immigrants": immigration hospitality must be expressed by the majority of the native population in order to encourage the enactment of fair immigration regulations and sympathetic media coverage of immigrant issues. When adopted by groups that are targeted with restriction, as was the case with Max Kohler, such criticism of restriction is easily rejected by the public because it emanates from the same "undesirable" groups excluded in immigration coverage and regulations.

In sum, media coverage in the 1920s reinforced and justified restrictive immigration policy by connecting immigrants to multiple ills, including inebriation and disease, lowered intelligence, and radical political ideologies. In so doing, media coverage supported the passage of restrictive immigration policy that declared the "era of the immigrant" ended. Once the National Origins Act was passed, media coverage justified legislation as a necessary policy in response to the ills of immigration. In this fashion, the 1920s exemplifies the ways in which media and regulatory hospitality mutually reflected the nativism that undercut the degree of hospitality immigrants from southern and eastern Europe were accorded.

Home-Building Efforts of Immigrants

In spite of the media hostility toward immigrants and the national immigration policies passed in the 1920s to limit and control immigration, immigrant groups continued to resist expressions of inhospitality in media and policy with practices of home-building. First and foremost, an important avenue of home-building for immigrants was the flourishing ethnic press in the United States. As Robert Park noted, European immigrants were generally not allowed to publish in their own languages in their countries of origin, where they had not experienced free speech. Thus, they had strong attachments to printing and reading news in their native languages in America (Park 1922, 9). At the same time, immigrants could not rely on the American press for their news because the "immigrant intellectual [had] a very poor opinion of the American newspaper . . . , with its local news, its personal gossip, and its human-interest anecdotes, [it was] not his conception of journalism" (Park 1922, 69).

American press of the time focused on local rather than international news, ignoring political developments taking place in immigrants' countries of origin. As Park argued, immigrants during this period gravitated toward newspapers written in their native languages as they navigated their new belonging to the United States, connecting with immigrants from similar backgrounds scattered across the nation and maintaining a bond to their countries of origin through language and cultural practices. Immigrant bulletins and newspapers focused on homeland political and economic developments as well as foreign relations with the United States ("Italy-America Society" 1920). They also introduced immigrants to the technological developments taking place in the United States, whether in engineering, transportation, or other realms of daily life (Park 1922, 104–106).

Occasionally, the immigrant press would console immigrants targeted by discriminatory and unjust policies, restoring and reaffirming their faith in the promise of their adopted nation and invoking and reinforcing the myth/trope of hospitality. Edward Bierstadt noted that after Russian and Ukrainian societies were raided and their members were attacked or even killed, the foreign-language press reiterated again the appeal to its readers that these injustices were committed by individuals and that "they did not represent the nation" (Bierstadt 1921).

As a result, the immigrant press of the 1910s and 1920s flourished at a time that American English-language presses were transforming from their once intensely participatory positions as public fora into commercial enterprises. Immigrant readers bolstered the development of ethnic presses into a participatory forum (Nord 2001) for democratic debate with ethnic editors and the larger immigrant community by writing readers' letters (Jaroszyńska-Kirchmann 2015, 2).

Immigrants also used food as an important arena of home-building in the 1920s. Italian immigrants in particular found culinary ways to bypass the restriction on the production and distribution of alcohol during the Prohibition era. As Harvey Levenstein wrote in *Paradox of Plenty*, a history of eating in the United States, Italian restaurateurs "who regarded Prohibition as some kind of a sick joke—continued to serve their homemade wine, beer, and . . . fiery grappa" along with affordable meals to Italian immigrants. These restaurants also attracted a broader American clientele searching for venues that served alcohol (Levenstein 1994, 51).

In so doing, Italian immigrants transformed the restrictions of Prohibition, which they perceived to be anti-immigrant and anti-Catholic, into opportunities to promote and market Italian food and culture. As Baughman reflected, "If the Yankee elite had not left the East side in search of a cocktail back in the 1920s, they might never have learned the joys of a good marinara sauce of a veal saltimbocca" (Baughman 2006, 385). In fact, Levenstein marveled, "by the time Prohibition ended in 1933, the cozy little restaurant in Little Italy with checkerboard tablecloths, candles in wine bottles, and reasonably priced food and drink was already on its way to becoming a cliché" (Levenstein 1994, 51).

Another avenue for home-building among immigrants of the 1920s period was education. Eager to integrate into the United States citizenry and to acquire necessary language and technical skills to enter the workforce, immigrants created foreign-language schools that provided necessary classes in the English language to adult immigrants who had found American adult education programs propagandistic and unhelpful (Bierstadt 1921). Russian immigrants established universities, including the Russian People's University and the Russian Collegiate Institute of New York, that enrolled a few hundred students in vocational subjects such as English language and grammar, automobile repair, blacksmith work, and the use of machinery in farming. Attendance at such schools declined dramatically after the Palmer Raids in 1919, as Russian immigrants avoided gathering for fear of accusations of Bolshevism.

In 1919, fifteen states established English-only instruction laws targeting the education of newly arrived immigrants and their children. These laws banned bilingual education and even the use of a foreign language to support the education of immigrant children. English-language instruction was seen as a means to mitigate the radical and anarchist ideologies brought ashore by immigrants (Crawford 2000, 21). Countering efforts to stifle immigrants' native languages at schools, immigrant groups created familial and immigrant-group education and cultural programming, a pattern replicated among Slavic Americans, Italian Americans, and Jewish American Yiddish speakers. Moreover, they encouraged a limited level of residential and cultural segregation, which supported native-language maintenance during this period (Sawaie and Fishman 1985). In spite of the difficulties that regulations represented, these educational institutions continued throughout the 1920s to provide much-needed adult- and child-educational services to immigrants when the existing educational programs had neglected them.

Finally, immigrants appealed to the law to contest the immigration restriction as well as the dehumanizing statements made by journalists and policymakers describing them. They also connected the dehumanizing rhetoric to a wave of anti-immigrant violence throughout the country. On April 29, 1929, Senator David Reed of Pennsylvania declared on the Senate floor that Syrians were the "trash of the Mediterranean," implying that they were a mongrelized, impure race, part of "all the Levantine stock that churns around through there and does not know what its own ancestry is" (Cong. Rec. 71 [1929]).

Less than a month later, a Syrian, Nola Romey, was lynched in Lake City, Florida, after his wife, Fannie, was murdered by a cop ("White Man Lynched" 1929). In response, Syrian Americans wrote a number of opinion pieces in two prominent Syrian American publications: *Syrian World* and *ash-Shaab*. Their articles compared the plight of Syrian

WHITE MAN LYNCHED BY MOB IN FLORIDA

Taken from Jail After Wife Is Killed by Policeman She Had Wounded

FIG. 4.5 "White Man Lynched," *Reading Times*,
May 18, 1929.

Americans to that of African Americans, and they pondered how Syrians fit into the complex racial politics of 1920s America. Community leaders also wrote to their senators and sought legal counsel to respond to Senator Reed's comments. The efforts of the Syrian community in this instance were moderately successful: they encouraged Senator Reed to retract his remarks, and they convinced other senators to raise the concerns of Syrian Americans for debate in Congress (Gualtieri 2009, 111). It is telling that although Syrian Americans recognized their shared struggle with African Americans in newspaper articles addressing the immigrant community, they employed a very different strategy when raising their concerns to politicians by affirming their racial purity and "Whiteness" and highlighting their efforts to Americanize and assimilate into society (111). To some extent, this effort succeeded, as media coverage in the *Reading Times* recorded the incident as one of the lynching of a "White man," illustrating how Syrian immigrants' arguments succeeded somewhat at labeling the community as "White."

The strategies immigrants adopted to adapt and resist discriminatory rhetoric and regulation during the 1920s reveal one key limitation of the "nation of immigrants" narrative. In each of these strategies, immigrants creatively adapted to their alienation and othered status in the American public sphere, at times turning discriminatory policies into economic and cultural opportunities. Nevertheless, their inability to directly overturn discriminatory policies reveals the power dynamics at the heart of American immigration hospitality, wherein solidarity efforts of the majority group are necessary to adequately contest and overturn policy. Moreover, the case of

Syrian Americans demonstrates that immigrants sought to overcome dis-crimination through reasserting their racial Whiteness or their proximity to Whiteness as a testament of their belonging to the population. In so doing, immigrants' efforts indirectly reaffirmed the primacy of White belonging to the American nation, to which one may only truly belong by becoming White. The unquestionable and unquestioned belonging of White Prot-estant immigrants to the nation and the value of proximity to Whiteness also reveals a central contradiction at the heart of hospitality. As Derrida notes, hospitality may also involve episodes of xenophobic material or sym-bolic violence to secure the belonging and authority of a native population and hence their capacity to extend welcome. In valorizing their belonging through their proximity to Whiteness, Syrian immigrants recognize the belonging and authority of White people as they advocate for greater hos-pitality in both media and politics. It is important to take note of these pat-terns to reckon with the limitations and risks inherent to even hospitality as an approach to immigration.

While this strategy may have succeeded at labeling the victim White ex post facto, the mere labeling of a community as White, whether in the media or law, did not protect it from racial violence and hostility. The futil-ity of immigrants' efforts to align themselves with Whiteness is exemplified in the contradictory news headline, "White Man Lynched," announcing the lynching of Nola Romey. If indeed Nola was White, how could he have been "lynched," a term at the time that was almost exclusively reserved for media coverage of racial violence against Black victims? And if Nola had been lynched, was he still White? In fact, the use of the term *lynched* seems to put Nola's Whiteness into question. Simultaneously, the use of the term *White* to identify Nola seems to put the act of lynching into question. All these fruitful contradictions point yet again to the limitations of hospitality if one takes the supremacy of White belonging for granted. The lasting threat of this deficiency can also be noticed in the chilling comments of Nola and Fannie Romey's daughter, who said in 1968, "All my life I still live in fear. I look over my shoulders thinking are they looking for the survivors of my family?" (as quoted in Gualtieri 2009, 113).

These examples point to the limitations of the nation of immigrants nar-rative and of the contestations of restrictive policy when they are adopted solely by immigrants who are deemed undesirable. Instead of contesting the grounds of restriction, the opposition to immigration restriction often indirectly reaffirms the belonging and authority of the dominant group of White Protestant European immigrants rather than extending belonging to new immigrant groups.

Conclusion

This chapter has argued that—thanks to the eugenics movement, the KKK, discriminatory immigration policy, and anti-immigrant media coverage— the 1920s embodied immigration inhospitality, not hospitality. Importantly, the central immigration policy of this period—the 1924 Immigration Act—would remain in place almost unchanged for four decades. More importantly, this chapter has sought to identify yet another set of lessons and recommendations that can be gleaned from reviewing immigration and media coverage using the lens of hospitality.

The conditions that emerged in the 1920s provide several insights into the impact of xenophobic racist political organization and thought on immigration hospitality. For instance, in the matter-of-fact media coverage of some of the most nefarious media and academic texts of the period, from *The Passing of the Great Race* to *Birth of a Nation*, the media granted a shroud of legitimacy and acceptability to racist, anti-immigrant rhetoric. Moreover, due to the uncritical coverage of facile arguments that center immigrants at the heart of all the nation's ills—from alcoholism, disease, and unemployment to radicalism—media coverage contributed to lasting suspicions toward immigrants as more prone to criminality and immoral behavior. These patterns in media hostility toward immigrants echo through the decades and provide valuable lessons as to how media hospitality may be better practiced when covering crime, disease, and other social concerns in contemporary journalism.

Crucially, it demonstrates how a focus on national origin and narratives of desirable and undesirable immigrants serves to restrict U.S. immigration hospitality and encourage limits and bans to restrict the arrival of "undesirable" immigrants. The influence of racist and eugenicist concerns surrounding the desirability of certain groups of migrants stretches from the national quotas of the 1920s to the Muslim Travel Ban of the 2010s, illustrating the value of addressing this issue in order to encourage immigration hospitality.

This chapter shows how the 1920s marked a crucial period of U.S. immigration restriction, embodying the conditions under which immigration hospitality shrinks. It allows us to trace the continuities between periods of immigration hostility, as the 1920s marked an intensification of the medicalized nativism that began in the Chinese exclusion era. Moreover, the "Red Scare" of the 1920s exemplified a pattern of accusing immigrants of harboring radical views and sympathies that continues to restrict immigration hospitality to this day. The period also shows the dynamics through which media and policy interact to create a climate of nativism and hostility toward immigrants, in ways—and using slogans—that continue to find resonance to this day. Thus, the 1920s offers lessons in how a short period of anti-immigrant furor can drive the creation of discriminatory policies with a lasting impact on immigration hospitality that remains far after the antimigration lobbying groups and movements subside. The chapter also demonstrates how nativist anti-immigrant sentiment and slogans may be reused in later eras. As noted earlier, the 1920s (fig. 4.4) was the first time the slogan "America First" emerged in media coverage of immigration policy. The slogan would be resurrected in the 2016 presidential election by republican candidate Donald Trump, who successfully campaigned on an anti-immigrant stance and an "America First" platform, exemplifying the contemporary echoes of the nativist anti-immigrant fervor of previous eras.

5

The Shift to National
Security: Patriot Act
(2000s)

• •

The late twentieth and early twenty-first centuries add another period to the story of U.S. immigration hospitality. This chapter begins by illustrating the impact of mid-twentieth-century legislation and the civil rights movement in the 1960s in helping dismantle the national origins quotas set by the 1920s immigration laws. Though this created a temporary platform for immigration hospitality to flourish for various immigrant groups arriving in the United States, this chapter shows how its potential was offset by the Bush and Obama administrations at the turn of the 2000s. The 9/11 attacks and their aftermath resulted in a strong diminution of immigration hospitality, justified by an impetus to protect national security from foreign threats—namely, terrorism. Media coverage of Muslims in the aftermath of 9/11 reinforced the tightening immigration restrictions then targeting Muslim immigrants.

Turn of the Twenty-First Century in Context

The civil rights movement, perhaps more than any other forum, played an important role in changing immigration policy. Its success in delegalizing discrimination in housing, education and employment, and federal services guaranteed equal access to opportunities to all citizens regardless of race (Civil Rights Act 1964). In so doing, the Civil Rights Act conferred upon African Americans in the United States quasi-full and equal treatment almost a century after the end of the commercial slave trade that had brought Africans to the shores of the United States. The Voting Rights Act of 1965 went further, outlawing prerequisites or conditions that would "deny or abridge the right of a citizen to vote on account of race or color."

As indicated in the introduction to this book, African American immigration to the United States represents the first wave of forced displacement and involuntary migration arriving at the nation's shores, under the auspices of a brutal slave trade that predestined this community to exploitation and persecution. Emancipation and the civil rights movement therefore represented a fundamental transformation to U.S. immigration hospitality by forcing the nation to reckon with past wrongs, finally allowing the recognition of a community that had until then been relegated to a hostage position in the framework of hospitality. Repercussions of this movement toward racial equality among U.S. citizens gradually spilled over into reevaluations of racial discrimination in immigration law. This is particularly due to the connections between discrimination against African American forced immigrants and subsequent waves of "undesirable" immigrants. Consider the regular comparisons between immigrant groups and African Americans, who were deemed the epitome of undesirability—"Irish immigrants often found themselves compared to blacks" Takaki noted (Takaki 1994, 141). Such comparisons established African Americans as the standard for racially "inferior . . . savages" that were to remain subservient to Anglo-Saxon Americans (141). The institution of slavery had devastating consequences for the treatment of many groups deemed racial "Others" alongside African Americans. For example, Irish immigrants were often hired by slave masters to do hazardous jobs they wouldn't give their slaves because, as Takaki quoted a Southern planter, "if a negro dies, it's a considerable loss, you know" (142). Once a society accepts the ownership and commodification of human life on the basis of racial, ethnic distinctions, it has already accepted the disregard for all human life that is deemed racially inferior. It is because of these reasons that civil rights are important elements of the story of immigration hospitality in the United States.

Parallels between immigrant rights and civil rights activists also emerged in another key arena: the quest for expanded access to education. As noted in chapter 2, Chinese Americans were the first group to contest Jim Crow laws in federal courts to obtain equal access to primary education. Similarly, Takaki observed that African Americans and Jews faced similar barriers to university employment and that the antidiscrimination achievements of the civil rights movement helped both groups enter academic fields. In housing, Jewish immigrants in the United States became the first group to use antidiscrimination laws to overcome discriminatory housing practices, demonstrating that "the frontline of the battle for equality for everyone, including the Jews, was the civil rights struggle for the blacks" (Takaki 1994, 143).

Most importantly, the overlooked connection between the civil rights movement and immigrant rights rested upon acknowledging the immigrant history of African Americans, who had been brought to the United States during the slave trade as the nation's first forced migrants, although conversations on forced migration often restricted their focus to contemporary contexts. Moreover, African American immigrants experienced multiple waves of forced migrations, as Ira Berlin noted in *Generations of Captivity*, whereby they were cyclically displaced as part of a domestic slave trade that responded to changes in labor demand (2004, 131). Ethnomusicologist Ingrid Monson illustrated in her work that it was impossible to consider African musical contributions to American culture without first acknowledging that "African immigration to North America under the terms of chattel slavery must be described as completely involuntary or forced migration" (2003, 22).

Thus, the abolition of slavery, the Civil Rights Act, and the Voting Rights Act were three accomplishments of African American rights that would recognize African Americans as full citizens and grant them equal political rights, releasing them from the bondage and subjugation that had greeted them when they first arrived in America. It is important to note that in finally acknowledging the rights of African Americans to equal citizenship and treatment, U.S. policy embraced the responsibility of hospitality. This, in turn, encouraged more recognition of the rights and liberties of a broader spectrum of newcomers, regardless of race, religion, ethnic background, or any other marker of difference.

In addition, African immigrants' continued struggle against unequal treatment of citizens on the grounds of race resonated beyond the context of voting and segregation debates to make possible the broader acceptance of racial diversity in American politics and society. It was in this vein that President Lyndon Johnson, in his State of the Union address to Congress in 1964, called for the end of discrimination against all categories of citizens in the United States while also "lifting by legislation the bars of discrimination against those who seek entry into [the] country" (Johnson 1965).

The abolishment of racially discriminatory immigration legislation brought the history of U.S. immigration policy full circle from the 1700s to the twentieth century, because it represented a small period of hope in which immigration hospitality could finally be extended to all immigrant groups arriving in the United States. This sentiment motivated Johnson to sign into law the 1965 Hart-Celler Act (H.R. 2580; Pub. L. No. 89–236, 79 Stat. 911), enacted June 30, 1968, effectively putting an end to the 1924 Immigration Act. Under the watchful gaze of Lady Liberty—the enduring image of American immigration hospitality—he delivered a speech declaring the 1924 act "un-American in the highest sense, because it has been untrue to the faith that brought thousands to these shores even before we were a country" (H.R. 2580; Pub. L. No. 89–236, 79 Stat. 911).

The Hart-Celler Act enshrined the value of immigration hospitality as central to American identity and culture, and it rewrote the history of racial discrimination and immigrant inhospitality as a mere lapse in America's welcoming ethos rather than the norm.

Johnson considered the signature of the Hart-Celler Act as "one of the most important acts of [his] Congress and administration" because, in his words, "it does repair a very deep and painful flaw in the fabric of American justice. It corrects a cruel and enduring wrong in the conduct of the American nation" (Johnson 1965). The enactment of the Immigration and Nationality Act of 1965, which was another name for the Hart-Celler Act, ended the national origins formula in favor of prioritizing family reunion for immigration and naturalization, a move that promised to transform American immigration policy from that point onward (Halter and Capozzola 2014, 3).

For several decades, the Hart-Celler Act continued to dramatically transform the country's demographic makeup (Takaki 1994, 13). The post-1965 "New American Immigration" reflected a diversity new to American society, a phenomenon *Time* magazine called "the Coloring of America" ("America's Changing Colors" 1990). The era of post-1965 immigration policy ushered in an age when immigration hospitality would offer a moderated welcome to European, Asian, Arab, and African immigrants alike. It was in this context that the first mass refugee crisis struck American policymakers, and it was against this context that a response on forced migrants seeking refuge in the United States would subsequently emerge.

This policy shift directly affected forced migrants as well, whose arrival in the United States was equally governed by the existing national origins quotas. First among them was the Displaced Persons Act, in which U.S. Congress recognized eligible displaced persons as anyone who had entered Germany, Austria, and Italy between September 1, 1939, and December 22, 1945. It also encompassed displaced persons residing in the postwar territories governed by the American, French, or British allied forces. The act also included residents of Germany or Austria who had fled Nazi persecution and had not been resettled in their country of origin. It entitled all "eligible displaced persons" permanent residence in the United States, according to the constitution of the United Refugee Organization, of which the United States was a member at the time. Significantly, the Displaced Persons Act was passed in a postnational origins quota policy environment, where the measure cemented a position for refugee policy as a humanitarian commitment that the United States acknowledged, unlike the nation's national origins quotas, which had allowed immigration officials to turn back many Jewish refugees in the 1920s and 1930s because quotas had been satisfied (Friedman 1973).

Secondly, the United States became a signatory to the International Geneva Convention in 1951, as well as to the convention's revisions and amendments in the 1970s. As a result, international humanitarian law (anchored in the Geneva Convention) guaranteed protection to refugees and stateless persons resulting from a conflict. Articles 44 and 45 also defined the right of refugees to migrate to another state of residence as well as the rights of refugees and stateless persons within their "state of refuge" (Article 73, Geneva Protocol). Thus, refugees and asylum seekers arriving in the 1980s onward benefited from substantially increased rights to refuge vis-à-vis earlier waves of forced migration in the United States.

Yet another seminal moment in U.S. immigration policy toward refugees came in 1981, when the United States found itself for the first time a country of mass asylum for immigrants fleeing their countries (U.S. Congress 1981). This occurred when an unprecedented 125,000 Cubans entered the United States between April and September of 1980. Faced with a stark change in the international position toward forced migrants and the new conditions following the 1951 convention, U.S. immigration policy was no longer able to bar forced migrants as it had done in the aftermath of World War II. At the same time, the passage of the Hart-Celler Act limited the ability of the United States to restrict forced migrants by claiming that national origins quotas had been satisfied (as it had done in the past).

These new immigration imperatives revealed contradictions in the hospitality ethic. Tellingly, then-president Ronald Reagan claimed that the Mariel boatlift brought home to most Americans the fact that the United States immigration policy was out of control as America's commitments to several international conventions precluded the possibility of turning the Cuban refugees away. This put the United States in a position that resonates with the contemporary treatment of the "refugee crisis" of 2016 and 2017. Just as in 1968, these agreements did not prevent the United States from accepting the smallest possible number of refugees. As chairman of the Subcommittee on Immigration and Refugee Policy, Alan Simpson noted that although the United States was a signatory of the 1968 United Nations Protocol Relating to the Status of Refugees, that did not mean that the country "must accept for permanent resettlement each legitimate asylee who arrives on [its] shores" (U.S. Congress 1981, 2).

Nevertheless, the increased opening of both immigration policy as a whole and refugee policy in particular signaled an era of growing hospitality and heightened diversity in the demographic makeup of the American citizenry that promised to foster positive public responses to proimmigration policies. This was evident in the changing demographic makeup of the American immigrant population over the several decades following the Hart-Celler Act. Pew Research showed that the foreign-born share of the population grew from 5 percent in 1960 to 13 percent in 2013 as a result of the Hart-Celler Act. It also projected in 2015 that the combined proportion of first- and second-generation immigrants within the American population would rise to 37 percent by 2050, compared with 15 percent back in 1965 (Kohut 2015). Indeed, by 2013, the census showed that half of the immigrant population was Latin American/Caribbean and 27 percent was Asian, while the European share of the immigrant population had fallen to 13 percent.

The polls also suggested a pattern of rising positive public opinion on immigration as a result of the growing numbers of immigrants among the voting public. Thus, while only 7 percent of the American public favored increasing immigration in 1960, that figure rose to 25 percent by 2014 (Kohut 2015). In addition, first- and second-generation immigrants tend to favor proimmigration policies. According to Pew Research, Latinos represent the largest ethnic or racial minority group, at 13 percent of the voting-eligible population, and they tend to vote for presidential and local government candidates who possess positive stances on immigration (Cilluffo and Fry 2019). By 2020, one-in-ten eligible voters is born outside the U.S., suggesting that future electorates will increasingly favor candidates who support reforming immigration law and providing greater pathways to citizenship and a clear resolution to the status of undocumented immigrants (Barreto 2018).

Thus, the combined effect of the Displaced Persons Act, the Geneva Convention, the Hart-Celler Act, and the civil rights movement all represented a moment of hope for immigration hospitality in the United States, providing the conditions for positive immigration reform; promising growing diversity in the public as immigration hospitality was extended to newcomers regardless of their race, ethnicity, or creed; and providing the conditions for increasingly positive public opinion on immigration. However, all of this would change in 2001, in the wake of the events of 9/11.

Regulatory Hospitality after 9/11

The hope represented by the late twentieth century came to a halt in the aftermath of the September 11 attacks. Responding to news circulating that terrorists had entered the United States on visitor visas, Congress and the Bush administration mobilized quickly to transform U.S. immigration policies and institutions, with the aim of restricting immigration hospitality toward immigrants and refugees from Muslim-majority countries. The impact of these changes can still be felt today by immigrants across the spectrum, producing multiple waves of immigration restriction and hostility from counterterrorism initiatives that target Muslim immigrants to the United States and the Muslim community as a whole. This extends to the registry of Muslim immigrants that operated from 2001 to 2017 as well as the surveillance, detention, and deportation efforts underway in the early 2000s.

During this most recent period of immigration restriction, opposition to immigration restriction was stifled under the imperative of protecting national security and combating extremism, and contestations of policies often sought to divert attention from one immigrant group to another rather than contest the suitability of immigration restriction overall. This section tracks anti-Muslim immigration policy across the early 2000s, connecting two previous eras of restriction—that of the Chinese Exclusion Act of the 1880s and the deportations and raids of the 1920s—with immigration policy of the 2000s. In connecting the contemporary manifestations of immigration restriction to periods of exclusion and nativism, this section illustrates yet another set of conditions under which U.S. regulatory hospitality shrank.

The 9/11 attacks had a profound impact on U.S. immigration policy. Fourteen months after the attacks, Congress enacted the Homeland Security Act (Pub. L. No. 107–296), which reorganized many agencies and their policies regarding immigration. The act created the Department of Homeland Security (DHS), and it brought twenty-one federal agencies, including the Immigration and Naturalization Service (INS), the Federal Emergency Management Agency (FEMA), and the Transportation Security Administration (TSA) all under the umbrella of the newly created body: DHS. The movement initiated a new era in American policy, one in which the policymaking and administration of immigration fell under a national security framework, where immigrants were regarded with caution and suspicion.

This new directive was openly outlined by U.S. immigration agencies. Typical was this overview of U.S. immigration policy priorities post-9/11, taken from the USCIS website: "The events of September 11, 2001 injected new urgency into INS' mission and initiated another shift in the United States' immigration policy. The emphasis of American immigration law enforcement became border security and removing criminal aliens to protect the nation from terrorist attacks" (USCIS 2012, 11).

During this period, the Bush administration also created the National Security Entry-Exit Registration System (NSEERS). The program collected data on immigrants from Pakistan and Bangladesh along with other Muslim countries from 2011 onward. It was envisioned as an antiterrorism registry of males over the age of sixteen from those countries who were fingerprinted, photographed, and interviewed at the point of registry and required to check in with Immigration and Customs Enforcement (ICE) on a periodic basis. Not only did the program criminalize Muslim men and treat them with suspicion, but NSEERS created an environment that was hostile toward Muslim Americans and Muslim immigrants. One survivor, Mohammad Jafar Alam, expressed, "I know exactly what a program like NSEERS does to a person and their family. The extreme mental, emotional distress, the financial problems, the pressures on a family and the isolation that happens is a punishment not just for one person, but everyone involved" (quoted in Sohrabji 2017).

NSEERS also paved the way for a frenzy of detentions, deportations, and other measures taken against Muslim immigrants. As Deepa Fernandes wrote in her groundbreaking research on U.S. immigration detention centers post-9/11, the aftermath of 9/11 had terrifying and often deadly consequences for Muslim immigrant noncitizens living in the United States. Many Muslim immigrants, whether they were illegal immigrants, green card holders, students, or tourists, were rounded up and put in detention centers in the aftermath of 9/11, without due process or clear accusations justifying their detention. The registry enabled the rounding up of up to five thousand Muslim male immigrants in what became known as the Ashcroft Raids, during which the government deprived these individuals of their due process rights (Fernandes 2007).

In these cases, court rulings were important sources of precedent that compounded the single-minded security framework of government immigration policies. Thus, in the *Turkmen v. Ashcroft* case in 2006, when Muslim detainees after 9/11 sued the U.S. government over abuses endured during their detention, a New York judge ruled that the government had the right to detain noncitizens on the basis of their religion, race, or national origin and to hold them indefinitely without explanation. Federal judge John Gleeson's ninety-nine-page ruling argued that such singling out on the basis of race or religion was possible for noncitizens. However, he added, "If applied to citizens, [it] would be highly suspicious," a position that Rachel Meeropol, a lawyer representing the Muslim male plaintiffs, called "profoundly disturbing," because it gave the green light for the government to detain noncitizens "at the whim of the President" while placing them outside of constitutional protection (Rothschild 2006). Law professor David Cole, who was co-counsel to the plaintiffs in the case, wrote an article in the *Los Angeles Times* in the aftermath of the decision saying that his clients asked him, "What will they do to us if there is another attack? Will they intern us like they interned the Japanese?" (Cole 2006). The concerns of immigrants revealed that immigrant communities sensed the continuities between the U.S. immigration hostility of the past and the present with an acuity and clarity that slipped by many Americans in communities not targeted by counterterrorism programs. Moreover, these concerns showed that targeted immigrant groups in one period of restrictiveness recall the treatment of other immigrant groups in earlier eras (Bernstein 2006).

Gleeson's decision had a large impact on immigration hospitality in the United States, setting a frightening future precedent in the United States for the complete disregard of the basic rights of noncitizen immigrants residing on American soil. It signaled the precarity and volatility of their position in the United States as aliens with unrecognized rights. As Gerald Neumann argued, the decision hinted that "the next time there is a terror attack, the government is free to round up every Muslim immigrant in the U.S., based solely on their ethnic and religious identity, and hold them on immigration pretexts for as long as it desires" (quoted in Bernstein 2006).

Existing immigration policies were also modified to create stringent criteria for people residing in the United States on various kinds of visas. Overnight, international students in the United States found themselves in violation of their visa status for having dropped a credit that semester (Fernandes 2007, 30). In turn, the criteria for deportation expanded dramatically after 9/11 to make such lapses in immigrant status punishable with deportation (Kurzban 2008, 6). This also paved the way for racial-ethnic profiling by law enforcement in order to distinguish Americans from "aliens" (Kurzban 2008, 336). At the same time, opportunities for permanent residence shrank, instead paving way for the proliferation of temporary visas that allowed people to live, study, and work in the United States while preventing them from applying for permanent residence (Kurzban 2008, 6).

In conjunction with the changes in immigration laws that impacted the status of immigrants residing in the United States, Congress increased the budget allocation thirtyfold for ICE's Criminal Alien program, rising from $6.6 million in 2004 to $180 million in 2008 and resulting in a ballooning of the organization during that time. In fiscal year (FY) 2013, Congress began to funnel the funding of other programs toward ICE's Criminal Alien Capture program, resulting in a 64 percent increase in funding, from $196.7 million in FY 2012 to $322.4 million in FY 2015 (Cantor, Noferi, and Martinez 2015). Yet again, these choices reflected a criminalization of immigration and the broad acceptance and financial support of initiatives that targeted immigrants and detained, abused,[1] and deported them.

In other instances, laws were changed so that immigrants convicted of petty crimes could be detained indefinitely as "criminal aliens." Rather than deporting immigrants detained for crimes, these changes required that INS imprison them indefinitely on American soil. Yet another change of policy fostered the use of the term *excludables*, referring to noncitizens on U.S. soil in detention centers as legally nonexistent, as if they had never set foot in the country. Malone argued that the anxiety displayed in the nomenclature of detained immigrants reflected a discomfort of a "nation of immigrants" that prevented policymakers from addressing detained immigrants directly and "prevents us from describing them [detained immigrants] as human beings and what happens to them in simple, straightforward terms" (Malone 2008, 47). Complicating matters further, in the case of detained immigrants whose nations refused to accept repatriation, immigrants were forced into detention centers until a resolution for their status could be determined (Malone 2008, 47). This provided the pretext for the detention of numerous asylum seekers in the United States, as the law placed the burden of proof on applicants for asylum and on those who fled their countries without satisfactory documentation (Malone 2008, 51).

Patriot Act of 2001

In conjunction with changes in immigration policy, legislative changes that governed how law enforcement could operate and the circumstances under which it could surveil or follow citizens changed. The most significant of these legislative changes was the passage of the Patriot Act. In 2001, Congress enacted the Uniting and Strengthening America by Providing Appropriate Tools Required to Intercept and Obstruct Terrorism Act (which has since been known as the Patriot Act). The Patriot Act passed with overwhelming bipartisan margins in Congress, passing quasi unanimously in the Senate with a 98–1 margin, as well as passing by a wide margin in the House with 357–66 (Department of Justice 2001). It was intended to enhance the capabilities of law enforcement and multiple government agencies to prevent future attacks on American soil. However, several civil rights organizations noted abuses of citizens' rights as a result of the powers given to law enforcement to surveil and harass journalists, activists, and immigrant groups. Most importantly, the narrow definition of what constituted terrorism according to the Department of Justice allowed for the targeting of immigrants of Muslim-faith or those coming from Muslim-majority countries.

Officially, government bodies were careful to avoid connecting the Patriot Act with Islam. The act allowed several government agencies to bypass stringent permissions needed to wiretap, monitor, and surveil subjects, so long as these operations were conducted with the purpose of "preventing another terrorist attack on U.S. soil" (Patriot Act 2001). Thus, it was telling that government agencies were careful to provide definitions of terrorism according to the act in their mission statements that avoided any mention of religion or Islam. Instead, terrorism is defined as "premeditated, politically motivated violence perpetrated against noncombatant targets by subnational groups or clandestine agents" (CIA); as "the unlawful use of force or violence against persons or property to intimidate or coerce a government, the civilian population, or any segment thereof, in furtherance of political or social objectives" (FBI); and as "activity that—(A) involves an act that—(i) is dangerous to human life or potentially destructive of critical infrastructure or key resources; and (ii) is a violation of the criminal laws of the United States or of any State or other subdivision of the United States; and (B) appears to be intended— (i) to intimidate or coerce a civilian population; (ii) to influence the policy of a government by intimidation or coercion; or (iii) to affect the conduct of a government by mass destruction, assassination, or kidnapping" (DHS). The only definition of terrorism that mentions religion is that given by NATO, which states that terrorism is "unlawful use or threatened use of force or violence against individuals or property in an attempt to coerce or intimidate governments or societies to achieve political, religious or ideological objectives."

Nevertheless, the enforcement of the Patriot Act as well as the United States war on terror clearly targeted Muslim communities. Evidence of the targeting of Muslim communities pointed to a far narrower and more discriminatory definition of terrorism among these agencies, and media coverage gradually took note of this shift. A series of leaked documents by the *New York Times* reported that the CIA and NYPD had been collaborating on a surveillance program that targeted all Muslim Americans living in New York and that they inserted agents in Muslim student associations, mosques, and even Muslim barbershops to listen to conversations taking place in the Muslim community (Apuzzo and Goldman 2014). Operating under the auspices of the Patriot Act, the program used census data to map where Muslims in New York lived, and it classified all Muslim youth as susceptible to radicalization and all mosques as "terrorism enterprises" (Apuzzo and Goldman 2014, 180). The impressive investigative report earned the Associated Press a Pulitzer Prize in 2012 (Associated Press 2012) and resulted in an archive of leaked documents that revealed extensive surveillance of all aspects of Muslim American life. Ultimately, Apuzzo and Goldman went on to write a 336-page book to fully address the leaks (Apuzzo and Goldman 2014).

Following upon these institutional changes, the language used by the office of the U.S. president reinforced the suspicions leveled at Muslims. Even as presidential speeches by George W. Bush continued to stress that "Muslims are not *our* enemy," many of President Bush's speeches in the aftermath of 9/11 emphasized that "the war against terrorism is not a war against Muslims. . . . It's a war against evil people who conduct crimes against innocent people" (Bush 2001). Yet in many of these reiterations, President Bush articulated a dichotomy of the "our" of the American public, institutions and government—who were combatting terror—and Muslims who may or may not be the enemy but were certainly not part of the "our" of the American fabric (Bush 2002).

Take, for example, the statement he made at the annual White House Iftar dinner in 2002, where he said, "America treasures the relationship we have with our many Muslim friends, and we respect the vibrant faith of Islam which inspires countless individuals to lead lives of honesty, integrity, and morality. This year, may Eid also be a time in which we recognize the values of progress, pluralism, and acceptance that bind us together as a Nation and a global community. By working together to advance mutual understanding, we point the way to a brighter future for all" (Bush 2002). Statements like this one placed Muslim American community members in attendance as "friends" rather than compatriots and citizens. In conjunction, despite Bush's repeated assertions that "Muslims are not our enemy," his definition of the war on terror identified Muslim history as the core target of its project. Take, for example, this statement: "They [the terrorists] hope to establish a violent political utopia across the Middle East, which they call a 'Caliphate' where all would be ruled according to their hateful ideology. Osama bin Laden has called the 9/11 attacks 'a great step towards the unity of Muslims and establish the Righteous Caliphate.' This Caliphate would be a totalitarian Islamic empire encompassing all current and former Muslims lands, stretching from Europe to North Africa, the Middle East, and Southeast Asia" (Bush 2006). Moreover, Bush often expressed that at the core of the terrorist project was a concept integral to Islamic history and Muslim Weltanschauung: a historical form of Muslim rule known as the caliphate (Zuhur 2008, 6). The caliphate in Muslim history corresponds to a relatively long period in which the disciples of the Prophet Mohammad (PBUH) governed Muslim communities in the Middle East. By attacking the caliphate without qualifying that the expansionist, violent expression of the concept in the fundamentalist rhetoric used by bin Laden is the specific target of these critiques, Bush's speeches against the caliphate alienated Muslim communities and pointed out that their history and faith were considered dangerous political projects according to the president.

Despite widespread criticism of the Patriot Act and the war on terror's disproportionate burden on Muslims, both the Bush and Obama administrations did not acknowledge or respond to these calls for a review of the act and its implementation. In response to the critiques surrounding the Patriot Act, the Justice Department issued a document titled "Dispelling Myths about the Patriot Act" that addressed the many criticisms of the act. In the document's twenty-six sections that responded to critiques ranging from the targeting of peaceful activists to the widespread use of wiretapping, the department did not mention the words "Muslim" or "religious organization" once, thereby failing to respond to mounting evidence that the Patriot Act disproportionately targeted Muslim Americans and Muslim immigrants living in the United States because of its narrow definition of terrorism.

Finally, under the guise of national security concerns, refugee policy was drastically revised in a move that, while hidden under other national security imperatives in the nation's highest courts, was most plainly explained by George W. Bush, who stated, "We will turn back any refugee that attempts to reach our shore" (Human Rights Watch 2004). The Bush administration had finally found a way to dispense with legal and ethical obligations required by the International Convention on Refugees, and that was by criminalizing the act of crossing borders in order to reach a country of asylum and apply for resettlement. Essentially, as Mark Dow pointed out, "if you categorize a person in a certain way, that person's rights and protections are gone; if you categorize the place where you hold that person in a certain way, that person's rights protections are gone; and by using the pretext of war or national security— you can do anything at all to a person—certainly a noncitizen" (2008, 35). Moreover, the criminalization of border crossing resulted in a ballooning of the number of immigrants being held in national detention centers without public information being shared on detainee numbers or the charges on which they were being held. The most important thread that wove through all these policies and their implementation was one of public knowledge and public consent. As Malone pointed out, for as long as the information on whether and how many asylum seekers, immigrants, and foreigners were held by the United States was concealed, it was impossible for the public to tell whom it has deprived of liberty and dignity or the conditions of their detention, and "without that knowledge, consent is meaningless" (Malone 2008, 59).

Thus, the post-9/11 policy responses of the Bush and Obama administrations highlighted that from 2001 onward, the United States, for reasons of security, would severely restrict the hospitality extended toward immigrants and asylum seekers, particularly those from Muslim-majority countries or of the Muslim faith. They also demonstrated that the United States would no longer acknowledge and respect migrants' basic human rights. The implicit contract made between each American administration and the American public, in return for protection and security, would soon pave the way for the Muslim travel ban of 2017.

Media Hospitality

Media coverage during the post-9/11 period intensified the hostile environment created by immigration policies toward Muslim communities, a fact that has been well documented in a growing field of studies on media representations of Muslim communities post-9/11 (Bayoumi 2015; Alsultany 2012; Grewal 2014). This section begins by analyzing media coverage of Muslim immigrants and American Muslims in the *New York Times*, the *Wall Street Journal*, and the *Washington Post* from 2001 to 2015. It identifies several dominant trends in media coverage during this period that cemented a perceptual linkage of Muslims to violence and terrorism, justifying the passage of restrictive immigration policies and extrajudicial surveillance, detention, and deportation of Muslim immigrants. Moreover, the coverage repeatedly positioned Muslims as dangerous Others who carried out attacks on "Western" citizens because of their incomprehensible and unpredictable religious dogma. This analysis illustrates the role of the media in alternately justifying or questioning inhospitable discriminatory policy.

Journalism scholars have pointed to several trends in media coverage after 9/11, noting that the period following the attacks became a time of "rallying around the flag" as critical coverage of the national war on terror policies prompted/invited accusations of "giving aid and comfort to the enemy" (Navasky 2011, xix). Journalists resorted to common Western media tropes of "Islamic peril," which echoed the tropes once used to represent Chinese immigrants. This approach rested on simplistic generalizations of an entire faith that was practiced differently as the majority religion in forty-nine countries and observed by the citizens of numerous countries on every continent (Desilver and Masci 2017). Post-9/11 media coverage primarily followed the formula set by U.S. presidential speeches, presenting the post-9/11 era as a battle between "good vs. evil" in which derogatory stereotypes of Muslim communities formed the "evil" side of this dichotomy, securing the American position as morally righteous.

Dominant Media Tropes

Three main media tropes characterized representations of Muslim communities during this period. I concur with scholars who have argued that media coverage post-9/11 overlooked systematic violence taking place in global geopolitics and the role that U.S. military involvement in the Middle East may have played in destabilizing the regions now considered terrorist hotbeds (Karim 2011, 131–132). However, what follows focuses specifically on the dominant representation of Muslim immigration and Muslim American communities living in the United States. It explores the emphasis on Muslims as a "hard" and intractable enemy and the construction of an apparent pattern of Muslim violence against "soft targets," rendering this enemy all the more frightening. Finally, it examines how the media constructed all Muslims as impossible victims. Rendering all Muslims, moderate or violent, as complicit, the media precluded the representation of innocent Muslims, let alone victims, of the war on terror.

"Hard" Enemies

The first prevalent trope that emerged in post 9/11 media coverage was the emphasis on Muslims as a "hard enemy" whose motivations, language, religion, and culture could not be understood by the American public or political and military elite, making Muslims a hard enemy to defeat.

Such a sentiment was reflected in a front-page article in the *New York Times* on September 12, 2001, entitled "U.S. Attacked; Hijacked Jets Destroy Twin Towers and Hit Pentagon in Day of Terror," and it reflected the confusion and trauma that many witnesses to the 9/11 attacks experienced. While most of the quotes collected from onlookers relayed the shell-shocked experiences of New Yorkers on the day, one particular utterance began to synthesize the direction the *New York Times* took from the earliest moments: "It's like Pearl Harbor. It's war." The newspaper signaled a war that would unfold between the United States and an unnamed adversary (Kleinfeld 2001).

Another article in the *New York Times* responded to this sentiment with the headline "U.S. ATTACKED; President Vows to Exact Punishment for 'Evil'" (Schmemann 2001). The dialogical nature of the two articles, reflected in the construction of their titles, pointed to a cause-effect dyad, wherein the

9/11 attacks represented an assault on the United States, thereby eliciting retaliation. However, the U.S. reprisal following 9/11 was directed at an amorphous enemy described using the morally absolutist category of "evil" inspired by Manichean religious traditions. The flattening and oversimplification of extremist groups' motivations in this fashion invited overgeneralization of attitudes toward all Muslims following 9/11, as they were thought to be bearers of an "evil" religious ideology. These two front-page articles illustrate the pattern of American journalistic response to the traumatic events of 9/11 in which, as Karim argues, American journalists recovered from the confusion of the event to fall back on prescribed news-gathering procedures and existing cognitive frameworks about Islam, violence, and terrorism (Karim 2011, 131–132). They regarded the inconceivable and incomprehensible "Muslim terrorism" as a threat to Western societies. In conjunction, George W. Bush's quoted statements, such as, "We will make no distinction between the terrorists who committed these acts and those who harbor them," consolidated this elision (Schmemann 2001). Thus, Islamic terrorists, as well as the vague category of "those who harbor them," could easily be interpreted by some readers as everyone who shared the Muslim faith.

In fact, as the scholar Lila Abu Lughod reflected in an autobiographical account of her numerous invitations to lectures, news interviews, and other public outreach opportunities post-9/11, the period that followed the initial confusion often saw journalists seeking culturalist explanations to extremism, operating on the assumption that if only American leadership understood Islam better, the tragedy and loss of life on 9/11 could have been prevented (Abu-Lughod 2002, 784). Instead, this search for culturalist explanations reinforced the assumption that violence was inherently tied to the Muslim faith.

The menace of Islam was connected to reporting on immigration from Muslim-majority nations, as reporters began to question how, and even if, Muslim immigrants could be integrated into American society, using headlines such as "Defining the 'All-American Muslim'" (Schaefer Riley 2012), "Muslim Melting Pot" (Manji 2007), or "Are Muslims Integrating or Are They 'Taking Over'?" ("Are Muslims" 2010). These articles echoed many tropes of foreign race invasion that had appeared in previous eras of U.S. media history, calling for the need to tighten "lax immigration" policies that were allowing Muslim immigration to continue unfettered or citing the threat that a relatively higher "Muslim birth rate" posed to the demographic makeup of European and Northern American societies ("Are Muslims" 2010). Even articles adopting a more positive stance acknowledged the permanent "foreignness" of Muslim immigrants in Western society (Fredette 2014), illustrating the difficulty of assimilating Muslim immigrants. Moreover, efforts to include seemingly positive voices on Islam overwhelmingly relied on figures that Hamid Dabashi has called "native informers," who derive their authority from being "natives" while being "reformed" or "recovering" members of the Muslim community (2011, 22–23). Individuals such as Ayaan Hirsi Ali, who describes herself as a heretic to this day, or Irshad Manji, the Bengali-Canadian gay rights activist who claims to hope to "reform" Islam, were consulted as "native informers," but as scholars have pointed out, they were used to reinforce bias because their outspoken stances against their own communities confirmed the racial and cultural inferiority of Muslim immigrants (Dabashi 2011, 23; Grewal 2014, 18).

According to media coverage, the Muslim enemy was also ubiquitous. In the wake of the terrorist attacks on the World Trade Centers in New York City, the *New York Times* embarked on a global coverage campaign pinpointing Muslim groups and individuals accused of inciting or planning terrorist attacks in Indonesia (Bonner and Perelz 2002), China (Eckholm 2002), the U.K. (Cowell 2002), and the Philippines (Schmitt 2002). This international laundry list of militant acts suggested that all Muslim-majority countries were dangerous places teeming with terrorists and their sympathizers. The clear implication flowed that multinational companies, expatriate workers, and financial investors should abandon these locations. Indeed, the *New York Times* marveled that "despite the apparently globe-girdling reach of Islamic terror groups, some of the biggest Western multinational corporations are holding fast to their investments in most Muslim countries." More significantly, the article referred to "Islamic terror groups," thereby associating Islam as a whole with the violence carried out by a small fraction of believers in its name (Altman 2002).

These representations of Muslim-majority countries as bustling with terrorist activity and terrorism sympathizers facilitated the characterization of immigrants from Muslim-majority countries as undesirable national security threats. In fact, these arguments resurfaced in support of President Trump's proposal for a travel ban restricting the arrival of immigrants from Muslim-majority countries. Thus, the emphasis on an "Islamic threat" facing American values justified a media consensus on the need for immigration restriction. As I will show below, this coverage also legitimized the existing policies of surveillance, harassment, detention, and deportation of Muslim immigrants studying or working in the United States.

"Soft" Targets

Often, coverage of the threat of extremism also emphasized the vulnerability and gullibility of the American public and political elite. It repeatedly alluded to the American civilians, institutions, and values as being put at risk by the incoming migration of communities with incompatible values. Journalists characterized well-intended hospitality and generosity shown to Muslim immigrants as naive, invoking a history of Muslim violence directed at "soft targets." This trope portrayed Muslims as terrifying, merciless enemies who targeted unarmed civilians, women, and children.

News outlets attributed the vulnerability of the American public to its lack of knowledge and understanding of the Muslim faith. Thus, media coverage in the 9/11 era struggled to explain the basic principles of the religion it had pronounced as "evil." To address this need to understand Islam, the *Wall Street Journal* organized a symposium titled "What Is Moderate Islam?" Although the query may have been fitting in the immediate aftermath of 9/11, the intervention almost a decade after 9/11 indicated how little knowledge news media had gained over the span of nine years ("Symposium" 2010). In fact, as late as 2010, media coverage across all major newspapers continued to feature articles such as "What Is Moderate Islam?" (Hussain 2010).

Several articles emphasized that the American leadership and public lacked the understanding of Muslim ideology that would have enabled it to foresee and prevent a Muslim threat. Key were suggestions of the inevitability of Muslim violence and the misguidedness of generous perspectives on Muslim immigrants' intentions. A *Wall Street Journal* article criticized a sympathetic report by Brian Williams and Ron Allen that portrayed a Muslim cleric's blissful family life, pointing out that the cleric abruptly beheaded his wife after she asked for a divorce (Stephens 2010). The article cited yet another example of the unpredictability of Muslim attackers: a 1993 controversy over the closure of a Washington, D.C., mosque that was criticized for demonstrating discrimination against Muslims. Later, the article noted, the mosque would become known as "none other than . . . 'the 9/11 mosque,'" infamous for inspiring several terrorist attacks over the years. These examples posited that Americans' ignorance and misunderstanding of Islam was detrimental because it left them vulnerable to the threat that Muslims posed rather than because this ignorance fueled bigotry and discrimination against Muslims. Skewed conceptualizations of Islamic belief and practice were deployed against Muslims themselves, as is reflected in the largely rhetorical question underlining much reportage: "Is it bigoted to oppose bigots?" (Stephens 2010).

Moreover, media coverage criticized the perceived naive response of American leadership, and particularly President Obama, to emphasize that not all Muslims were terrorists and that America was not at war with Islam. For example, in the wake of the November 2015 Paris attacks, well-known *Washington Post* columnist Colbert I. King ridiculed the Muslim community's response, suggesting it rehearsed to the point of insincerity. Similarly, other articles blamed Muslim migrants in the immediate aftermath of the attack (Landauro, Dalton, and Entous 2015). King then criticized President Obama for eschewing the phrase "Islamic terrorism," asking the president "whose feelings are being spared?" He quoted Aretha Franklin saying, "Who's zoomin' who? Who's being fooled" to criticize the naïveté of American politicians and the American public in responding to the threat of Islam (King 2015). He also suggested that the American public was being fooled by its leadership's false rhetoric of Islam as a peaceful religion, which left it vulnerable to the danger Muslims posed.

American society's vulnerability was depicted as the consequence of Muslim immigrants' inability or unwillingness to integrate. Journalists questioned the ability of Muslim immigrants to become Americans in light of the tenants of the Muslim faith, and their incompatibility with ideals of free speech, individual freedom, or human rights. They cited the ghettoization of European societies as an example of the problems posed by Muslim immigrants internationally (Johnson 2005), suggesting that Muslim immigrants were unable to integrate into American society and institutions and put these institutions and values at risk. Consider, for example, coverage of Muslim responses to several offensive cartoons that the press deemed protected free speech, which privileged violent over peaceful protest. To counter the news media's defamation, Muslim scholars and professionals often responded to these reports. For example, Muslim attorney Qasim Rashid was featured in a series of articles and televised interviews in the *New York Times*, *Huffington Post*, the Fox News Network, and *USA Today*, stressing that free speech was one of the fundamental tenants of Islam. Rashid argued that the religion instructed its followers to respond to offensive messages with peaceful dialogue (Rashid 2015).

Moreover, newspaper coverage amplified and celebrated the voices of known Islamophobes to support illustrations of Islam as a vindictive religion that attacks peaceful individuals with critical views. For example, in November 2002, Marlise Simons from the *New York Times* wrote a fawning article commending the infamous Islamophobe Ayaan Hirsi Ali, proclaiming her a visionary for seeking to "reform Islam." Simons marveled at Ali's bravery in telling reporters that the prominent gay politician Pim Fortyun was justified in calling Islam "backward" (Simons 2002). The article also highlighted the death threats, enhanced security, and other consequences that Ali had faced for expressing her views. Such reporting drew broad conclusions about Islam, flattening the complexity of a religion practiced differently by many different cultures across the world; it also relied on a few prominent commentators known for their controversial and incendiary anti-Muslim rhetoric, representing an editorial strategy to characterize Islam as a whole as an oppressive and unjust religion and a vindictive ideology that motivated its followers to violently attack peaceful critics.

Finally, the coverage of violence inspired by radical interpretations of Islam often emphasized a willingness to attack "soft targets," signaling the brutality and inhumanity of Muslim violence. A search for the key words "soft targets" in the *New York Times*, *Washington Post*, and *Wall Street Journal* retrieved 443 results of articles that had used the term to identify terrorists' merciless targeting of innocent and helpless civilians. One article stressed that terrorists were beginning to target a terrifying list of leisure locations such as "shopping malls, sports arenas, hotels, restaurants, bars, nightclubs, movie theaters, [and] housing complexes," maximizing the pain and suffering inflicted on "us infidels" (Ervin 2006). Other articles noted that Al Qaeda's history of picking "soft targets" necessitated terror alerts that inconvenienced citizens and disadvantaged businesses (Kehaulani Goo and Mintz 2003; Henkel 2004). Focusing on terror alerts, other articles portrayed how even those who escaped terror attacks remained traumatized by the constant change in terror alert statuses from orange to yellow to red (Rashbaum and Flynn 2003).

Impossible Victims

Another trend in media coverage during this time period was the emphasis on the impossible position of Muslims as innocent victims of discrimination in immigration policy and law enforcement's war on terror. This was rooted in the persistent accusation that moderate Muslims did not condemn terrorist attacks, as well as in the fact that the monitoring, surveillance, detention, and deportation of Muslim immigrants were all necessary procedures in the war on terror.

The presumed guilt of moderate Muslims because they shared the Muslim faith of terrorists was reinforced by the public speeches made by the office of the president and quoted widely across news media. On one occasion, the *New York Times* quoted George W. Bush's statement saying, "We will make no distinction between the terrorists who committed these acts and those who harbor them" (Schmemann 2001). Thus, Islamic terrorists, as well as the vague category of "those who harbor them"—which could be interpreted by readers to encompass everyone who shared the Muslim faith—were pronounced the enemy. From that moment, media coverage post-9/11 adopted the rhetoric of the war on terror wholesale, replicating the narrative espoused by George Bush's administration with little critique. This pattern would continue across the coverage of the early 2000s.

Suspicion of all members of the Muslim faith because of their acceptance of what was deemed a violent religion obscured repeated statements by the Muslim American community to disavow terrorism, therefore cementing their guilt. For instance, the *Washington Post* reported that Muslim leaders in Canada and the United States had issued a "fatwa" against terrorism that prohibited Muslims from "giving any support to terrorist groups who have carried out attacks against unarmed civilians" (Murphy 2005). However, coverage by *USA Today* dismissed the role of American clerics in drafting the fatwa and instead criticized the "deafening silence among American Muslim leaders when it comes to denouncing extremists who terrorize in the name of Islam" (2005). These discussions across several news outlets illustrated the intertextual relationships between articles that covered Islam and terrorism and the power of each article at reinforcing the existing bias against the community. In response to these repeated criticisms of inaction from 2001 onward, Muslim Americans wrote opinion pieces communicating their dismay at the continuous promotion of the narrative of complacency among Muslims, citing the example of the Council on American Islamic Relations' (CAIR) petition against terrorism, which received several hundreds of thousands of signatures from Muslim supporters (Kemp 2004). In another article where CAIR publicized the launch of a multiplatform media campaign against terrorism spanning newspapers, radio, billboards, mosque sermons, and all forms of communication in the community, one spokesperson for a religious organization complained that "the most frequent criticism that's tossed at the American Muslim community is, 'You never denounce terrorism,' ignoring the fact that we've denounced terrorism every which way from Sunday. I don't know what more we can do, and that is part of why we launched these initiatives" (Murphy and Cooperman 2004). Articles in the *Washington Post* that were critical of the Republican stance that saw Islam and terrorism as interchangeable were also guilty of connecting Muslims with terrorism in more indirect ways, arguing that although Islam was not a violent religion, "terrorism is the expression of a violent ideology that has, disturbingly, taken root among some Muslims" (Gerson 2013).

Because so much media coverage focused on Muslims as aggressors and criminals, media outlets covering the global war on terror completely overlooked the injustices and terrors inflicted on the Muslim American and international Muslim populations. Thus, in focusing on attempted embassy bombings or potential threats of groups around the world, newspapers failed to cover the unjustified detainment, surveillance, deportation, torture, or extrajudicial killings taking place. Analyses of media coverage of immigrant detainees, for example, pointed to the severely reduced examples of journalism questioning the practices of Republican or Democratic administrations vis-à-vis immigrants (Kurzban 2008, 71). In fact, the push toward entertainment pieces and sensationalist coverage as well as the turn toward uncritical coverage relying on TV pundits allowed the Bush and Obama administrations to dictate coverage and to continue to conceal information regarding the number of immigrants detained and where they were being held. Instead, by insisting that such information was classified for national security or prisoner privacy reasons, government officials received the tacit consent of the public to detain particularly Muslim or Muslim-looking detainees because they were protecting the public from potential terrorism (Sheikh 2008, 81).

These portrayals of a global network of terrorist organizations planning coordinated and concurrent attacks on Western embassies conjured an image of an unprecedented security threat that would justify draconian security measures and discrimination against Muslim Americans and Muslim immigrants. Thus, when the *New York Times* reported that a new policy "quietly imposed by the Bush administration" prevented "tens of thousands of Muslim men, from more than 26 countries" from obtaining U.S. visas, it dismissed the move as an inconvenience that was "causing headaches for American diplomats" (Bonner 2002), leaving the policy's legitimacy and morality unquestioned. Instead, it represented restrictions on immigrants from Muslim countries—including Middle Eastern countries and Pakistan, Malaysia, and Indonesia—as necessary security measures. Moreover, the general portrayal of Islam as threatening and the populations of Muslim-majority countries as suspected terrorists dampened the impact of critical coverage in American media of the abuses of power at the heart of the war on terror that unfairly discriminated against Muslim immigrants. Thus, a series of articles in the *Washington Post* highlighted the use of "immigration policy as a weapon" in the war on terrorism (Sheridan 2005), with a specific focus on deporting Muslim immigrants and stripping citizenship from Americans with Muslim backgrounds. Citing the example of a Saudi immigrant who was detained on false charges of supporting terrorism, the newspaper demonstrated how the targeting of Muslim immigrants over minor issues, such as buying supplies for a social event at a mosque or misunderstanding official forms, resulted in their deportation (Sheridan 2005). This illustrated how immigrants from Muslim-majority countries felt intimidated and scared after their experiences in being detained and deported by ICE. Another example from the *Washington Post* quoted a Pakistani journalist-fellow at the Brookings Institute who was detained and deported for not registering within forty days of his arrival, part of an entry-exit registration system in place for immigrants from Muslim majority countries such as Syria and Pakistan. He had in fact been wrongly advised that this measure was no longer necessary by INS officials, who later put the fellow in prison for the mistake (Lardner 2003). In response, the journalist expressed that he "cannot wait to leave and, if such policies continue, will never come back" (Lardner 2003). However, this coverage of the degree of scrutiny and unjustly disproportionate consequences to any gaffe in filling immigration forms because of immigrants' religious background was repeatedly justified as "understandable" in light of law enforcement's need to combat terrorism (Thibodeau 2002).

Yet another article from 2002 illustrated journalists' tacit acceptance that violations of constitutional rights were necessary in the war on terror. When James Ujaama was held for a month without charge (in violation of his constitutional rights as an American citizen), the press justified this decision as necessary because he was "designated a material witness to terrorist activity, which allows the authorities to detain him indefinitely" ("Lawyer" 2002). These trends in coverage demonstrated an acceptance of the suspected illicitness of

Muslim Americans, as well as the need to violate their constitutional rights in order to prevent further attacks from happening. Thus, the dominant themes in American press coverage of Muslim immigrants and American Muslim communities have been those that adopted the national security lens of the war on terror, drawing attention to Muslim men in particular as aggressors and dangerous threats and justifying discrimination against the community as a necessary step in the global war against terrorism.

The activism of Muslim civil rights groups somewhat helped shift the media conversation and political environment in the war on terror. Beginning immediately after the attacks, Muslim groups such as CAIR encouraged voting registration among eligible Muslim American citizens ("Muslim Group" 2002). Moreover, Muslim civil rights groups allied with other civil rights advocates and began to advocate for acknowledgment and reparations for the abuses of Muslim citizens' constitutional rights in the wake of 9/11. For example, the Center for Constitutional Rights accused the government of arbitrarily holding Muslim detainees in prison for months on minor immigration violations with no hearings to determine whether the government had probable cause to hold them. One article in the *New York Times* covered a class-action lawsuit filed by the families of Muslims who had been wrongfully detained in the wake of 9/11 (Sachs 2002). Although the article was flanked by other pieces that focused on assistance to the families of victims of 9/11 (Wald 2002), the article initiated an acknowledgment of the newsworthiness of the civil rights activism of Muslim rights groups. Such a perspective, however, was not dominant.

Thus, the years following 9/11 witnessed an overall negative portrayal of Muslim immigrants and Muslim Americans in the American news media. This portrayal was dominated by a framework of national security concerns regarding a suspect Muslim population, a focus on Muslims in the United States as immigrants or citizens as internal threats, and a portrayal of Muslims abroad as potential threats to the United States if they decided to immigrate. The coverage stressed the "softness" of the American public in responding to the threat of terrorism and the vulnerability of the American public and political and social institutions. Meanwhile, coverage of injustices toward Muslims was muted and often coupled with several articles that reiterated Muslim terrorism threats justifying the abuse of power by the Bush and Obama administrations.

The patterns of media coverage following 9/11 exhibited a hostility toward Muslim Americans and Muslim immigrants that branded the group as violent criminals, complicit in the crimes committed by extremists in the name of their faith. It thus became very difficult for media coverage to adequately respond to the onslaught of anti-Muslim rhetoric that would emerge during the 2016 election or the transition period that followed. Instead, the lack of sufficient critical examination on the use of immigration policy as a weapon in the war on terror undermined the ability to adequately respond to the

Republican candidates who expressed intentions to limit or even halt immigration from Muslim-majority countries. Moreover, the tacit agreement in media coverage that the surveillance and detention of Muslim immigrants were necessary procedural steps in the war on terror prevented media coverage from responding to proposals to create a Muslim registry or other discriminatory policies targeting immigrants from Muslim-majority countries.

In sum, media coverage in the post-9/11 period was by and large inhospitable. It continued to emphasize the threat of Muslim terrorism, thereby justifying the surveillance, detention, deportation, and torture of Muslim immigrants as well as American citizens with Muslim backgrounds. The coverage emphasized that Muslims were difficult enemies that targeted the "softness" of American citizens' generosity of spirit and ignorance of the true danger of Muslim terrorism. It also continuously painted Muslims as guilty even when they condemned terrorist attacks and extremism, making it impossible to portray them as victims of the civil rights abuses of the post-9/11 era. These dominant tropes in media coverage would become instrumental in the 2016 election and Trump administration that would follow.

The 2016 Election and Its Aftermath

The 2016 presidential election represented a culmination of anti-Muslim hysteria on the American political stage. Among the Republican presidential candidates, Dr. Ben Carson likened Muslim refugees arriving from Syria and Iraq to "rabid dogs running around your neighborhood" (Wise and McPike 2015). Meanwhile, then-presidential candidate Donald J. Trump said he would "absolutely" require the creation of a Muslim registry. When asked how this registry would differ from the former Jewish registry created by Nazi Germany to record "persons undesirable to the National Socialist Regime" (Monroe-Sheridan 2018, 2), Trump responded by flippantly challenging the reporter, saying, "You tell me" (Gabriel 2015).

These incidents reflected a general shift in American politics from administrations that created policies that indirectly discriminated against Muslims to the potential rise to the presidency of individuals who openly expressed hostility toward Muslims. This both took the form of dehumanizing and threatening characterizations, such as those of Carson, and the form of potential surveillance and control programs, such as the Muslim travel ban and registry policies suggested by Trump. Ironically, the traumatic experience for multiple immigrant and minority communities in the United States of witnessing the electoral win of candidate Trump was likened to the experience of witnessing 9/11, with intervention-inspired public fora created to discuss the election among college students and community members (Skalka 2016; Dremann 2017; Li 2016) or newspaper articles that referenced the difficulty of this moment for these communities. In relaying the election results, some broadcasters reacted emotionally on-air (Grynbaum 2016), and late-night television hosts announced the results with visible consternation and concern (Yahr and Butler 2016).

The record levels of xenophobic and anti-immigrant sentiments expressed by presidential candidates in the 2016 election corresponded with a rise in hate crimes and incidents throughout 2016. On the University of Pennsylvania's campus following the 2016 election, Black freshmen students were invited to a daily lynching event on a social media platform. Noted Penn student Maya Arthur, in a statement that crystallized the fears that people of color, religious minorities, and the LGBTQ+ community were having, said, "If this is the start, . . . the next four years will be a continued struggle and continued othering of a part of a community that's already marginalized" (Dent 2016).

After the election, President-elect Trump proceeded to assemble a government that promised to act upon these hostile stances toward Muslims. The media took note. Take, for example, CNN's coverage of Trump's nomination of Mike Pompeo for the position of secretary of state: noting Pompeo's distinction during his studies at West Point, Carol Costello mentioned more "controversial" moments of the nominee's career, including his involvement in the Benghazi committee and his criticism of Hillary Clinton's handling of the crisis, as well as his history of saying "critical things about Muslims." In fact, after the Boston marathon bombing, Pompeo declared on the House floor that "leaders in the Islamic faith who are not out there condemning it are potentially complicit in it as well" (Boorstein 2018). The statement reflected Pompeo's views that Muslim immigrants and Muslim Americans were legitimate objects of suspicion who must constantly condemn the actions of Muslim attackers in order to disprove their complicity. In spite of his Islamophobic remarks, CNN argued that Pompeo possessed "a stainless reputation," pointing to the tacit acceptance of Islamophobia throughout government and media ("Trump Fills Three Key Positions" 2016).

Costello predicted that the nominee would be "grilled" on his anti-Muslim rhetoric by Democrats in the Senate, suggesting that Pompeo's views might be more acceptable to Republican senators, but concluded that Democratic resistance to the candidate would be motivated more by his criticism of former secretary of state and Democratic presidential nominee Hillary Clinton than by disagreement with his position on Muslims. Thus, after a perfunctory citing of Pompeo's anti-Muslim sentiment, CNN concluded that Pompeo's Islamophobic and xenophobic comments did not disqualify him for the position and that in fact he possessed a "stainless reputation" ("Trump Fills Three Key Positions" 2016). The Muslim community's anxieties about the formation of a government that was hostile to their existence in the United States was thereby overlooked. Similarly, media coverage of Kris Kobach's involvement in the Trump transition team and in drafting a future Muslim registry program minimized the hostility of the former Kansas secretary of state toward Muslims. This pattern would continue for many cabinet appointments made by the Trump transition team.

Another fundamental shift in media ecology during the 2016 election and the transition period was the increased ability and acceptability of the presidential candidate (later the president-elect) as well as his cabinet nominees to directly address the public via Twitter. For example, Flynn expressed opinions condemning the Muslim faith and not just radical Muslims as a violent ideology, tweeting after an attack in Paris: "In the next 24 hours, I dare Arab & Persian world 'leaders' to step up to the plate and declare their Islamic ideology sick and must B healed" (Kaczynski 2016).

Although mainstream media outlets featured numerous articles covering the "outrageous" statements made by the president-elect and his cabinet nominees on Twitter, this coverage was usually within the context of other issues, such as attacks on journalists, the CNN news outlet, and Jews (Anapol 2017; East 2016; Kaczynski 2016). Only a handful of articles across all online and offline media honed in on officials' statements against the Muslim community (Piggott 2016). Meanwhile, the coverage of the formative period of the Trump government in the national South East Asian immigrant newspaper *India-West*, a paper read primarily by Muslim immigrants, noted that "Trump has surrounded himself with people with unusual ideas who may support a ban on Muslims from any country," referencing the nominations of Michael Flynn and Mike Pompeo (Sohrabji 2017). This coverage noted the NSEERS registry enacted by the Bush administration and enforced by the Obama administration until December 22, 2017, as precursors to the potential registry that could be created by the Trump administration. This connection exemplified the consciousness of Muslim communities in the United States about the connection between past discriminatory government policies and the proposals of a Muslim travel ban and registry made during the Trump campaign, a teleological link that was often overlooked by reporters from outside the community (Sohrabji 2017).

Equally, mainstream coverage of the president-elect's choices in creating his government did not connect facts regarding the officials and policies of previous administrations and the appointees and proposed policies of President Trump's future administration. For example, just as newspapers condemned the Muslim travel ban, they failed to connect the ban and the registry to policies enforced by the Bush and Obama administrations, which only ended on December 22, 2017, a few days before Obama left office. Instead of acknowledging how the ongoing enforcement of NSEERS throughout the Obama administration provided a legal precedent as well as an infrastructure to support future legislation targeting immigrants from Muslim-majority countries,

Vox News simply congratulated Obama on "making it more difficult for Trump to build his Muslim registry" (Lind 2016). Yet again, discussions of current and future policy measures did not reckon with a history of injustice toward immigrant communities, thereby retarding any effort to dismantle immigration hostility toward Muslim immigrants.

Moreover, the coverage did not critically examine the motivations expressed by the Obama administration in terminating NSEERS, which revealed that in the era of the National Security Agency, such an antiquated registry was no longer necessary. Consider, for example, the statement published by the Department of Homeland Security during the dismantling of the NSEERS program: "DHS ceased use of the National Security Entry-Exit Registration System (NSEERS) program in 2011 after finding that the program was redundant, captured data manually that was already captured through automated systems, and no longer provided an increase in security in light of DHS's evolving assessment of the threat posed to the United States by international terrorism" (Department of Homeland Security 2016). The declaration demonstrated firstly that the NSEERS program, throughout its many years in operation, never acknowledged that it targeted arrivals from Muslim-majority countries, choosing instead, even when dismantling the program, to call it a "registration process for *certain* nonimmigrants," a wording that allowed a lack of accountability or critique because of its ambiguity. Another important reveal of this statement was the fact that the violations of basic rights of immigrant communities were made possible by the classification of such groups as "nonimmigrant" (Department of Homeland Security 2016). Considering the broad powers granted to the government to arrest and detain immigrant noncitizens indefinitely, the choice to define immigrants to the United States (according to U.N. definitions of immigration) as nonimmigrants denied these subjects the minimal rights provided to noncitizen immigrants.

Conclusion

The post-9/11 era demonstrated the volatility of American immigration hospitality, as it flourished from the 1960s onward due to the passage of the Hart-Celler Act, only to abruptly and dramatically decline after the September 11 terrorist attacks. Indeed, the regulatory and media environments of this era showed that immigration hospitality shrinks once a threat by part of an othered community is perceived.

This chapter traces cyclical patterns of anti-immigrant hostility that emerge with increasing intensity from one period to the next. Just as the medicalized nativism of the late 1880s intensified in the 1920s with the targeting of immigrants as vectors of disease, the Red Scare of the 1920s resurfaced with a vengeance post 9/11 in what I refer to as the "green threat" of Islam. The association of immigrant groups with radical ideologies and sympathies in the 1920s was heightened during the post-9/11 period, when Muslim American communities were suspected of extremist views and activities. Moreover, the tendency to paint all immigrants of a community with the same brush, first seen in narratives of the Chinese coolie addressed in chapter 3, collectively blamed all Muslims residing in the United States for each and every terrorist attack.

Noting this, Muslim comedian Bassem Youssef pointed out that all it takes is a terrorist attack to worsen the situation for Muslims in the United States. In response, he facetiously created a "vaguely Muslim looking morning after kit" for Muslim-looking Americans to use the day after any terrorist attack, wherein they can practice "sounding white" with a CD and have an automated condemnation statement literally at hand with a keychain that recited "I hereby condemn yesterday's terrorist attack" (Maldonado 2017). In fact, a common joke among Muslim immigrants became praying at each juncture that the next attack is not committed by a Muslim so that they may avoid having to repudiate extremism yet again.

Bassem Youssef's humorous advice points to the media and regulatory inhospitality that characterized the turn of the twenty-first century, as Muslim immigrants and Muslim-presenting Americans were vilified and represented as dangerous and suspected radicals in the media and as immigration and law enforcement policies targeted these groups under the guise of protecting national security. In turn, this environment was crucial to foregrounding and foreshadowing the policies and rhetoric that would define the Trump administration after the 2016 election.

6

Conclusion: The Future of American Hospitality

●●●●●●●●●●●●●●●●●●●●●●●

Muslim Travel Ban

On January 27, 2017, less than ten days after taking the oath of office, President Donald Trump enacted an executive order indefinitely halting the entry of Syrian refugees into the United States. It also placed a ninety-day ban on the entry of visitors from seven Muslim-majority countries: Iran, Iraq, Libya, Somalia, Sudan, Syria, and Yemen (Trump 2017). Instantaneously, travelers who were suspended midair as the ban went into effect suddenly found their visas invalidated and were detained upon arriving at their U.S. destinations. In the meantime, protests broke out throughout the country, from New York to California (McGurty and Frandino 2017).

The period immediately following the signing of this first executive order exhibited many of the characteristics Charles Tilly (2017) identifies with social movements: It entailed the activation of multiple civil society associations and coalitions in response (Mitchell 2017), including statements from CAIR, the ACLU, and SPCA protesting the order (ACLU 2017). The aftermath of the order produced rallies, demonstrations, and protests nationwide, with protestors marching at international airports and in city streets and public squares. The ban's enactment also sparked a number of donation drives enabling civil society organizations to fight the ban in court. This grassroots mobilization influenced the ensuing regulatory and media hospitality toward Muslim immigrants after the ban was issued, as the following sections will show. Moreover, it points to the important tension that occurs when journalists and members of the public express hospitality in the absence of regulatory hospitality, resulting in a contradiction in the migrant experience as they experience exclusion in immigration policy and welcome in media coverage of immigration and immigrants. As such, this example illustrates the possibility of these tensions at encouraging greater immigration hospitality.

The enactment of the Muslim travel ban is important for a discussion of immigration hospitality because it points to the possibility of grassroots responses to many of the perceived injustices and inadequacies of not only the Trump administration's policies toward Muslim immigrants but more broadly the historical treatment of immigrants in American immigration policy and its possible change in the future. In tracing the grassroots responses to the enactment of the Muslim travel ban, this chapter raises the possibility that a sense of public hospitality can not only challenge many of the perceived injustices toward Muslim immigrants but also rectify the inequities in the treatment of immigrants in the United States. Indeed, the public mobilization against the Muslim travel ban surprised Muslim communities in the United States that had experienced demonization and suspicion after 9/11. Any Muslim who has navigated an airport in the United States post-9/11 will understand the shock with which Muslims viewed images of protestors at airports across the nation shouting, "Let them in!"

Regulatory Hospitality and the Muslim Travel Ban

The public mobilization against the executive order resulted in a number of contestations and temporary suspensions of the order in 2017 and 2018. Civil rights organizations followed much of the American public's grassroots response to the Muslim travel ban: The National Immigration Law Center collected a list of the officially declared protests in thirty-two cities following the executive order (Trump 2017). Similarly, several regional chapters of the American Civil Liberties Union (ACLU) connected these protests to the challenges of the executive order in the American judicial system, seeing the protests as crucial factors supporting the civil rights groups' efforts to counter the decision ("Timeline of the Muslim Ban" n.d.; Trump 2017).

Thus, on February 3, 2017, the ACLU took the matter to court. Strengthened by the position that much of the public was taking against the ban, the ACLU obtained a temporary stay on the deportation of visitors detained under the executive order until June 27, 2017, while the legality of the order was in debate. A week later, the Ninth Circuit Court of Appeals upheld the decision to put a temporary stay on the order's enforcement. At every hearing of the case in court, and even when the cases were dismissed, protestors gathered outside chanted, "No Muslim Travel Ban ever" and "No ban no wall," strengthening civil rights groups' resolve to appeal unfavorable court decisions (Gandy 2017; Pieklo 2017).

The executive order was heard again in Virginia on December 8, 2017, as arguments were put forth against the Trump administration's third attempt to enforce the ban. After the failure of two attempts at a temporary ban, Deputy Assistant Attorney General Hashim Mooppan argued that a third executive order differed significantly from the original in that it provided evidence-based research that recommended prohibiting immigration from countries that did not provide sufficient information and documentation for its citizens. Having blocked the executive order three times, Doug Chin, the attorney general of Hawaii, recognized the peril of national origin and religious discrimination, issuing a statement saying, "This is the third time Hawaii has gone to court to stop President Trump from issuing a travel ban that discriminates against people based on their nation of origin or religion" (Kelsey 2017).

However, the judicial obstruction of the executive order failed to deter President Trump, who had promised throughout his campaign to achieve a "total and complete shutdown of Muslims entering the United States," even going as far as asserting that Muslim American citizens traveling outside the country would not be allowed to reenter the United States if he were elected president (Johnson 2015). These declarations, which were published on the then-presidential candidate's campaign website, were later removed because they presented evidence of Trump's unconstitutional intention to target individuals with the Muslim travel ban because of their religion. Thus, each challenge to the executive order forced the administration to issue a new iteration of the policy, reaching a third iteration in September 2017.

In the final Supreme Court decision made regarding the third iteration of the executive order on June 26, 2018, Supreme Court justices ruled 5–4 for upholding the policy, choosing to evaluate the thrice-revised order for its explicit language while disregarding the rhetoric of the administration and its key officials during the campaign and the drafting of the policy. Interestingly, the choice to disregard comments made by officials to evaluate whether a policy was discriminatory was a departure from the choice the Supreme Court had taken in *Masterpiece Cakeshop v. Colorado Civil Rights Commission* a few days earlier, where the court ruled 5–4 that the comments made by Colorado officials characterized a hostility toward Christianity (U.S. Supreme Court 2018, 14–15). The coverage of the decision yet again pointed to another instance during the discussions of the Muslim travel ban in which the levels of regulatory and media hospitality diverged from each other, allowing media hospitality to extend welcome to immigrants when regulations did not.

While many had hoped that the Supreme Court's decision to consider comments made by Colorado officials during hearings of the Masterpiece case suggested an opening for overturning the Muslim travel ban (Jacoby 2018), the court decided to take the opposite stance in its ruling on the ban. In spite of the unfavorable Supreme Court decision, the ongoing discussions and protests surrounding the Muslim ban and its multiple court hearings reveal the conditions under which regulatory hospitality shifts in the United States. It both contracts to near-extinction and balloons to surprising dimensions depending on the circumstances. In propelling public mobilization for political and legislative efforts that might enact more inclusionary and hospitable policies toward immigrants and refugees, it paradoxically draws attention to the potential of the myth of the "nation of immigrants" in inspiring greater immigration hospitality and in critiquing earlier restriction and discrimination.

The Muslim travel ban drew its support from the patterns of and arguments made for immigration restriction in other eras examined in earlier chapters of this book. Just as earlier eras had argued that immigrants should be banned because they brought with them threatening behavior such as opium smoking, diseases such as typhoid, or dangerous radical ideologies such as anarchism and socialism, contemporary debates on immigration continue to justify immigration restriction because immigrants threaten to import various social ills—namely, religious radicalism and terrorism.

Consider, for example, a brief filed by the Zionist Organization of America (ZOA) in support of the Muslim travel ban, which justified the restriction of any immigrants arriving from war-torn countries because they were "infested with terrorist groups and sympathizers," neglecting the American commitment to accept refugees escaping violence (Berney 2018, 3). This statement both neglected the American commitment to accept refugees fleeing violence at home and revealed outright support for a discriminatory policy by an organization that claims to lobby against religious and ethnic discrimination; it also demonstrated verbatim use of the Geneva Convention for refugees to justify exclusion. Here refugees' escape from war-torn countries was used to defend policies of restriction rather than defend the ability to flee violence as a protected human right. Positions similar to that of the ZOA were put forth by multiple organizations that adopted a "national security" framework, including national security experts from the Center for Security Policy, Citizens United, the Conservative Legal Defense and Education Fund, Gun Owners of America, Inc., and the English First Foundation (Berney 2018).

These discussions recall the conditions under which immigration hospitality has shrunk in multiple periods of American history, where security and safety concerns positioned immigrants as vectors of disease and perpetrators of violence and other undesirable social behaviors. They also demonstrate how the dehumanization of specific categories of immigrants—Chinese, Eastern and Southern European, or Muslim—hinders the recognition of both their capacity to integrate and their right to migrate to safer and more prosperous countries.

Arguments in support of the executive order directly reference other periods of history during which immigration restriction was enacted under similar concerns (Lee 2016). For example, in the aftermath of the June decision, *National Review* wrote that the executive order fell within the authority of the president (Berney 2018). Opponents of the ban criticized this connection to historical parallels of discriminatory policy as indicative of the policy's moral paucity. For instance, Congressman Ted Lieu issued a statement following then-candidate Donald Trump's suggestion of a ban during his presidential campaign, dismissing the move as an attempt "to justify [his] bigoted proposal based on policies the U.S. enacted in World War II" (Lieu 2015). As Lieu indicated, the replication of the World War II policies was unacceptable because "the racist internment of Americans of Japanese descent represented some of the darkest moments in American history—when we betrayed our most sacred values" (Lieu 2015). Similarly, Representative Judy Chu, chair of the Congressional Asian Pacific American Caucus (CAPAC), criticized the Trump proposal because of its resemblance to Japanese internment policies during World War II, saying that "like Japanese incarceration, imposing a registry upon American Muslims is not only unconstitutional, but it goes against our very principles as a nation" (Lee 2016). Thus, just as earlier periods of immigration restriction are invoked to justify discriminatory policy in later periods, they also open these policies to critique because of the critical retrospective view of discriminatory policy.

What is most compelling about the Muslim travel ban for the study of immigration hospitality, however, is that it demonstrates a moment in which the discriminatory exclusion of one group from hospitable welcome can invite public appraisal. Take, for instance, *USA Today*'s discussion of the Muslim travel ban in April 2018. The article noted that although several Supreme Court justices appeared to favor upholding the ban, "only one side of the argument over President Trump's travel ban was well represented outside court" (Wolf 2018). Pointing to the numerous protestors gathered outside the hearing, the article accompanied this observation with several images of peaceful protestors standing in front of the court building (fig. 6.1).

From the earliest period of its history, the United States has rested upon the prejudicial exclusion and systematic oppression of Native Americans and African Americans as Others. These two groups were not given immigrant status but treated in ways that anticipated the later treatment of new arrivals to the United States. As the country developed, it fostered a bifurcated immigration environment that extended hospitality to White, mostly Protestant, northern European settlers and immigrants while excluding particular categories of immigrants—Chinese, southern and eastern Europeans, and Muslims—from this welcome. In this sense, the opposition to the Muslim travel ban illustrates continuities in the contradictions of American hospitality, highlighting the

FIG. 6.1   Protesters with placards gather at the U.S. Supreme Court in Washington, D.C., April 25, 2018. AstridRiecken, EPA-EFE.

need to address the Muslim travel ban as part of a continuum of restrictive inhospitable immigration policies. But it also illustrates a crucial mechanism through which immigration hospitality might be expanded, as public awareness of these continuities increases and the acceptance of discriminatory policy diminishes.

This sentiment is noticeable in a brief put forth by the Japanese American community that highlighted the endurance of immigration restriction and discrimination against communities. Submitted by the Korematsu Center for Law and Equality, a brief by the children of the famous interned Japanese American Fred Korematsu maintained that they felt compelled to respond to this case, as they recognized the disturbing relevance of this Court's decisions in their fathers' infamous cases challenging the mass removal and incarceration of Japanese Americans during World War II (Korematsu 2017, 2). The children highlighted their father's legacy in fighting against the incarceration of Japanese Americans and his efforts to prove that "military necessity" did not justify the deprivation of innocent Americans of their constitutional rights because of their race and national origin. They reminded the court that the United States had since admitted that the internment of Japanese Americans was wrong, awarding their father the Presidential Medal of Freedom for his "work advancing civil and human rights" (Korematsu 2017, 2). What the responses of the Korematsus and others reveal is that for immigrant communities targeted by discriminatory policies and immigration hostility, the continuities between past injustice and contemporary policy are vivid and palpable. This renders the current imperative to combat these injustices more pressing.

All in all, the legal arguments surrounding the Muslim travel ban reveal a few common tropes in American regulatory hospitality that I have identified. First, the arguments supporting the ban reveal that the precedent of previous restriction is used to justify later discriminatory policies. They relatedly demonstrate the cyclical resilience of the conditions that cause immigration hostility, such as security concerns, religious intolerance, and racial and ethnic Othering. For example, multiple sources supporting the ban describe it as a "necessity" that is similar in other bans to Chinese, Iranian, and other immigrants in earlier periods of American history.

Second, proponents of the ban continuously defend the need to exclude by nation of origin as acceptable, thereby alluding to the national origins quotas of the 1920s as precedents. Thus, just as this period characterized a shrinkage of American regulatory hospitality, it also reveals the conditions of national security that instigate the contraction of hospitality as well as the cyclical patterns that illustrate the way immigration hospitality regresses to discrimination and restriction.

But most importantly, and more so than in other periods, discussion of the ban points to the capacity of social movements to express a sense of public welcome and hospitality to transform the policymaking environment at the grassroots level. While the three iterations of court hearings did not prevent the Muslim travel ban from being upheld by the Supreme Court in June 2018, they had impact in tempering its scope, severity, and influence. Not only does discussion enable discriminatory policies to be heard and contested in court, but it also promises that such movements can foster an environment for greater immigration hospitality.

Media Hospitality and the Muslim Travel Ban

Just as the judicial response to the executive order reflects a reaction to the public opposition to the policy, the media coverage of the executive order issued by Trump on January 27, 2017, continues to respond to the dramatic shift in public attitudes regarding discrimination against Muslim immigrants and Muslim Americans. First exemplified by the protests that swept through the nation in the wake of the executive order, media coverage of public protests online and offline directly addresses the mechanisms through which media hospitality has shrunk in the past. Unlike in the past, however, it also tackles the particular manifestations of media inhospitality toward Muslim immigrants by critiquing them.

Because the executive order and the protests occurred simultaneously, the media often addressed protests of the ban as part of their coverage of the ban itself. For instance, while the executive order was first being contemplated by the Trump administration, the *New York Times* enthusiastically reported that New Yorkers were wasting "no time in protesting whatever [is] next" (Robbins 2017). The *Washington Post* ran one article titled "No Ban No Wall, Justice for All" (Ribas and Micaya 2018) and another proclaiming "Love the Neighbor" (McCrummen 2017). Such coverage of the protests helps make it possible for public expressions of hospitality to invigorate the media's immigration policy discussions from the bottom up. In that light, it is important to note how often images captured at protests accompany the news articles reflecting on the executive order. This has included numerous articles by the *New York Times* featuring pictures of protest banners accompanying reflections on the legality and constitutionality of the Muslim travel ban (Gladstone and Sugiyama 2018; Liptak and Shear 2018).

Criticism of the executive order has been particularly evident in social media postings. For example, one sign (fig. 6.4) posted by the Women's March Twitter account on January 25, 2017, stated that "immigrants make America great" (Women's March 2017). The same sign was recirculated on other Twitter accounts and in blog posts (Baftijari 2017).

These efforts are helping enhance media hospitality in mainstream news coverage. As news outlets reflect on the ban by replicating many of the tropes of solidarity, hospitality, and welcome that are emerging in user-generated content in social media, articles portraying Muslim immigrants as victims of discrimination, injustice, and violence are reversing the post-9/11 trend that primarily portrayed Muslims as criminals and perpetrators of violence and terrorism. The *Washington Post* boldly stated that the "U.S. is still harsh to Muslims, no matter how the travel ban case goes" (Yasin 2018). Other articles pointed out that "US bigotry didn't start with Trump" (Essa 2017), reminding the public of the past treatment of Muslim immigrants. Finally, a stream of articles reflected upon the Supreme Court's "indefensible double standard" in considering the anti-Christian rhetoric in one case and overlooking anti-Muslim rhetoric in another, suggesting that Muslims suffer disproportionately when such imbalances of judicial oversight occur (Somin 2018; Aziza 2018). In this way, media coverage harnessing the messages being circulated in public protests and online responses, which affirm the American identity of Muslim Americans, reflects a shift toward greater hospitality after a period of Othering and exclusion following 9/11. Thus, the aftermath of the ban is producing media coverage that affirms the belonging of Muslim Americans and combats the Othering of Muslims that had taken place in the past, particularly due to media coverage that had emphasized criminality or terrorism. It also is challenging news outlets to provide more compassionate and objective coverage of Muslim immigrants, enhancing media hospitality.

Resonant with this more hospitable coverage is the fact that the media are recirculating images created by activists, artists, and community leaders that directly address immigration hostility of the past and counter past media coverage's tendency to emphasize the Otherness and foreignness of immigrant groups. One example of this trend can be seen in Shepard Fairey's poster project responding to the Muslim travel ban (fig. 6.5). Fairey used his iconic style, previously used to create the "Hope" posters that defined the Obama campaign and administration, to create an image of a Muslim woman veiled in the American flag, weaving the community into the nationalist symbol to proclaim it as part of the nation.

The image, recirculated in news outlets such as *USA Today*, *Huffington Post*, and CNN online, became emblematic of the belonging of Muslim immigrants that defied the exclusionary policies of the Trump administration (Wolf 2018). Thus, as Fairey told CNN, his "We the People" poster series would convey a "simple message" that depicted the diversity of the American people in the face of Trump's xenophobia and Othering (Schwarz 2017).

The circulation of the image in the media also complemented its circulation in offline protests. One scholar of Muslim media representations described her experience at the Women's March in 2016, where she noticed Fairey's then-iconic image of a Muslim woman wearing the American flag as a headscarf (fig. 6.5) and marveled, "Wow, people care about Muslims all of the sudden!" (Halabi and Peterson 2018). Muslim immigrants are commenting on the greater public understanding of Muslim rights as part of the broader movement for civil rights in the country (Snow and Banks 2017).

Efforts such as these have produced memorable images that testify to the intersectionality of the post–Muslim travel ban civil rights movement, such as this now-iconic image of two Muslim and Jewish fathers hoisting their children on their shoulders during an airport protest in Chicago. The image, taken by photographer Nuccio DiNuzzo, was shared in numerous outlets, including CNN online, Quartz, ABC News online and the *New York Times* (Aberra 2017; Crespo, 2017; Quito 2017; Burton 2018). It was also republished alongside articles pertaining to the Muslim ban, as debates surrounding the order continued (Kristof 2017).

Indeed, the media positioned public mobilization in the immediate aftermath of the ban as evidence of a dramatic transformation in public opinion toward Muslims: *Vox* cited a study by three political scientists—Loren Collingwood, Nazita Lajevardi, and Kassra Oskooii—concluding that "the national discourse on the Muslim Travel Ban" repeated statements that the policy conflicted with "American values" and changed public opinion on the matter of Muslim immigration (Burton 2018). Such media coverage revealed an uncharacteristic awareness of news outlets regarding the shifting attitudes of the American public toward Muslim immigrants.

Alongside critical coverage of the executive order and public protests, media coverage also demonstrated a shift from its post-9/11 focus on Muslims as criminals and terrorists to a growing recognition of Muslims as victims of discrimination and violence. Thus, articles after the ban focused on Muslim victims of hate crimes, such as a stream of articles in the *Washington Post* that followed the case of a Muslim teenager who was assaulted and killed as she was leaving her mosque (Siddiqui, Zauzmer, and Pulliam Bailey 2017). The articles criticized law enforcement and the regulatory infrastructure that had resulted in cases of hate crimes being prosecuted as "road rage" incidents in spite of race and religion motivating the attacks (Stack and Mele 2017). One pointed out that a similar concurrent attack on Muslim mosque-goers in London, which had killed one Muslim and left ten injured, was being investigated by London police as "terrorism against Muslims" (Bilefsky 2017), suggesting a critique of the lack of adequate response by Virginia police in the case of the slain Muslim American teenager.

Additionally, media hospitality is also manifested in the inclusion of Muslim voices and perspectives in media coverage that allows audiences to understand the struggles of a minority community. As such, articles in the *New York Times*, *Wall Street Journal*, *Washington Post*, and other outlets have since enlisted Muslim bloggers, imams, and prominent activists to reflect on the impact of the ban (Umar 2018; Hawgood 2018). An opinion piece in the *New York Times* by an Iranian blogger pointed out the "reductive media representations" of Muslims in American media and provided her insight not only on Muslim American lifestyles and belonging but also on the repercussions of discriminatory policies for Muslim American communities (Hawgood 2018). An opinion piece by Iranian American scholar Samira Rajabi reflected on the traumatic impact of the executive order on herself and her family, providing a humanizing perspective of how such policies affect universally joyous occasions such as weddings (Rajabi 2018). Finally, in an article in the *New York Times*, Muslim imam Mustafa Umar suggested that since Islam teaches us that life is a struggle to do good and overcome divine "tests" of one's faith, the Trump presidency represents a test of faith for the Muslim community, challenging its resolve and willingness to advocate for greater justice (Umar 2018).

The introduction of Muslim voices in mainstream media also impacts the patterns of media coverage. The *New York Times*, for instance, highlighted the change brought about by the greater diversity of writers and opinion leaders invited to opine on issues in the news, when, in the aftermath of one terrorist attack, it invited Muslim community members to reflect on the dangerous and alienating impact of news coverage patterns that follow terrorist attacks in the United States (Barone 2017). Such conversations reflect efforts by news outlets to provide fairer and more ethical coverage of Muslim Americans. They also point toward efforts to elucidate past wrongs.

One consequence of the Muslim travel ban has been vibrant discussions among journalists and editors regarding the ethical coverage of the debate over the executive order. For instance, in January 2017, a directive sent by the editor of the *Wall Street Journal* was leaked to *Politico*, in which the editor berated journalists for portraying the executive order as a Muslim travel ban rather than a general travel ban and instructed them to describe the countries included in the ban as "states that pose significant or elevated risks of terrorism" (Perlberg 2017; Pompeo 2017). The incident sparked a debate in many other news outlets—the *Washington Post*, *Politico*, and *Huffington Post*—and even broadcast news such as CNN and alternative news sites such as BuzzFeed. When the editor claimed that his choices were motivated by the need to focus reporting on facts and thus to not call falsehoods that the president stated "lies" or to not call the order a Muslim ban, these choices were labeled "deeply disturbing" (Herrerla 2017). Similarly, journalists speaking on condition of anonymity told *Politico* that "for the editor-in-chief of a major American newspaper to go out of his way to whitewash [this] is unconscionable," pointing to the nefariousness of ambiguous language that normalizes and disguises discrimination against Muslims (Pompeo 2017). These responses suggested that while American mainstream media had plainly and uncritically reported discriminatory policy in the past, it would no longer necessarily do so in the aftermath of the Muslim travel ban.

Finally, media responses to the executive order have produced a reemergence of Lady Liberty as a dominant trope in critiques of the policy particularly as a betrayal of American values and American hospitality. Replicating images and tropes that were used before during the Chinese exclusion era (fig. 6.3), cartoonists and online activists drew images of a compassionate and indignant Lady Liberty protecting members of a community that had been discriminated against.

Examples of this trend emerged in several Twitter threads reflecting on the policy. In the wake of the ban, writer Hank Green challenged Twitter artists to create hand-drawn cartoons about the ban, and the result was a series of tweets. One such image (fig. 6.2) portrayed an indignant Lady Liberty, who with knitted brow and a mouth pursed as if to say a calming "shush," consoled a brown-skinned veiled Muslim woman. Here, the skin tone and headscarf that had previously been used as symbols of the Otherness of Muslims were shown empathetically. This iconic image was shared thousands of times online and carried at protests across the country, becoming emblematic of resistance to the ban. Jamie Hu, the artist who created the illustration, told *Vice* that he was proud this illustration was his most recognized piece of art because "Muslims and refugees deserve just as much protection and love in America as anyone" (Mufson 2017).

Other images featured an angry Lady Liberty protecting Muslim immigrants. One such image portrayed the Statue of Liberty holding a Syrian

FIG. 6.2 Lady Liberty protecting Muslim woman. Jamie Hu, @quiversarrow on Instagram, 2017.

refugee child who carried the torch in her hand. The drawing directly connected the betrayal of what the Statue of Liberty stood for to the Muslim travel ban, as Columbia's angry raised eyebrow mirrored the child's concerned lowered brows. These images portrayed women and children, perceived to be the most vulnerable populations in forced displacement.

The messages in contemporary artistic responses to the Muslim travel ban resurrected many of the images of the Chinese exclusion era and other periods

FIG. 6.3 "Justice for the Chinese." Thomas Nast, March 27, 1886. Museum of Fine Arts Houston. Shared under public domain license.

of restriction. They portrayed the statue protecting immigrants and opposing bigotry and violence against immigrants. They also replicated the tenderness of Lady Liberty from previous images.

These images also portrayed immigrants as the bearers of Lady Liberty's torch, thereby connecting the position of immigrants in American society with the resonance and reach of American ideals. In this image by Karen Hallion (fig. 6.4), Lady Liberty supportively embraced a Muslim woman who holds the flaming torch not high above her head but solemnly, clasping both hands at her waist as if in prayer. Images like these suggested the faith of immigrants in the promise of the United States and how that faith sustained America's image as a land of immigrants.

Images circulating in social media platforms thus influenced the level of media hospitality as exhibited by mainstream outlets. They also prompted

FIG. 6.4 "Mother of Exiles." Karen Hallion, @Khallion, Twitter, 2017.

conversations in mainstream media about how hospitality belonged within American identity and values. For instance, *Vox* reported that the Muslim travel ban instigated a conversation about what American values stood for and how the travel ban conflicted with Americans' perception of their own values (Burton 2018). Similarly, in the *Washington Post*, images of the Statue of Liberty held by protestors at marches accompanied a reflection on what American values meant for immigrants in the United States (Hauslohner 2018).

This theme has been noticeable in many of the images portraying "American values" and Lady Liberty following the executive order. The myth of the nation of immigrants implicitly ties hospitality to America's identity, culture, and values. Thus, responses to the Muslim travel ban highlight the ideal of hospitality personified by Lady Liberty and connect this ideal to American values. Similarly, critiques of the order focus on the visual portrayal of the death of hospitality that this executive order accomplished and the betrayal of American ideals that this death entailed.

From the words of Emma Lazarus to the years of standing witness to Ellis Island, the Statue of Liberty has come to emblematize America's vision of itself as a welcoming nation, portrayed in some artistic reflections of 2017. Another response to Hank Green's invitation to reflect on the Muslim travel ban through art is this illustration by Nica Andor, which proclaims "all are welcome," showing Lady Liberty affectionately embracing a Muslim child who returns her embrace (fig. 6.5)

The importance of the myth of the nation of immigrants is evident in the messages portrayed in these cartoons, which elaborate on a perceived set of American ideals that place immigration hospitality and welcome at the center of American values, a portrayal that would be echoed in the slogans and banners of the public mobilization against the travel ban. Within hours of its proclamation, an estimated ten thousand protestors marched in Battery Park, New York, facing the Statue of Liberty, while another eight thousand marched at the Capitol steps (McGurty and Frandino 2017). At airports across the United States, protestors congregated and shouted, "Let them in!" In Philadelphia, over six thousand flocked to the airport. Another two thousand protestors occupied San Francisco Airport with signs stating, "Muslims welcome here." Throughout the country, tens of thousands took to Twitter and the streets to express their discontent with the policy, all maintaining one core argument in common: the United States has always been a nation of immigrants and a welcoming country for refugees from around the world. Faced with the reality of an immigration policy that withheld welcome to Muslim immigrants, protestors filled airport arrivals halls chanting to remove barriers to immigrants and extend them direct welcome.

These responses connect the welcome extended to Muslim immigrants to the perceived ideals of the nation of immigrants. A sampling of the protest chants recited at demonstrations throughout the country also echoes these trends, as protestors shouted, "This is what America looks like," in reference to the racial and ethnic diversity that define contemporary American society. Other chants included "We are all immigrants" (Sinnar 2017). Another powerful chant was "Let them in," chanted by protesters to extend welcome to

FIG. 6.5 "All Are Welcome." Nica Andor, @NicaMinoru. Twitter, 2017.

Muslim immigrants detained at airports, even when the authorities could not. Often, these chants could be heard from a distance. But they were certainly heard by immigrants as they were detained.

In light of these images and protest slogans, it is clear that the opposition to the executive order offers a glimmer of hope for the prospects of immigration and media hospitality in the United States. It demonstrates the impact of the demographic change brought about by the Hart-Celler Act in inspiring an empathetic public view of immigrants. For example, the Muslim travel ban sparked a trend online that highlighted the immigrant history of those who opposed the order, as prominent personalities, such as Reza Aslan, tweeted, "My family fled Iran for a better life in US," alongside a photograph of his family. These responses by accomplished American citizens highlight that their contribution to the United States was made possible by their family's migration ("#MyMuslimAmericanFamily" 2018).

In sum, the aftermath of the Muslim ban has thus far pointed toward greater media hospitality toward Muslim immigrants and immigrants in general. While it is too soon to predict how lasting the effect of the Muslim travel ban will be, this period points to the capacity of public expressions of hospitality to inspire a shift in mainstream news media toward accommodating greater media hospitality. It is also prompting the media to reevaluate the hostility expressed toward these communities in past periods.

A Future for American Hospitality?

Roger Silverstone distinguished between "media morality" and media ethics, explaining that while the latter concerned the practical application of certain ideals in professional spheres such as journalism, the former referred to the moral worldview represented in the media (2013, 7). Silverstone was concerned with the role the media plays in constructing a moral order, particularly as it concerned the appearance of the Other (2006, 8). In this book, I have offered an analysis of media morality in relation to multiple communities of racialized immigrant groups in three different eras of U.S. immigration.

With this historical approach, this project seeks to advance a crucial argument regarding Silverstone's concept of "media morality" as well as morality *of the* media. Borrowing from a continuing debate within history as a discipline, I concur that "the value of history is . . . moral: by liberalizing the mind, by deepening the sympathies, by fortifying the will, it enables us to control not society, but ourselves" (Becker 1915, as cited in Sheehan 2005). As such, I present this interrogation of the history of media and immigration policy to offer a deeper understanding of the factors limiting immigration hospitality and how future media coverage and policymaking may better address them. Moreover, I consider how media and immigration hospitality converge to impact immigrant lived experiences alongside the efforts each wave of immigrants has made to confront hostility and build a sense of home in their adopted country. I hope that this account, with its difficult position between the fields of history and communication and immigration and media studies, may open up fruitful avenues of future research on hospitality as a moral position within these two areas.

This history shows that particular ethnic, racial, and religious communities have been systematically excluded from the embrace of American immigration hospitality. Yet, the passage of the Muslim travel ban and the public, media, and regulatory responses to it points to one potential avenue in which hospitality may still have a future: host populations living up to the promise of America as a nation of immigrants.

Throughout this book, I have argued that hospitality describes a relationship between a host who has developed an identity that is spatially anchored—and is thus seen as belonging to a place and possessing authority over it—and a guest whose identity is perceived as tied to other places and who enters the host's domain. This relationship combines notions of home and identity, host and belonging, and guest and Other/stranger. In it, the host grants access to potential places of belonging, often providing food, drink, and shelter, and welcomes the guest by cultivating a relationship of openness and understanding.

This book identifies hospitality as an important and relevant ethical intervention in both the study of immigration history in the United States and the study of media coverage of immigrant communities and immigration. I illustrate how media coverage and immigration regulation express hospitality toward immigrants in American society. Focusing on three periods of immigration restriction, I present the conditions under which American hospitality is extended or denied to immigrants and how we may better account for them to extend the hospitality we show future newcomers.

Admittedly, this book notes that hospitality remains an unequal relationship, and one that shrinks periodically in the face of compounding variables that distinguish immigrants from the native population, including perceived visible racial difference, religious diversity, and ethnic, linguistic, and socioeconomic differences between incoming immigrants and the settled population. The analysis has thus attended to the power dynamics through which immigration policy and media discourses about immigration have mutually constructed an inhospitable environment for immigrants. Though this stops short of attributing causal impact in the relationship of media and policymaking, it does suggest a joint interaction of media and regulation on the immigrant experience. Their combined presence helps explain how hospitality impacts immigrants' lives.

By invoking the context of hospitality as both a concept and a relationship governing immigration, my argument unsettles the assumption that White, predominantly Protestant Americans of European ancestry constitute a "native" population that belongs to the United States and thereby exert greater authority over its territory. Additionally, it expands the phenomenon of American hospitality by accommodating the cases of slavery and Indigenous genocide and expropriation as examples of the nascent and periodic degeneration of the host-guest relationship. That relationship's denigration to one of host-guest or host-hostage, respectively, reveals the racial discrimination at the core of the nation's model of immigration.

This pattern of hospitality—in which notions of "hostage" taint both the host and guest roles relevant to the relationship—continues to impact more current periods of history. It reserves the activities of belonging and ownership—characteristics of the host community—to one racial category, foreshadowing the racial discrimination and exclusion that would befall other racial, religious, and ethnic groups over time. Such was the case with Chinese immigrants in the 1880s, southern and eastern European immigrants in the 1920s, and finally immigrants from Muslim-majority countries in the 2000s. It also reasserts itself in the Muslim travel ban. Thus, the historical grounding of this analysis points to the racial injustice embedded in American immigration hospitality and illustrates the consequences of this past on the practice of hospitality in later periods.

Thirdly, this project addresses the dissonance between the restrictive immigration history of the United States from the 1880s onward and the myth of the "nation of immigrants" that is often evoked in political or media debates on immigration. Most clearly illustrated in the treatment of the Muslim ban in this chapter, this dissonance undercuts aspirations of immigration hospitality. Yet the latter remains immensely powerful as an ideal that guides policymakers, activists, journalists, and members of the public in navigating constructs of self and other. At the heart of this myth is a conception of American identity that centers on the just treatment of the newcomer who arrives at the nation's airports, shores, and borders.

The surfacing of these tropes across the most widely circulated national newspapers during these historical periods shows that although criticism of restrictive policies may be prevalent in the news of each period, hospitality relies on a welcome from the majority of the population. This suggests that critiques of regulation are only successful at resisting, changing, or dismantling policies when they are adopted by large segments of the public rather than simply the immigrant communities that the regulation targets. This is exemplified in the 1880s failure of the Chinese immigrant community to reverse the Exclusion Act or any of its conditions as well as in the ineffectiveness of Max Kohler's activism against 1920s immigration policies that were discriminatory toward Jewish immigrants. But this dynamic is reversed in the current resistance to the Muslim travel ban, which encompassed a broad spectrum of American society and resulted in critical coverage in several of the leading mainstream news outlets of the period. The latter example proved successful at repealing two versions of the ban and requiring the third iteration of the Muslim travel ban to be heard at the Supreme Court. Thus, history yet again points to the importance of a majority-group adoption of hospitality for discriminatory regulation to be critically examined and overturned.

Indeed, the contrast between the public response to the immigration restriction discussions of the 1880s, 1920s, and 2000s and the contemporary debate surrounding the Muslim ban reveals that, as Martin Luther King Jr. once stated, "the arc of the moral universe is long, but it bends toward justice" (Denzel Smith 2018). Unlike the periods of intense restriction analyzed in previous chapters, which witnessed strong bipartisan support for the policies that regulated and limited immigration and widespread public support across media outlets and platforms for the negative rhetoric surrounding immigration, the Muslim travel ban was countered by vibrant bipartisan debates surrounding American values, as this chapter has illustrated. It is telling that reflections on the Muslim ban have centered on the precise ethical lens of hospitality, evoking religious and nationalistic rhetoric to suggest that the hospitable treatment of refugees and immigrants reflects the moral rectitude of American society and that discriminatory policies betray America's identity as a "nation of immigrants."

Inspired by the "universal normatively positive position" that hospitality occupies across the world (Bulley 2016, 3), the centrality of hospitality to American national identity, as demonstrated by the defining myth of the "nation of immigrants," illustrates the potential of the "nation of immigrants" myth—if incongruous with American immigration history—to ethically inspire more inclusive policy in the future. Indeed, I argue that the myth becomes all the more significant during periods of restriction and discriminatory policy.

Ultimately, the treatment of hospitality is crucial to examine how extending welcome impacts the immigrant experience and how immigrants navigate home-building, particularly in periods of restriction. Home-building requires the perception of a welcoming host nation and a newcomer willing to join the new nation. The words of one recently naturalized citizen, interviewed by *The Nation* at an anti-ban protest, encapsulate the importance of perceptions of welcome and hospitality to immigrants and new citizens: "I was really excited to become American. And now I'm sad. I'm sad that America is being affiliated with people who don't believe it's a welcoming place, who feel like they can close our borders. That's not what America believes in. I've lived here for 15 years now, and this is the first time I've felt legitimately scared—scared for the country, scared for my friends, scared for people like me who come here for a better life and we're being turned away. *That's not what this country stands for*" (Kane 2017, emphasis added).

Community efforts at home-building appear repeatedly in immigrants' efforts for equal rights and positioning of their history at the core of a nation's development. Thus, the mobilization of Chinese immigrants to defy Jim Crow laws was crucial to their home-building. The arguments put forth by 1920s immigrants regarding the inhumane nature of national origins quotas was an

example of home-building. Finally, home-building is evident in the mobilization of Muslim immigrants following the Muslim ban, producing the hashtag
#MyMuslimImmigrantFamily to document their stories as Muslims in the
United States. Sharing their collective history represents a crucial dimen-
sion of home-building that highlights a community's position as part of the
national community. These efforts assert the belonging of immigrant communities within the nation, transforming their position from that of a guest/
other to that of the host.

Home-building also materializes in immigrant activism against bigotry and
discrimination. In April 2018, for example, a Muslim civil rights group publicly demanded an apology from a Louisiana elected official who had posted
an Islamophobic tweet accusing Muslims of unhygienic toilet practices with
a photo of a bearded man on the toilet claiming that Muslims use their hands
instead of toilet paper ("Muslim Group Asks Official to Apologize" 2018).
These public declarations and denunciations shape the political environment
and policymaking. When Patrick Colbeck, a Michigan elected official began
peddling conspiracy theories contending Muslims planned to hijack American politics by running for office, the public denunciation of his Islamophobic
remarks elicited a wider condemnation by fellow politicians, with Michigan
senate minority leader Jim Ananich arguing that Colbeck continued "to prove
that he's an ass," while Senator David Knezek, a Democrat from Dearborn
Heights, called him a coward and a bully (Yin 2018). All of these condemna-
tions were reported in the local and national press and circulated among the
American public. Such public contestations and denunciations of discriminatory rhetoric allow immigrant communities to mobilize to lower the acceptability of discrimination.

The contestation against the Muslim travel ban holds significance for the
future of immigration hospitality. It demonstrates that public response to
discriminatory policy is effective in curbing even the authority of the executive branch at enforcing discriminatory policy. At the same time, it signals a
public rejection of discriminatory rhetoric and a more sympathetic view of
the plight of Muslims after the ban. As a result, the period following the Muslim travel ban reflects a potential reversal of many of the dominant tropes in
coverage of Muslim immigrants during the post-9/11 era, as news articles are
publishing images proclaiming that Muslims are neither terrorists, nor un-
American (fig. 6.5), nor security risks who deserve to be banned (Gani 2017).

This policy and media analysis of American immigration hospitality demonstrates that the myth of the "nation of immigrants" diverges from the exclusionary, racist, and inhospitable nature of immigration policy or discourse.
However, at the same time, the myth remains a powerful metaphor that continues to inspire activism toward greater immigration hospitality. It endures
as an important point of mobilization for immigrants who rely on its promise

and retains its power to symbolically project welcome, especially in periods of restriction. It thereby examines media and policy as two areas where American immigration hospitality is expressed and where the welcome extended or denied to immigrants affects their mission of building a sense of home in their adopted country. Its analysis of media and policy addresses the creative ways immigrants adapted to inhospitable policies to create a sense of feeling at home in the United States, from Chinatown laundromats to Italian restaurants. In each period, the chapters of this book show how strong dissenting voices—those as widely known as Emma Lazarus or as little known as Max Kohler—continued to champion the moral responsibility of the United States as a receiving country even in periods of restriction.

In pointing to the important caveat to the promise of the "nation of immigrants" myth, exemplified by the opposition to the Muslim travel ban in 2017 and 2018, this book suggests that the myth is most powerful as a vehicle for positive change in media representation and in reversing discriminatory policy when it is widely embraced by a large swath of society rather than by a narrow group of immigrants targeted by exclusion. This seemingly fraught act of welcome surpasses any simplistic measure of its importance, as it continues to impact the various ways in which immigrants sense welcome and proceed to build a sense of feeling at home in their adopted countries. Just as Lady Liberty symbolically embraced and protected newcomers from the Chinese exclusion era to the time of the Muslim travel ban, the #NoBan-NoWall movement represents a moment of opportunity to foster mobilization toward greater immigration hospitality in the United States, now and in the future.

Appendix A: Note on Reflexivity and Methods

The polemical nature of the debate on forced migrants in the United States over the past two decades makes research on the topic difficult, as it is assumed that the researcher possesses a particular stance regarding not only the debates surrounding refugees in host nations but also the heated debates within one's own communities. In my case, the debate within the Syrian diaspora regarding the justification of the Syrian regime or its opposition adds a layer of complexity to the study of migration and forced migration. Certainly, my position both as a Syrian and as a member of a family from which many have become refugees during the current crisis is worthy of note from the outset of this research. Thus, this research is performed with the understanding that complete objectivity is impossible under any circumstance (Armitage 2008). Rather, objectivity in research may be approximated via a number of strategies that protect the integrity of the data. This includes the application of the procedures of grounded theory (Glaser and Strauss 2009) to allow the systematic collection, organization, and interpretation of the press articles and policy documents that compose the core of this study.

It is important to transparently note my involvement with the topic at hand. In 2015, in the midst of my PhD studies at the University of Pennsylvania, my parents applied for asylum in the United States. Given my involvement throughout the process, owing to a relatively stronger command of the English language and greater proximity to legal counsel, the years 2015 and 2016 left me acutely aware of the intricacies of U.S. immigration policy, or as aware as one can be in such a labyrinth, particularly one that is constantly in flux. It became clear to me at the time how the narratives of the United States as a "nation of immigrants" and a "nation of exiles," often staples of media coverage on immigration policy public debates, conflict with the restrictiveness, complexity, and growing closure of its immigration and refugee and asylum policy. Equally, it became clear that immigration policy is rarely historically contextualized in journalistic, academic, or even legal discourse, allowing for a simplification of the debate that flattens historical nuances that impact the immigrant experience. It is as a result of these ponderings that I decided to undertake this project, and thus it is important to note as part of my methodological choices.

Appendix B:
Regulatory Documents

A list of all the immigration policies and regulatory documents consulted in preparing this book is included below.

Acts of Congress

A Bill to Grant to the Chinese Rights of Entry to the United States and Rights to Citizenship. 1943. Pub. L. No. 1882, Statute at Large. https://congressional.proquest.com/congressional/Docview/t01.d02.78_hr_1882_ih_19430217?accountid=14707.

U.S. Cong. 1748 Transcript of Alien and Sedition Acts. 5th Cong. 2nd sess. U.S. Immigration.

U.S. Cong. 1790 Naturalization Act. 1st Cong. 2nd sess. chap. 3, 1 Stat. 103. U.S. Immigration Legislation Online. University of Washington Bothell.

U.S. Cong. 1795 Naturalization Act. 3rd Cong. 2nd sess. chap. 19, 20, 1 Stat. 414. U.S.

U.S. Cong. 1798 Naturalization Act. 5th Cong. 2nd sess. Accessed February 1, 2017. https://www.ourdocuments.gov/doc.php?flash=true&doc=16&page=transcript.

U.S. Cong. 1819 Steerage Act. 15th Cong. 2nd sess. chap. 47, 3 Stat. 488.

U.S. Cong. 1847 Passenger Act. 29th Cong. 2nd sess. chap. 17, 9 Stat. 128.

U.S. Cong. 1855 Passenger Act. 33rd Cong. 2nd sess. chap. 213, 10 Stat. 715.

U.S. Cong. 1864 Immigration Act. 38th Cong. 1st sess. chap. 246, 13 Stat. 385.

U.S. Cong. 1870 Naturalization Act. 41st Cong. 2nd sess. chap. 252–254, 16 Stat. 254. University of New Mexico. Accessed February 1, 2017. https://repository.unm.edu/bitstream/handle/1928/3592/16%20Stat %20254%20(1870).pdf?sequence=5.

U.S. Cong. 1875 Page Law. 43rd Cong. 2nd sess. chap. 141, 18 Stat. 477.

U.S. Cong. 1882 Chinese Exclusion Act. 47th Cong. 1st sess. chap. 126, 22 Stat. 58.

U.S. Cong. 1882 Immigration Act. 47th Cong. 1st sess. chap. 376, 22 Stat. 214.

U.S. Cong. 1885 Contract Labor Law. 48th Cong. 2nd sess. chap. 164, 23 Stat. 332.

U.S. Cong. 1891 Immigration Act. 51st Cong. 2nd sess. chap. 551. 26 stat 1084.

U.S. Cong. 1892 Geary Act. 52nd Cong. 1st sess. chap. 60.

U.S. Cong. 1902 Scott Act. 57th Cong. 1st sess. chap. 641, 32 Stat. 176.

U.S. Cong. 1903. "An Act to Regulate the Immigration of Aliens into the United States." 57th Cong. 1st sess. chap. 1012, 32 Stat. 1222.

U.S. Cong. 1907 Immigration Act. 59th Cong. 1st sess. chap. 641, 34 Stat. 898. Accessed February 1, 2017. https://archive.org/stream/ cu31924021131101/cu31924021131101_djvu.txt.

U.S. Cong. 1917 Immigration Act. 64th Cong. H.R. 10384, Pub. L. No. 301, 39 Stat. 874. U.S. Immigration Legislation Online. University of Washington Bothell. Accessed February 1, 2017. http://library.uwb.edu/ Static/USimmigration/1917_immigration_act.html.

U.S. Cong. 1918 Wartime Measure. 65th Cong. H.R. 10264, Pub. L. No. 65– 154, 40 Stat. 559. U.S. Immigration Legislation Online. University of Washington Bothell. Accessed February 1, 2017. http://library.uwb .edu/Static/USimmigration/1918_wartime_measure.html.

U.S. Cong. 1921 Emergency Quota Law. 67th Cong. H.R. 4075, Pub. L. No. 67–5, 42 Stat. 5.

U.S. Cong. 1924 Immigration Act. 68th Cong. H.R. 7995, Pub. L. No. 68– 139, 43 Stat. 153.

U.S. Cong. 1940 Nationality Act. 76th Cong. H.R. 9980, Pub. L. No. 76– 853, 54 Stat. 1137.

U.S. Cong. 1941 Wartime Measure. 77th Cong. S. 913, Pub. L. No. 77–113, 55 Stat. 252.

U.S. Cong. 1943 Magnuson Act. 78th Cong. H.R. 3070, Pub. L. No. 78– 199, 57 Stat. 600.

U.S. Cong. 1945 War Brides Act. 79th Cong. H.R. 4857, Pub. L. No. 79– 271, 59 Stat. 659.

U.S. Cong. 1946 Alien Fiancées and Fiancés Act. 79th Cong. S. 2122, Pub. L. No. 79–471, 60 Stat. 339.

U.S. Cong. 1948 Displaced Persons Act. 80th Cong. S. 224, Pub. L. No. 80–774, 62 Stat. 1009.

U.S. Cong. 1950 Act on Alien Spouses and Children. 81st Cong. S. 1858, Pub. L. No. 717, 64 Stat. 464.

U.S. Cong. 1952 Immigration and Nationality Act. 81st Cong. S. 1858, Pub. L. No. 717, 64 Stat. 464.

U.S. Cong. 1965 Immigration and Nationality Act. 89th Cong. H.R. 2580, Pub. L. No. 89–236, 79 Stat. 911.

U.S. Cong. 1968 Armed Forces Naturalization Act. 90th Cong. H.R. 15147, Pub. L. No. 90–633, 82 Stat. 1343.

U.S. Cong. 1975 Indochina Migration and Refugee Assistance Act. 94th Cong. H.R. 6755, Pub. L. No. 94–23, 89 Stat. 87.

U.S. Cong. 1982 Amerasian Immigration Act. 97th Cong. S. 1698, Pub. L. No. 97–359, 96 Stat. 1716. U.S.

U.S. Cong. 1986 Immigration Reform and Control Act. 99th Cong. S. 1200, Pub. L. No. 99–603, 100 Stat. 3359.

U.S. Cong. 1990 Immigration and Nationality Act. 101st Cong. S. 358, Pub. L. No. 101–649, 104 Stat. 4978.

U.S. Cong. 1991 Armed Forces Immigration Adjustment Act. 102nd Cong. S. 296, Pub. L. No. 102–110, 105 Stat. 555.

U.S. Cong. 1996 Illegal Immigration Reform and Immigrant Responsibility Act. 104th Cong. H.R. 3610, Pub. L. No. 104–208, 110 Stat. 3009–546.

U.S. Cong. 2002. Enhanced Security and Visa Entry Reform Act. 107th Cong. H.R. 3525, Pub. L. No. 107–173. U.S. Citizenship and Immigration Services. Accessed February 1, 2017. https://www.uscis.gov/ilink/docView/PUBLAW/HTML/PUBLAW/0-0-0-24919.html.

Government Documents

"An Act to Establish a Bureau of Immigration and Naturalization, and to Provide for a Uniform Rule for the Naturalization of Aliens throughout the United States. Approved June 29, 1906." 1907. *American Journal of International Law* 1 (1): 31–47.

"A Bill to Amend the Immigration Act of 1924." 1925. 68th Cong. 2nd sess. H.R. 12430.

Bush, President George W. 2001. "Remarks by President George W. Bush and President Megawati of Indonesia." White House: President George W. Bush. September 19, 2001. https://georgewbush-whitehouse.archives.gov/infocus/ramadan/islam.html.

Bush, President George W. 2002. "Presidential Message Eid al-Fitr." White House: President George W. Bush. December 5, 2002. https://georgewbush-whitehouse.archives.gov/infocus/ramadan/islam.html.

Bush, President George W. 2006. "Statement of President Bush." U.S. Government Publishing Office. https://www.govinfo.gov/content/pkg/CRECB-2006-pt13/html/CRECB-2006-pt13-Pg17222-10.htm.

Cleveland, President Grover. (1886) 2013. "Dedication of Lady Liberty Enlightens the World." Speech, October 28, 1886. In *Presidential Documents: The Speeches, Proclamations, and Politics That Have Shaped the Nation from Washington to Clinton*, edited by Thomas McInerney and Fred Israel, 147. New York: Routledge.

Department of Homeland Security. 2016. "Removal of Regulations Relating to Special Registration Process for Certain Nonimmigrants." Federal Register. December 23, 2016. https://www.federalregister.gov/documents/2016/12/23/2016-30885/removal-of-regulations-relating-to-special-registration-process-for-certain-nonimmigrants.

Department of Justice. 2001. "The USA PATRIOT Act: Myth vs. Reality." https://www.justice.gov/archive/ll/subs/add_myths.htm#s.

"41st Congress, 3rd Session." Congressional Globe. Accessed July 5, 2022. https://memory.loc.gov/ammem/amlaw/lwcglink.html#anchor41.

Grant, President Ulysses S. 1874. "Sixth Annual Message." UC Santa Barbara: The Ameri can Presidency Project. December 7, 1874. https://www.presidency.ucsb.edu/documents/sixth-annual-message-3.

"The Immigration Act of 1924 (The Johnson-Reed Act)." 2016. Office of the Historian: Milestones in the History of U.S. Foreign Relations. https://history.state.gov/milestones/1921-1936/immigration-act.

Johnson, President Lyndon B. 1965. "Remarks at the Signing of the Immigration Bill, Liberty Island, New York." UC Santa Barbara: The American Presidency Project. October 3, 1965. https://www.presidency.ucsb.edu/node/241316.

National Archives and Records Administration. 1776. "Declaration of Independence: A Transcription." Last modified October 7, 2021. https://www.archives.gov/founding-docs/declaration-transcript.

———. 2002. "Census Records 1790–1950." Accessed July 1, 2022. https://www.census.gov/library/publications.html.

———. 2016. "Records of the Immigration and Naturalization Service." Record Group 85, bulk 1882–1957. Last updated August 15, 2016. https://www.archives.gov/research/guide-fed-records/groups/085.html.

"Records of the Immigration and Naturalization Service." 1995. Record group 85, bulk 1882–1957. National Archives. https://www.archives.gov/research/guide-fed-records/groups/085.html.

Trump, D. J. 2017. "Executive Order 13769 of January 27, 2017: Protecting the Nation From Foreign Terrorist Entry Into the United States." *Federal Register* 82, no. 20 (February 1, 2017). https://www.govinfo.gov/content/pkg/FR-2017-02-01/pdf/2017-02281.pdf.

UNHCR. 1951. "Convention and Protocol Relating to the Status of Refugees" (Geneva Convention). Accessed June 18, 2022. http://www.unhcr.org/en-us/3b66c2aa10.

———. 1997. "Fact Sheet No.9 (Rev.1), The Rights of Indigenous Peoples." July 1997. https://www.ohchr.org/sites/default/files/Documents/Publications/FactSheet9rev.1en.pdf.

USCIS. 2012. "Overview of INS History." USCIS History Office and Library. https://www.uscis.gov/sites/default/files/USCIS/History%20and%20Genealogy/Our%20History/INS%20History/INSHistory.pdf.

USCIS. 2014. "USCIS Revises Form N-400, Application for Naturalization." Last modified February 4, 2014. https://www.uscis.gov/archive/uscis-revises-form-n-400-application-for-naturalization.

U.S. Census Bureau. 1880. "Population by Race, Sex and Nativity." *1880 Census: Volume 1*. Statistics of the Population of the United States.

U.S. Government Publishing Office. 1882. "47th Congress, 1st Session." 13 Cong. Rec. (Bound). Senate, July 14, 1882. https://www.govinfo.gov/app/details/GPO-CRECB-1882-pt6-v13/GPO-CRECB-1882-pt6-v13-18-1.

Court Cases and Briefs

"Affidavit and Flyers from the Chinese Boycott Case." n.d. National Archives. Last modified October 11, 2017. https://www.archives.gov/education/lessons/chinese-boycott.

"Brief of Amici Curiae of the Fred T. Korematsu Center for Law and Equality et al. in Support of Plaintiffs, Arab American Civil Rights League v. Trump, No. 17-cv-10310."

Berney, A. 2018. "Brief Amicus Curiae by the Zionist Organization of America (Zoa) in Support of Petitioners Donald J. Trump, President of the United States, et al." Supreme Court. https://www.supremecourt.gov/DocketPDF/17/17-965/37139/20180228180326118_Trump%20v%20Hawaii%20-%20ZOA%20Amicus%20-%20Feb%2028%202018-No%2017-965%20pdf%20Berney.pdf.

Korematsu, K. 2017. "Amici Brief of Karen Korematsu, Jay Hirabayashi, Holly Yasui, the Fred T. Korematsu Center for Law and Equality, Civil Rights Organizations, and National Bar Associations of Color in Support of Plaintiffs-Appellees." Fred T. Korematsu Center for Law and

Equality. https://digitalcommons.law.seattleu.edu/cgi/viewcontent
.cgi?article=1062&context=korematsu_center.

U.S. Supreme Court. 2017. "Donald J. Trump, President of the United
States, et al., Petitioners v. Hawaii, et al." https://www.supremecourt
.gov/search.aspx?filename=/docket/docketfiles/html/public/17-965
.html.

———. 1898. "United States v. Wong Kim Ark, 169 U.S. 649." https://
supreme.justia.com/cases/federal/us/169/649/.

———. 1893. "Fong Yue Ting v. United States, 149 U.S. 698." https://
supreme.justia.com/cases/federal/us/149/698/.

———. 2018. "*Masterpiece Cakeshop v. Colorado Civil Rights Commission*.
Opinion of the Court." https://www.supremecourt.gov/opinions/
17pdf/16-111_j4el.pdf.

Acknowledgments

This book was written amid a series of constraints: A travel ban that limited my mobility as a scholar and therefore shifted the analytical focus of this project. An immigration policy of family separation and detention that symbolized the brutality of American immigration policies and underscored the importance of this project. It was written during a pandemic that forced humanity into self-isolation and compelled us to reimagine our connection to one another. This book evolved against the backdrop of a global movement for Black lives and dignity that mobilized citizens in the United States and around the world. Finally, it was written during a period of caregiving and bereavement that humbled me as an academic and reminded me of the immeasurable beauty and incalculable preciousness of our shared time. These extraordinary circumstances both disrupted and enriched the writing process; their impact weaves through the book and, I hope, through all my future research. This book departs from the basic premise that the dignity of human life requires a moral commitment from every immigration and media system. It explores the ways in which injustice and White supremacy are woven into the fabric of the nation, but they are nevertheless neither invincible nor irreversible.

The context I write in also highlights the role that intellectual community played in supporting the scholarly process. I would like to thank the community at the Annenberg School for Communication at the University of Pennsylvania, I could not have asked for a better first home in the United States. Barbie Zelizer, who in the short but intensely edifying time that she was my advisor has become the inner voice that constantly challenges me to be a better scholar and writer. Klaus Krippendorff, whose openness in sharing his personal reflections on displacement has helped me feel less lonely in the academy. Guobin Yang and Victor Pickard supported this project as it pivoted in response to travel restrictions. Entering and navigating academia without an understanding of many academic conventions is an almost impossible feat, and I could not have done it without Christa Salamandra, who has read and critiqued my work long before I could claim the title of PhD. The friends I have made along the way have provided invaluable moral support: Tim and Dana Libert, Vicki Gilbert and Elliott McCarthy, Muira McCammon, Cristoph Mergerson, and many more, thank you for your intellectual generosity and hospitality.

I have been fortunate to enjoy the collegiality of incredible scholars at University of Leeds. I must single out for thanks Yvonne Tasker, who mentored me through the vagaries of the academic publishing world. I am also grateful to Joanne Armitage, Sally Osei-Appiah, Pablo Morales, and Holly Steel, for the many coffee dates at Opposite—and virtual chats—talking about the ethical ramifications of research, scholarship, and pedagogy and the moral injury of the engaged scholar.

Above all, I would like to thank two important figures in my life: My father, Issam Halabi, who armed me with an education and great pride in being his beloved daughter, a pride I carry with me into every venture, academic or otherwise. And my partner, Sam Kilani, whose love and compassion remind me to look at the universe in bewilderment and joy.

This book is above all else a labor of love, dedicated to our immigrant families (past and future) who have come a great distance to build a life on these shores. It was written as I navigated my own naturalization and is dedicated to my newly adopted country and the Indigenous people and immigrant-settlers who call it home. May it inspire a continuous reflection on hospitality to the stranger in *our* midst and beyond *our* shores.

Notes

Chapter 1

1 Quotations were taken from publicly available transcripts of the National Cable Satellite Corporation (TGRANE 2020).

2 W. E. B. Du Bois's career offers a mirror to the Amy Wax anecdote that opens this book. It also raises a compelling historical precedent through which one can examine the moral responsibility of academic institutions vis-à-vis antiracist research. After completing his book *The Philadelphia Negro*, Du Bois was disappointed that his publication did not earn him a permanent position at the University of Pennsylvania, where he was employed as a "trained observer" of African American issues (PENN Today 2016). The failure of the university leadership to see the value in Du Bois's scholarship resulted in the loss of a scholar whose work would "outlast any other scholar in the history of the department." Among his many achievements, Du Bois's study of over five thousand individuals "opened up entirely new ways of conducting sociological research," solidifying his position as one of the pioneers of urban ethnography (Scott Holloway 2015, xvi). This precedent, contrasted with Amy Wax's numerous violations of students' privacy and teaching ethics, should raise important questions on the moral responsibility of the academy.

3 This does not suggest that Christian theological thought is emblematic of a universal acceptance of hospitality. It suffices to consider the pervasive image of the legend of the wandering Jew to illustrate the inhospitable history of Christian thought toward the traveler and stranger. According to the legend, the wandering Jew was condemned to homelessness for his sins and was destined to wander the earth in repentance. Such images ascribe blame to displaced communities in the past and ground such prejudice in religious narratives. For a more detailed account, see Leschnitzer's "The Wandering Jew" (1971).

Chapter 2

1 I argue that forced migration in which one retains some residual agency in fleeing differs from the conditions of abduction and kidnapping prevalent during the slave trade. This distinction provides a fruitful avenue to explore the degrees of agency and self-determination within forced migration.

2 The Passenger Act (1847) provided more detailed regulation of incoming immigration, including a tax of ten dollars levied per passenger. Most importantly, however, the act was the first to acknowledge the African slave trade and to make specific requirements regarding the transportation of slaves into the United States. The Passenger Act followed the Steerage Act and allowed regulators to include the slave trade within immigration regulations.

Chapter 3

1 See *Chinese in the Post–Civil War South: A People without a History* by Lucy M. Cohen (1984), which details the struggle of Chinese laborers brought to replace newly emancipated slaves in the South. The book, as well as other work by Cohen, illustrates how Chinese immigrants were not "docile" workers and how they endeavored to contest racial discrimination against them.

2 Long believed to mate for life, *yuanyang* or Mandarin ducks are a metaphor for harmonious and faithful marriage in Chinese popular culture.

3 I examined both the *New York Times* coverage of Chinese immigration from 1882 to 1920 and, considering the particular importance of the West Coast to this issue, several West Coast publications, including the *San Francisco Tribune*, the *Oakland Tribune*, and the *Record-Union* as well as select coverage from other publications. Moreover, as highlighted by journalistic historian Thomas Leonard, political cartoons and particularly the highly influential lithographs of Thomas Nast provided a mechanism of "visual thinking" in an environment of low literacy, where there was a thirst for pictures at a time when the public would wait years to see the likenesses of politicians (Leonard 1986, 98, 127). As such, I included political cartoons in this sample, drawing from the archives of *Harper's Weekly* and *The Wasp* as well as secondary research on the topic.

Chapter 4

1 Open-gate immigration is a myth often evoked to denote eras of relative immigration openness that bypassed its selective application, as discussed in the previous chapter on Chinese exclusion.

2 The myth of America's moral decay is a powerful and persistent one, evidenced by its resurgence again and again in American history in response to television, social media, LGBTQ+ rights, and any number of great shifts in national policy. For contemporary treatments of the phenomenon, see Pavlovitz's "The Christian Myth of America's Moral Decay" (2017).

3 The decision to exclude Mexico from immigration quotas stemmed from the lack of attention toward Mexican immigrants as potential threats. As Mexican immigrants came to replace other groups during the period of restriction from the 1920s to the 1960s, the issue of restriction of Mexican immigration began to rise in policy discussions. For more on this shift, see Levenstein's "The AFL and Mexican Immigration in the 1920s" (1968).

4 This article appears earlier in the chapter to illustrate the threat of inebriation and other ills. The combination of multiple themes within each article illustrates the interconnected nature of the arguments against immigration at the time.

Chapter 5

1 Several investigative journalists have revealed a long-standing history of sexual abuse in ICE detention centers, transportation networks, and so on. For more, see Speri's "Detained, Then Violated" (2018).

References

Aarim-Heriot, N., and R. Daniels. 2003. *Chinese Immigrants, African Americans, and Racial Anxiety in the United States, 1848–82*, Vol. 124. Urbana-Champagne: University of Illinois Press.

Aberra, N. 2017. "How a Viral Protest Photo Gave This Rabbi a Chance to Spread a Message of Hope." *Vox*, February 1, 2017. https://www.vox.com/conversations/2017/2/1/14476824/trump-refugee-protest-viral-photo.

Abu Lughod, L. 2002. "Do Muslim Women Really Need Saving? Anthropological Reflections on Cultural Relativism and Its Others." *American Anthropologist* 104 (3): 783–790.

Acuña, R. 2012. "The Political Economy of Indigenous Dispossession: Bare and Dispensable Lives in the Andes." Critical Legal Thinking, October 9, 2012. http://criticallegalthinking.com/2012/10/09/the-political-economy-of-indigenous-dispossession-bare-and-dispensable-lives-in-the-andes/.

AFP. 2016. "Un réfugié syrien porte la flamme olympique dans un camp de migrants d'Athènes." *Le Journal de Montreal*, April 26, 2016. http://www.journaldemontreal.com/2016/04/26/un-refugie-syrien-porte-la-flamme-olympique-dans-un-camp-de-migrants-dathenes.

Ager, A., ed. 1999. *Refugees: Perspectives on the Experience of Forced Migration*. London: Pinter.

Ahmed, S. 1999. "Home and Away: Narratives of Migration and Estrangement." *International Journal of Cultural Studies* 2 (3): 329–347.

———, ed. 2003. *Uprootings/Regroundings: Questions of Home and Migration*. Oxford: Berg.

Ajrouch, K. J., and A. Jamal. 2007. "Assimilating to a White Identity: The Case of Arab Americans." *International Migration Review* 41 (4): 860–879.

Akenson, D. H. 2011. *Ireland, Sweden and the Great European Migration: 1815–1914*. Liverpool, U.K.: Liverpool University Press.

Al-Ali, N. S., and K. Koser. 2002. *New Approaches to Migration? Transnational Communities and the Transformation of Home*. London: Routledge.

Alba, R., and V. Nee. 1997. "Rethinking Assimilation Theory for a New Era of Immigration." *International Migration Review* 31 (4): 826–874.

Alcindor, Y. 2020. "Trump Insists on Using Racist Language. Will That Approach Win Him Support?" *PBS Newshour*, July 2, 2020. https://www.pbs.org/newshour/show/trump-insists-on-using-racist-language-will-that-approach-win-him-support.

Aldrich, T. B. 1892. "The Unguarded Gates." *Atlantic Monthly* 70:57.

"Aliens Eager to Immigrate Here." *Wall Street Journal*, May 10, 1921.

Alsultany, E. 2012. *Arabs and Muslims in the Media: Race and Representation after 9/11*. New York: New York University Press.

Altman, D. 2002. "Wary Companies Are Staying in the Muslim World." *New York Times*, October 24, 2002. https://www.nytimes.com/2002/10/24/business/wary-companies-are-staying-in-the-muslim-world.html.

"America No Asylum for Europe, Says Johnson." *Wall Street Journal*, November 19, 1920. ProQuest Historical Newspapers.

American Civil Liberties Union. 2017. "ACLU Comment on Trump Administration's New Travel Ban Restrictions." September 24, 2017. https://www.aclu.org/news/aclu-comment-trump-administrations-new-travel-ban-restrictions.

———. n.d. "Timeline of the Muslim Ban." Accessed July 2, 2022. https://www.aclu-wa.org/pages/timeline-muslim-ban.

"America's Changing Colors." 1990. *Time*, April 9, 1990. http://content.time.com/time/covers/0,16641,19900409,00.html.

Anapol, A. 2017. "Former Bush Speechwriter: Trump's Tweets Are a 'Direct Attack' on the Safety of Journalists." *The Hill*, November 25, 2017. http://thehill.com/homenews/administration/361828-atlantic-editor-trumps-tweets-are-a-direct-attack-on-the-safety-of.

Andersen, J. G. 2006. "Immigration and the Legitimacy of the Scandinavian Welfare State: Some Preliminary Danish Findings." iAMID Working Paper Series 53/2006. Aalborg University, Copenhagen, Denmark.

Anderson, B. 2006. *Imagined Communities: Reflections on the Origin and Spread of Nationalism*. London: Verso.

Anderson, K., M. Domosh, S. Pile, and N. Thrift, eds. 2002. *Handbook of Cultural Geography*. London: Sage.

Apuzzo, M., and A. Goldman. 2014. *Enemies Within: Inside the NYPD's Secret Spying Unit and Bin Laden's Final Plot against America*. New York: Simon and Schuster.

"Are Muslims Integrating or Are They 'Taking Over'?" 2010. *Wall Street Journal*. November 19, 2010. https://www.wsj.com/articles/SB10001424052748703326204575617103929968856.

Arendt, H. 1973. *The Origins of Totalitarianism*. New ed. New York: Harcourt Brace Jovanovich.

Armitage, J. S. 2008. "Persona Non Grata: Dilemmas of Being an Outsider Researching Immigration Reform Activism." *Qualitative Research* 8 (2): 155–177.

Arnesen, E. 2001a. "Whiteness and the Historians' Imagination." *Historically Speaking* 3 (3): 19, 22.

———. 2001b. "Whiteness and the Historians' Imagination." *International Labor and Working-Class History* 60:3–32.

Arnold, D., and Pickles, J. 2011. "Global Work, Surplus Labor, and the Precarious Economies of the Border." *Antipode* 43 (5): 1598–1624. https://doi.org/10.1111/j.1467-8330.2011.00899.x.

"Ask Drastic Change to Tighten Dry Law." 1924. *New York Times*, January 2, 1924.

"The Assessor's Strategy." 1882. *Oakland Tribune*, March 17, 1882.

Associated Press. 2012. "AP Wins Pulitzer Prize for Investigative Reporting on NYPD Surveillance." April 16, 2012. https://www.ap.org/press-releases/2012/ap-wins-pulitzer-prize-for-investigative-reporting-on-nypd-surveillance.

Aziza, S. 2018. "As Supreme Court Weighs Travel Ban, Trump's Wider anti-Muslim Agenda Proceeds Unchallenged." The Intercept, April 27, 2018. https://theintercept.com/2018/04/27/muslim-ban-supreme-court-trump-vetting-muslims/.

Baftijari, Y. 2017. "#NoBanNoWall Shows the Sobering Reality of Trump's Immigration Policies." Vivala. Accessed August 5, 2018. http://www.vivala.com/politics/nobannowall-tweets-trump-immigration-policies/6645.

Bahr, E. 2011. *Weimar on the Pacific: German Exile Culture in Los Angeles and the Crisis of Modernism*. Los Angeles: University of California Press.

Ballinger, P. 2003. *History in Exile: Memory and Identity at the Borders of the Balkans*. Princeton, N.J.: Princeton University Press.

Baptist, E. E. 2014. *The Half Has Never Been Told: Slavery and the Making of American Capitalism*. New York: Basic Books.

Barone, J. 2017. "Discussing Bias against Muslims after a Terrorist Attack: 'The Media Does Play a Role.'" *New York Times*, November 1, 2017. https://www.nytimes.com/2017/11/01/reader-center/new-york-attack-muslim-americans.html?rref=collection%2Ftimestopic%2FMuslim%20Americans.

Barreto, M. 2018. "Democrats Can Win on Immigration." *New York Times*, February 11, 2018. https://www.nytimes.com/2018/02/11/opinion/democrats-win-immigration.html.

Barrett, J., and D. Roediger. 1997. "Inbetween Peoples: Race, Nationality and the 'New Immigrant' Working Class." *Journal of American Ethnic History* 16, no. 3 (Spring): 3, 44.

"Bartholdi Day." 1886. *New York Times*, October 28, 1886.

Bauder, H. 2008. "Neoliberalism and the Economic Utility of Immigration: Media Perspectives of Germany's Immigration Law." *Antipode* 40 (1): 55–78. https://doi.org/10.1111/j.1467-8330.2008.00571.x.

Baughman, I. 2006. "Italian Food in America or How Prohibition Gave Us the Olive Garden." *Appetite* 47 (3): 385. https://doi.org/10.1016/j.appet.2006.08.008.

Baum, B. D., and D. Harris, eds. 2009. *Racially Writing the Republic: Racists, Race Rebels, and Transformations of American Identity*. Durham, N.C.: Duke University Press.

Bayoumi, M. 2015. *This Muslim American Life: Dispatches from the War on Terror*. New York: New York University Press.

"The Beacon of Liberty." 1882. *New York Times*, November 26, 1882.

Begley, S. 2015. "Brooklyn and the True History of Irish Immigrants in 1950s New York." *Time*, November 4, 2015. http://time.com/4097071/brooklyn-irish-immigrants-history/.

Behr, E. (1996) 2011. *Prohibition: Thirteen Years That Changed America*. New York: Arcade.

Bell, A. 2010. "Being 'At Home' in the Nation: Hospitality and Sovereignty in Talk about Immigration." *Ethnicities* 10 (2): 236–256.

Benson, R. 2014. *Shaping Immigration News*. Cambridge: Cambridge University Press.

Berger, P., and T. Luckmann. 1967. *The Social Construction of Reality: A Treatise on the Sociology of Education*. Dortmund, Germany: University of Dortmund.

Bergson, H. 1993. *Matière et mémoire*. Paris: Presses Universitaires de France.

Berlin, I. 1998. *Many Thousands Gone: The First Two Centuries of Slavery in North America*. Cambridge, Mass.: Belknap.

———. 2004. *Generations of Captivity: A History of African-American Slaves*. Cambridge, Mass.: Belknap Press of Harvard University Press.

Bernstein, N. 2006. "Judge Rules That U.S. Has Broad Powers to Detain Noncitizens Indefinitely." *New York Times*, June 15, 2006. http://www.nytimes.com/2006/06/15/nyregion/15detain.html.

Besharov, D. J., and M. H. Lopez, eds. 2015. *Adjusting to a World in Motion: Trends in Global Migration and Migration Policy*. Oxford: Oxford University Press.

Bierstadt, E. H. 1921. "Americanizing America." *The Reviewer*. Accessed June 30, 2022.

Biesen, S. 2016. "Re-imagining the Jazz Age: Nightclubs, Speakeasies and Shady Crime in Jazz Film Noir Musical Performances." In *Looking Back at the Jazz Age: New Essays on the Literature and Legacy of an Iconic Decade*, edited by N. Von Rosk, 159–178. Newcastle upon Tyne, U.K.: Cambridge Scholars.

Bilak, A., G. Cardona-Fox, J. Ginnetti, E. J. Rushing, I. Scherer, M. Swain, N. Walicki, and M. Yonetani. 2016. "Global Report on Internal Displacement." Internal Displacement Monitoring Centre. http://www.internal-displacement.org/globalreport2016/.

Bilefsky, D. 2017. "London Attack near Mosque Investigated as Terrorism." *New York Times*, June 19, 2017. https://www.nytimes.com/2017/06/19/world/europe/uk-van-attack -london-mosque.html?hp&action=click&pgtype=Homepage&clickSource=story -heading&module=photo-spot-region&region=top-news&WT.nav=top-news.

"Billy Sunday Speeds Barley Corn to the Grave; Preaches at Mock Obsequies, with Devil as Mourner, in Norfolk Tabernacle." 1920. *New York Times*, January 17, 1920.

"Blame Migrants for Own Hardships." 1923. *New York Times*, July 8, 1923.

Bluestein, G. 1962. "'The Arkansas Traveler' and the Strategy of American Humor." *Western Folklore* 21 (3): 153–160.

Blum, L. 2002. *"I'm Not a Racist, But . . .": The Moral Quandary of Race*. Ithaca, N.Y.: Cornell University Press.

Bonner, R. 2002. "Threats and Responses: Immigration; New Policy Delays Visas for Specific Muslim Men." *New York Times*, September 10, 2002. https://www.nytimes.com/ 2002/09/10/world/threats-responses-immigration-new-policy-delays-visas-for-specified -muslim-men.html.

Bonner, R., and J. Perelz. 2002. "Threats and Responses: Jakarta; Indonesia Links Muslim Group with Terrorism." *New York Times*, October 17, 2002. https://www.nytimes.com/2002/10/ 17/world/threats-and-responses-jakarta-indonesia-links-muslim-group-with-terrorism.html.

Boorstein, M. 2018. "Mike Pompeo, Trump's Pick to Replace Tillerson, Has Long Worried Muslim Advocates." *Washington Post*, March 13, 2018. https://www.washingtonpost .com/news/acts-of-faith/wp/2018/03/13/sweeping-comments-by-trumps-state-dept-pick -about-islam-have-long-worried-muslim-advocates/?utm_term=.e35d6b55dc87.

Borah, W. W., and S. F. Cook. 1963. *The Aboriginal Population of Central Mexico on the Eve of the Spanish Conquest*. Berkeley: University of California Press.

Briggs, V. M. 1984. *Immigration Policy and the American Labor Force*. Baltimore: Johns Hopkins University Press.

Brown, J. 1855. *Slave Life in Georgia: A Narrative of the Life, Sufferings, and Escape of John Brown, a Fugitive Slave, Now in England*. London: W. M. Watts.

Budiman, A. 2020. "Key Findings about U.S. Immigrants." Pew Research Center, August 20, 2020. https://www.pewresearch.org/fact-tank/2020/08/20/key-findings-about-u-s -immigrants/.

Bulley, D. 2016. *Migration, Ethics and Power: Spaces of Hospitality in International Politics*. London: Sage.

Burgess, J. A. 1985. "News from Nowhere: The Press, the Riots and the Myth of the Inner City." In *Geography, the Media and Popular Culture*, edited by Jacquelin Burgess and John R Gold, 192–228. London: Routledge.

Burton, T. I. 2018. "Study Suggests Trump's 'Muslim Ban' Actually Improved Attitudes toward Muslims." *Vox*, January 10, 2018. https://www.vox.com/identities/2018/1/10/ 16869424/trump-muslim-ban-patriotism.

Butler, S., trans. 1999. *Homer, The Iliad*. Mineola, N.Y.: Dover.

"Cabin Passenger Brings Typhus to the City." 1921. *New York Times*, February 6, 1921.

"Calls Quota Law Cruel." 1924. *New York Times*, January 27, 1924.

Canny, N. P. 1973. "The Ideology of English Colonization: From Ireland to America." *William and Mary Quarterly* 30 (4): 575–598. https://doi.org/10.2307/1918596.

Cantor, G., M. Noferi, and D. Martínez. 2015. "Enforcement Overdrive: A Comprehensive Assessment of ICE's Criminal Alien Program." American Immigration Council, November 1, 2015. https://www.americanimmigrationcouncil.org/research/enforcement-overdrive-comprehensive-assessment-ice's-criminal-alien-program.

Carter, G. F. 1952. "Interglacial Artifacts from the San Diego Area." *Southwestern Journal of Anthropology* 8 (4): 444–456. https://doi.org/10.1086/soutjanth.8.4.3628484.

Casas, M. R. 2007. *Married to a Daughter of the Land: Spanish-Mexican Women and Interethnic Marriage in California, 1820–1880*. Reno: University of Nevada Press.

Casas-Cortes, M., S. Cobarrubias, N. De Genova, G. Garelli, G. Grappi, C. Heller, S. Hess, et al. 2015. "New Keywords: Migration and Borders." *Cultural Studies* 29 (1): 55–87. https://doi.org/10.1080/09502386.2014.891630.

Castells, M. 1996. *The Rise of the Network Society*. The Information Age: Economy, Society, and Culture, vol. 1. London: Blackwell.

Castles, S. 2000. "International Migration at the Beginning of the Twenty-First Century: Global Trends and Issues." *International Social Science Journal* 52 (165): 269–281.

———. 2001. "Migration: Sociological Aspects." In *International Encyclopedia of the Social and Behavioral Sciences*, vol. 14, edited by N. Smelser and P. Baltes. Amsterdam: Elsevier.

———. 2003. "Towards a Sociology of Forced Migration and Social Transformation." *Sociology* 37 (1): 13–34.

Castles, S., and A. Davidson. 2000. *Citizenship and Migration: Globalization and the Politics of Belonging*. New York: Routledge.

Caves, K. 2012. "The Bottle and the Border: What Can America's Failed Experiment with Alcohol Prohibition in the 1920s Teach Us about the Likely Effects of Anti-Immigration Legislation Today?" *Economists' Voice* 9 (1): 1–4. https://doi.org/10.1515/1553-3832.1911.

Chae, D. H., et al. 2017. "The Role of Racial Identity and Implicit Racial Bias in Self-Reported Racial Discrimination: Implications for Depression among African American Men." *Journal of Black Psychology* 43 (8): 789–812. https://doi.org/10.1177/0095798417690055.

"Chamber of Commerce Meeting." 1922. *Wall Street Journal*, December 8, 1922.

Chambers, I. 1994. *Migration, Culture, Identity*. New York: Routledge.

Chan, S. 1998. *Claiming America: Constructing Chinese American Identities during the Exclusion Era*. Philadelphia: Temple University Press.

"Charges Ellis Island Passed in 9,799 Out of 10,002 Who Should Have Been Barred." 1921. *New York Times*, February 10, 1921.

Charmaz, K. 1990. "'Discovering' Chronic Illness: Using Grounded Theory." *Social Science & Medicine* 30 (11): 1161–1172.

———. 2000. "Constructivist and Objectivist Grounded Theory." In *Handbook of Qualitative Research*, vol. 2, edited by N. Denzin and Y. Lincoln. 509–535. London: Sage.

———. 2005. "Grounded Theory: Methods for the 21st Century." In *Handbook of Qualitative Research*, vol. 3, edited by N. Denzin and Y. Lincoln, 507–537. London: Sage.

———. 2014. *Constructing Grounded Theory*. London: Sage.

Charmaz, K., and R. G. Mitchell. 1996. "The Myth of Silent Authorship: Self, Substance, and Style in Ethnographic Writing." *Symbolic Interaction* 19 (4): 285–302.

Chin, J. 2021. "Covid Fueled Anti-Asian Racism. Now Elderly Asian Americans Are Being Attacked." *Washington Post*, February 9, 2021. https://www.washingtonpost.com/nation/2021/02/09/attacks-asian-american-elderly-/.

"China in the Senate." 1882. *New York Times*, March 4, 1882.

"Chinatown Area Plan." 1995. San Francisco Planning Department. July 6, 1995. https://generalplan.sfplanning.org/Chinatown.htm.

"Chinese Criminals." 1882. *Los Angeles Times*, January 26, 1882.

"Chinese from Hong Kong." 1883. *New York Times*, October 14, 1883.

"The Chinese Question." 1885. *New York Times*, November 27, 1885.

Chiu, P. 1960. *Chinese Labor in California, 1850–1880: An Economic Study*. Madison: University of Wisconsin Press.

Chou, C. 2014. "Land Use and the Chinatown Problem." *Asian Pacific American Law Journal* 19 (1): 29–75.

Churchill, W. 2002. *Struggle for the Land: Native North American Resistance to Genocide, Ecocide, and Colonization*. San Francisco: City Lights.

Cilluffo, A., and Fry, R. 2019. "An Early Look at the 2020 Electorate." Pew Research Center, January 30, 2019. https://www.pewresearch.org/social-trends/2019/01/30/an-early-look -at-the-2020-electorate-2/.

Cohen, L. M. 1984. *Chinese in the Post–Civil War South: A People without a History*. Baton Rouge: Louisiana University Press.

Cole, D. 2006. "Manzanar Redux?" *Los Angeles Times*, June 16, 2006. http://articles.latimes .com/2006/jun/16/opinion/oe-cole16.

Collier, A. 2021. "Through Gatsby's Eyes: New York's Jazz Age Gems." *Lonely Planet*, September 23, 2021. https://www.lonelyplanet.com/articles/gatsbys-greatest-places -exploring-new-yorks-jazz-age-gems.

Collins, P. H. 2000. "Gender, Black Feminism, and Black Political Economy." *Annals of the American Academy of Political and Social Science* 568 (1): 41–53.

"The Coming Coolie Cargo." 1882. *West-Coast Record-Union*, July 25, 1882.

"Congress to Tighten Immigration Curb." 1924. *New York Times*, January 27, 1924.

Cook, E. F. 2006. *The Odyssey in Athens: Myths of Cultural Origins*. Ithaca, N.Y.: Cornell University Press.

———. 2016. "Homeric Reciprocities." *Journal of Mediterranean Archaeology* 29 (1): 94–104. https://doi.org/10.1558/jmea.v29i1.31048.

Coolidge, M. 1909. *Chinese Immigration*. New York: Henry Holt.

Council, N. R., and C. de Balexert. 2008. "Guidelines on Profiling Internally Displaced Persons (IDPs)." Internal Displacement Monitoring Centre. April 2008. https://www .internal-displacement.org/publications/guidance-on-profiling-internally-displaced -persons.

Cowell, A. 2002. "Threats and Responses: The Investigation; Fugitive Muslim Cleric, an Outspoken Supporter of Al Qaeda, Is Arrested in London." *New York Times*, October 26, 2002.

Crawford, J. 2000. *At War with Diversity: US Language Policy in an Age of Anxiety*. Clevedon U.K.: Multilingual Matters.

———. 2015. *Place: A Short Introduction*. London: John Wiley.

Crespo, G. 2017. "Two Children, Two Faiths, One Message." CNN, February 1, 2017. https://edition.cnn.com/2017/01/31/us/muslim-jewish-children-at-protest-irpt-trnd/ index.html.

"Curb Immigration to Save the Nation." 1924. *New York Times*, January 26, 1924.

Curtin, P. D. 1969. *The Atlantic Slave Trade: A Census*. Madison: University of Wisconsin Press.

Dabashi, H. 2011. *Brown Skin, White Masks*. London: Pluto.

Daniels, R. 1995. *Asian America: Chinese and Japanese in the United States since 1850*, 3rd ed. Seattle: University of Washington Press.

———. 1997. *Not like Us: Immigrants and Minorities in America, 1890–1924*. Chicago: Ivan R. Dee.

———. 2002. *Coming to America: A History of Immigration and Ethnicity in American Life.* 2nd ed. New York: Perennial.

———. 2004. *Guarding the Golden Door: American Immigration Policy and Immigrants since 1882.* 1st ed. New York: Hill and Wang.

———. 2011. *Asian America: Chinese and Japanese in the United States since 1850.* Seattle: University of Washington Press.

———. 2016. *Franklin D. Roosevelt: The War Years, 1939–1945.* Urbana: University of Illinois Press.

Dayan, D. 2007. "On Morality, Distance and the Other Roger Silverstone's Media and Morality." In "Honoring Roger Silverstone." Special issue, *International Journal of Communication* 1 (1): 113–122.

Degler, C. 1966. Review of *The Political Economy of Slavery: Studies in the Economy and Society of the Slave South*, by E. D. Genovese. *American Historical Review* 71, no. 4 (July): 1422–1423. https://doi.org/10.1086/ahr/71.4.1422.

DeLaet, D. L. 1999. "Introduction: The Invisibility of Women in Scholarship on International Migration." In *Gender and Immigration*, edited by G. Kelson and D. DeLaet, 1–17. London: Palgrave Macmillan.

Deloria, V., Jr. 2003. *God Is Red: A Native View of Religion.* 30th anniv. ed. Golden, Colo.: Fulcrum.

"Denies Dry Law Failed." 1922. *New York Times*, January 9, 1922.

Dent, M. 2016. "'N—er Lynching' Group Text Shocks Penn Freshmen." *Billy Penn.* https://billypenn.com/2016/11/11/n-er-lynching-group-text-shocks-penn-freshmen/.

Denzel Smith, M. 2018. "Is King All That We Are Allowed to Become?" *The Atlantic.*

Deo, M. E., J. J. Lee, C. B. Chin, N. Milman, and N. W. Yuen. 2008. "Missing in Action: 'Framing' Race on Prime-Time Television." *Social Justice* 35 (2): 145–162.

"Deported Armenians Slain." 1924. *New York Times*, December 20, 1924.

Derrida, J. 1999. *Hospitality, Justice and Responsibility: A Dialogue with Jacques Derrida.* London: Routledge.

———. 2000. *On Hospitality: Anne Dufourmantelle Invites Jacques Derrida to Respond.* Stanford, Calif.: Stanford University Press.

Desilver, D., and D. Masci. 2017. "World's Muslim Population More Widespread Than You Might Think." Pew Research Center, January 31, 2017. http://www.pewresearch.org/fact-tank/2017/01/31/worlds-muslim-population-more-widespread-than-you-might-think/.

Deveau, J.-M. 1997. "European Slave Trading in the Eighteenth Century." *Diogenes* 45 (179): 49–74. https://doi.org/10.1177/039219219704517905.

Dixon, E. J. 2001. "Human Colonization of the Americas: Timing, Technology and Process." *Quaternary Science Reviews* 20 (1–3): 277–299.

Dixon, J., and K. Durrheim. 2000. "Displacing Place-Identity: A Discursive Approach to Locating Self and Other." *British Journal of Social Psychology* 39 (1): 27–44.

Douglass, F. 1854. *Narrative of the Life of Frederick Douglass, an American Slave.* Boston: Anti-slavery Office. Project Gutenberg, 1992. https://www.gutenberg.org/files/23/23-h/23-h.htm.

Douzinas, C. 2007. *Human Rights and Empire: The Political Philosophy of Cosmopolitanism.* Oxford: Routledge-Cavendish.

Dow, M. 2008. *American Gulag: Inside U.S. Immigration Prisons.* Berkeley: University of California Press.

Dremann, S. 2017. "Community Notebook: 'Immigrants and Allies' Forum on Jan. 19 in Palo Alto." Palo Alto Online, January 12, 2017. https://www.paloaltoonline.com/news/2017/01/12/community-notebook-immigrants-and-allies-forum-on-jan-19.

"Drops Subsidies to German Press." 1924. *New York Times*, January 8, 1924.

Du Bois, W. E. B. 1903. *The Souls of Black Folk*. Philadelphia: University of Pennsylvania Press.

Dumont, J. C., and G. Lemaître. 2005. "Counting Immigrants and Expatriates in OECD Countries." OECD Social, Employment and Migration Working Papers. OECD Library. https://doi.org/10.1787/1815199X.

Dunbar-Ortiz, R. 2014. *An Indigenous Peoples' History of the United States*. Boston: Beacon.

Duncan, J. 1993. "Sites of Representation: Place, Time and the Discourse of the Other." In *Place/Culture/Representation*, edited by J. Duncan and D. Ley, 39–57. London: Routledge.

Duncan, J., and D. Ley. 1993. "Introduction: Representing the Place of Culture." In *Place/Culture/Representation*, edited by J. Duncan and D. Ley, 1–25. London: Routledge.

Duyvendak, J. W. 2011. *The Politics of Home: Belonging and Nostalgia in Western Europe and the US*. Hampshire, U.K.: Palgrave Macmillan.

East, K. 2016. "Flynn Retweets Anti-Semitic Remark." Politico, July 24, 2016. https://www.politico.com/story/2016/07/michael-flynn-twitter-226091.

Eck, D. L. 2013. "The Religious Gift: Hindu, Buddhist, and Jain Perspectives on Dana." *Social Research* 80 (2): 359–379, 650.

Eckholm, E. 2002. "U.S. Labeling of Group in China as Terrorist Is Criticized." *New York Times*, September 13, 2002. https://www.nytimes.com/2002/09/13/world/us-labeling-of-group-in-china-as-terrorist-is-criticized.html.

"805,228 Immigrants Year Ending June 30." 1921. *New York Times*, August 31, 1921.

"1890 Census Urged as Immigrant Base." 1924. *New York Times*, January 7, 1924.

Eisenstein, S., 1949. *Film Form: Essays in Film Theory*. San Diego: Harcourt Brace Jovanovich.

Eltis, D., and D. Richardson. 2010. *Atlas of the Transatlantic Slave Trade*. New Haven, Conn.: Yale University Press.

"Emma Lazarus: Death of an American Poet of Uncommon Talent." 1887. *New York Times*, November 20, 1887.

"Entertaining Loh Fau Brigands." 1917. *Marshall County News*, October 12, 1917.

Entman, R. M. 1993. "Framing: Toward Clarification of a Fractured Paradigm." *Journal of Communication* 43 (4): 51–58. https://doi.org/10.1111/j.1460-2466.1993.tb01304.x.

Ervin, C. K. 2006. "Terrorism's Soft Targets." *Washington Post*.

Essa, A. 2017. "US Bigotry Didn't Start with Trump." IOL, February 1, 2017. https://www.iol.co.za/news/opinion/azad-essa-us-bigotry-didnt-start-with-trump-7574694.

Esses, V. M., S. Medianu, and A. S. Lawson. 2013. "Uncertainty, Threat, and the Role of the Media in Promoting the Dehumanization of Immigrants and Refugees." *Journal of Social Issues* 69 (3): 518–536. https://doi.org/10.1111/josi.12027.

"Eugenists Dread Tainted Aliens." 1921. *New York Times*, September 25, 1921.

"Excursions: Bartholdi Day." 1886. *New York Times*, October 24, 1886.

"Expects Our Curb on Aliens to Stay." 1924. *New York Times*, January 13, 1924.

Feagin, J. 1997. "Old Poison, New Bottles." In *Immigrants Out! The New Nativism and the Anti-immigrant Impulse in the United States*, edited by J. F. Perea, 13–43. New York: New York University Press.

Fernandes, D. 2007. *Targeted: Homeland Security and the Business of Immigration*. 1st ed. New York: Seven Stories.

Ferrell, R. H. 2006. "Immigration and the Red Scare." In *Who Belongs in America? Presidents, Rhetoric, and Immigration*, edited by V. B. Beasley, 134–148. College Station: Texas A&M University Press.

"First-Class Passengers Detained." 1921. *Wall Street Journal*, July 11, 1921.

Fitzgerald, F. S., and G. Reynolds. 2015. *The Great Gatsby*. London: Penguin.

Fong, E., and W. Markham. 1991. "Immigration, Ethnicity, and Conflict: The California Chinese, 1849–1882*." *Sociological Inquiry* 61 (4): 471–490. https://doi.org/10.1111/j.1475 -682X.1991.tb00174.x.

———. 2002. "Anti-Chinese Politics in California in the 1870s: An Intercounty Analysis." *Sociological Perspectives* 45 (2): 183–210. https://doi.org/10.1525/sop.2002.45.2.183.

"Foreign and Native Public Enemies." 1920. *Wall Street Journal*, January 29, 1920.

Foucault, M. 2009. *Security, Territory, Population: Lectures at the Collège de France 1977– 1978*, vol. 4. London: Palgrave Macmillan.

"Franklin on Immigration Restrictions." 1921. *Wall Street Journal*, December 20, 1921.

Fredette, J. 2014. "Are Muslims Permanent Foreigners in France?" *Washington Post*, October 2, 2014. https://www.washingtonpost.com/news/monkey-cage/wp/2014/10/02/are -muslims-permanent-foreigners-in-france/?utm_term=.03523fcb26b8.

Frichner, T. 2010. "The Preliminary Study on the Doctrine of Discovery." *Pace Environmental Law Review* 28 (1): 339–345.

Friedman, S. S. 1973. *No Haven for the Oppressed: United States Policy toward Jewish Refugees, 1938–1945*. Detroit: Wayne State University Press.

Gabriel, T. 2015. "Donald Trump Says He'd 'Absolutely' Require Muslims to Register." *New York Times*, November 20, 2015. https://www.nytimes.com/politics/first-draft/2015/11/ 20/donald-trump-says-hed-absolutely-require-muslims-to-register/.

Gandy, I. 2017. "The Supreme Court's Punt on Cases Could Affect Immigrants' Constitutional Rights." Rewire, June 28, 2017. https://rewire.news/article/2017/06/28/supreme -courts-punt-cases-affect-immigrants-constitutional-rights/.

Gani, A. 2017. "People Are Using the #NoBanNoWall Hashtag to Protest Trump's Border Wall." BuzzFeed News, January 26, 2017. https://www.buzzfeed.com/aishagani/no-ban -no-wall-tweets-trump?utm_term=.fxWE7ORqO#.pdKynRZGR.

Garcia, M., S. Garcia, I. Herrera, C. de León, M. Phillips, and A. O. Scott. 2021. "'In the Heights' and Colorism: What Is Lost When Afro-Latinos Are Erased." *New York Times*, June 21, 2021. https://www.nytimes.com/2021/06/21/movies/in-the-heights-colorism .html.

Genovese, E. D. 1989. *The Political Economy of Slavery: Studies in the Economy and Society of the Slave South*. Middletown, Conn.: Wesleyan University Press.

Gerson, M. 2013. "Tied in Knots by Radicalism." *Washington Post*, April 23, 2013.

Giddens, A. 1990. *Modernity and Self-identity*. Stanford: Stanford University Press.

Gilroy, P. 1991. "It Ain't Where You're from, It's Where You're At . . . the Dialectics of Diasporic Identification." *Third Text* 5 (13): 3–16.

———. 1993. *The Black Atlantic: Modernity and Double Consciousness*. Cambridge, Mass.: Harvard University Press.

———. 2013. *There Ain't No Black in the Union Jack*. London: Routledge.

Giovanni, J., A. A. Levchenko, and F. Ortega. 2015. "A Global View of Cross-Border Migration." *Journal of the European Economic Association* 13 (1): 168–202.

Gitlin, M. 2009. *The Ku Klux Klan: A Guide to an American Subculture*. Santa Barbara, Calif.: Greenwood.

Gladstone, R., and S. Sugiyama. 2018. "Trump's Travel Ban: How It Works and Who Is Affected." *New York Times*, July 1, 2018. https://www.nytimes.com/2018/07/01/world/ americas/travel-ban-trump-how-it-works.html.

Glaser, B. G., and A. L. Strauss. 2009. *The Discovery of Grounded Theory: Strategies for Qualitative Research*. London: Routledge.

Gold, M. 2012. *Forbidden Citizens: Chinese Exclusion and the U.S. Congress: A Legislative History.* Alexandria, Va.: Harper Perennial.

Goldberg, B. 1992. "Historical Reflections on Transnationalism, Race, and the American Immigrant Saga." *Annals of the New York Academy of Sciences* 645 (a): 201–215. https://doi.org/10.1111/j.1749-6632.1992.tb33493.x.

Goldberg, D. J. 1999. *Discontented America: The United States in The 1920s.* Baltimore: Johns Hopkins University Press.

Goldberg, R. A. 2003. *America in the Twenties.* 1st ed. Syracuse, N.Y.: Syracuse University Press.

Gompers, S. 1901. *Meat Vs. Rice: American Manhood against Asiatic Coolieism. Which Shall Survive?* Printed as Senate document 137 (1902); reprinted with intro. and appendices by Asiatic Exclusion League. San Francisco: American Federation of Labor.

Goodstein, L. 2005. "From Muslims in America, a New Fatwa on Terrorism." *New York Times.*

Gordon, C., ed. 1999. *Major Problems in American History, 1920–1945: Documents and Essays.* Boston: Houghton Mifflin.

Gordon-Reed, A. 2020. *Racism in America: A Reader.* Cambridge, Mass.: Harvard University Press.

Gramsci, A. 1971. *Selections from the Prison Notebooks of Antonio Gramsci.* New York: International.

Grant, M. (1916) 2016. *The Passing of the Great Race, or, the Racial Basis of European History.* New York: Ostara.

Grant, M., C. W. Gould, L. Howe, R. H. Johnson, F. H. Kinnicut, J. B. Trevor, and R. D. Ward. 1925. "Third Report of the Sub-Committee on Selective Immigration of the Eugenics Committee of the United States of America: The Examination of Immigrants Overseas, as an Additional Safeguard in the Processes of Enforcing American Immigration Policy." *Journal of Heredity* 16, no. 8 (August): 293, 298.

Green, H. 2017. "For every reply to this tweet with a hand-drawn message of support for immigrants, Muslims, and/or refugees, I will donate $5 to the ACLU." Twitter, January 28, 2017. https://twitter.com/hankgreen/status/825471810183503872.

Greenwood, M. J., and G. L. Hunt. 1989. "Jobs versus Amenities in the Analysis of Metropolitan Migration." *Journal of Urban Economics* 25 (1): 1–16.

Grewal, Z. 2014. *Islam Is a Foreign Country: American Muslims and the Global Crisis of Authority.* New York: New York University Press.

Grigg, D. B. 1977. "EG Ravenstein and the 'Laws of Migration.'" *Journal of Historical Geography* 3 (1): 41–54.

Grynbaum, M. 2016. "As Race Tightened, News Anchors Seemed as Stunned as Anyone." *New York Times,* November 9, 2016. https://www.nytimes.com/2016/11/09/business/media/media-coverage-election-day.html.

Gualtieri, S. M. A. 2009. *Between Arab and White: Race and Ethnicity in the Early Syrian American Diaspora.* Berkeley: University of California Press.

Gusfield, J. R. 1955. "Social Structure and Moral Reform: A Study of the Woman's Christian Temperance Union." *American Journal of Sociology* 61 (3): 221–232.

———. 1962. "Mass Society and Extremist Politics." *American Sociological Review* 27 (1): 19–30. https://doi.org/10.2307/2089715.

Guterl, M. P. 2003. "After Slavery: Asian Labor, the American South, and the Age of Emancipation." *Journal of World History* 14 (2): 209–241.

Gutiérrez, G. A. 1991. "The Displacement of Native Americans from Iowa." Master's thesis, Iowa State University. https://lib.dr.iastate.edu/rtd/17338.

Gyory, A. 1998. *Closing the Gate: Race, Politics, and the Chinese Exclusion Act*. Chapel Hill: University of North Carolina Press.

Hage, G. (1997) 2010. "Migration, Food, Memory and Home-Building." *Memory: Histories, Theories, Debates*, edited by S. Radstone and B. Schwartz, 416–427. New York: Fordham University Press.

Halabi, N., and K. Peterson. 2018. "Examining the 'Muslim Ban.'" March 23, 2018, Center for Media, Religion and Culture podcast, CU–Boulder. https://thirdspacesblog.com/2018/03/23/examining-the-muslim-ban-the-media-religion-podcast/.

Hall, P. 1898. "Immigration Restriction League (U.S.)." Records, 1893–1921; Series I, Correspondence to and from the IRL; B, Circular letters: 1898–1907. Jan. 25. MS Am 2245, folder 1046. Houghton Library, Harvard University, Cambridge, Mass. http://nrs.harvard.edu/urn-3:FHCL.HOUGH:959406?n=4.

Hall, S. 1980. "Cultural Studies: Two Paradigms." *Media, Culture & Society* 2 (1): 57–72.

———. 1981. "The Whites of Their Eyes: Racist Ideologies and the Media." In *The Media Reader*, edited by M. Alvarado and J. Thompson, 9–23. London: British Film Institute.

———. 1999. "A Conversation with Stuart Hall." *Journal of the International Institute* 7, no. 1 (Fall). http://hdl.handle.net/2027/spo.4750978.0007.107.

Haller, M. H. 1971. "Organized Crime in Urban Society: Chicago in the Twentieth Century." *Journal of Social History* 5 (2): 210–234.

———. 1976. "Bootleggers and American Gambling 1920–1950." In *Gambling in America—Commission on the Review of National Policy Towards Gambling—Final Report 1976*. Washington, D.C.: U.S. Department of Justice. https://www.ojp.gov/ncjrs/virtual-library/abstracts/gambling-america-commission-review-national-policy-toward-gambling.

———. 1990. "Illegal Enterprises: A Theoretical and Historical Interpretation." *Criminology* 28 (2): 207–236.

Halter, M., and C. Capozzola. 2014. Introduction to *What's New about the "New" Immigration? Traditions and Transformations in the United States since 1965*, edited by M. S. Johnson, K. P. Viens, and C. E. Wright. New York: New York University Press.

Hammond, L. 2004. *This Place Will Become Home: Refugee Repatriation to Ethiopia*. Ithaca, N.Y.: Cornell University Press.

Handlin, O. 1951. *The Uprooted: The Epic Story of the Great Migrations That Made the American People*. Boston: Little, Brown.

———. 1991. *Boston's Immigrants, 1790–1880: A Study in Acculturation*. 50th anniv. ed. Cambridge, Mass: Belknap.

Hanke, L. 1937. "Pope Paul III and the American Indians." *Harvard Theological Review* 30 (2): 65–102. https://doi.org/10.1017/S0017816000022161.

Harris, R. C., and E. Leinberger. 2002. *Making Native Space: Colonialism, Resistance, and Reserves in British Columbia*. Vancouver: UBC Press.

Hauslohner, A. 2018. "For Muslims, Supreme Court's Ruling on Entry Ban Will Be Statement of America's Values." *Washington Post*, April 24, 2018.

Hawgood, A. 2018. "A Muslim Fashion Blogger with a Fierce Message." *New York Times*, March 7, 2018. https://www.nytimes.com/2018/03/07/fashion/muslim-fashion-blogger-hoda-katebi.html?rref=collection%2Ftimestopic%2FMuslim%20Americans.

Hayden, B. 2006. "What's in a Name? the Nature of the Individual in Refugee Studies." *Journal of Refugee Studies* 19 (4): 471–487.

Heidegger, M. 1958. *The Question of Being*. New York: Rowman and Littlefield.

Held, D. 1999. *Global Transformations: Politics, Economics and Culture*. Stanford, Calif.: Stanford University Press.

Hellwig, D. 1981. "Black Leaders and the United States Immigration Policy, 1917–1929." *Journal of Negro History* 8:110–127.

Henkel, R. 2004. "Making Sense of Terror Alerts." *New York Times*.

Henriksson, A. 2017. "Norm-Critical Rationality: Emotions and the Institutional Influence of Queer Resistance." *Journal of Political Power* 10 (2): 149–165. https://doi.org/10.1080/2158379X.2017.1336339.

Henry, F. 1999. *The Racialization of Crime in Toronto's Print Media: A Research Project*. Toronto: Ryerson University Press.

Hermann, A. 2019. "Penn Professor Amy Wax: Determining Whether President Trump Is a Racist Is 'So Shallow.'" PhillyVoice, August 23, 2019. https://www.phillyvoice.com/penn-professor-amy-wax-racism-president-trump-interview-new-yorker-colonialism/.

Herrerla, C. 2017. "Wall Street Journal Editor Berates Reporters for Critical Trump Coverage." *Huffington Post*, August 24, 2017. https://www.huffingtonpost.com/entry/wall-street-journal-gerard-baker-leaked-emails-trump-phoenix_us_599e31d0e4b06d67e3351b00.

Hetherington, K. 1997. "In Place of Geometry: The Materiality of Place." *Sociological Review* 45 (S1): 183–199.

Higham, J. 1988. *Strangers in the Land: Patterns of American Nativism, 1860–1925*. New Brunswick, N.J.: Rutgers University Press.

Hitomi, K. 1994. "Automation—Its Concept and a Short History." *Technovation* 14 (2): 121–128. https://doi.org/10.1016/0166-4972(94)90101-5.

Hoerder, D. 1999. "From Immigration to Migration System. New Concepts in Migration History." *OAH Magazine of History* 14 (1): 5–11.

Hoffman, W. "Need to Select Immigrants." 1924. *New York Times*, January 27, 1924.

Holloway, J. S. 2006. "The Black Scholar, the Humanities, and the Politics of Racial Knowledge since 1945." In *The Humanities and the Dynamics of Inclusion since World War II*, edited by D. Hollinger, 217–246. Baltimore: Johns Hopkins University Press.

Hom, M. 1987. *Songs of Gold Mountain: Cantonese Rhymes from San Francisco Chinatown*. Berkeley: University of California Press.

Hoppenstand, G. 1992. "Yellow Devil Doctors and Opium Dens: The Yellow Peril Stereotype in Mass Media Entertainment." In *Popular Culture: An Introductory Text*, edited by J. G. Nachbar and K. Lausé, 277–291. Bowling Green, Ohio: Bowling Green State University Popular Press.

Hoppenstand, G., and Y. D. Doctors. 1983. "Opium Dens: A Survey of the Yellow Peril Stereotypes in Mass Media Entertainment." In *The Popular Culture Reader*, edited by C. D. Geist. Bowling Green, Ohio: Bowling Green State University Popular Press.

Houghton Library. n.d. *Immigration Restriction League (U.S.) Records, 1893–1921*. No. MS Am 2245. Harvard University. Accessed July 1, 2022. https://id.lib.harvard.edu/ead/hou00163/catalog.

"House Passes Immigration Bill." 1921. *Wall Street Journal*, May 14, 1921.

Hu-Dehart, E. 1993. "Chinese Coolie Labour in Cuba in the Nineteenth Century: Free Labour or Neo-Slavery?" *Slavery & Abolition* 14 (1): 67–86. https://doi.org/10.1080/01440399308575084.

Human Rights Watch. 2004. "U.S.: Don't Turn Away Haitian Refugees." February 25, 2004. https://www.hrw.org/news/2004/02/25/us-dont-turn-away-haitian-refugees.

"Hunting Chinamen." 1885. *New York Times*, September 4, 1885.

Huot, S. S., and D. L. Rudman. 2010. "The Performances and Places of Identity: Conceptualizing Intersections of Occupation, Identity and Place in the Process of Migration." *Journal of Occupational Science* 17 (2): 68–77.

Hussain, E. 2010. "What Is Moderate Islam?—Don't Call Me Moderate, Call Me Normal." *Wall Street Journal*, September 1, 2010.

"Hylan Asks Harding to Stop Klan Paper." 1922. *New York Times*, December 21, 1922.

Ignatiev, N. 1995. *How the Irish Became White*. New York: Routledge.

Ikuenobe, P. 2011. "Conceptualizing Racism and Its Subtle Forms." *Journal for the Theory of Social Behaviour* 41 (2): 161–181.

"Immigrants Deported under Restriction Laws." 1921. *Wall Street Journal*, August 1, 1921.

"The Immigrant's Statue." 2015. National Park Service. Last updated February 26, 2015. https://home.nps.gov/stli/learn/historyculture/the-immigrants-statue.htm.

"Immigration for Six Months Reaches Aggregate of 532,882." 1921. *Wall Street Journal*, September 20, 1921.

"Immigration Problem Affecting Industry." 1922. *Wall Street Journal*, October 25, 1922.

"Immigration Restriction." 1924. *New York Times*, January 13, 1924.

"Immigration Today Greater Than Any Time in U.S. History." 1924. *Washington Post*, December 15, 1924. ProQuest Historical Newspapers.

"Influence of Harper's Weekly." n.d. Illustrating Chinese Exclusion. https://thomasnastcartoons.com/the-chinese-cartoons/influence-of-harpers-weekly/.

International Commission on Intervention, State Sovereignty, & International Development Research Centre. 2001. "The Responsibility to Protect: Report of the International Commission on Intervention and State Sovereignty." Canada: International Development Research Centre.

Italy-America Society. 1920. "Bulletin of the Italy America Society." https://iiif.lib.harvard.edu/manifests/view/drs:6541692$6i.

"Italy Feels Hard Hit by Immigration Bill." 1924. *New York Times*, January 6, 1924.

"Italy Leads Immigration List." 1922. *Wall Street Journal*, October 6, 1922.

Jacobson, M. F. 1998. *Whiteness of a Different Color: European Immigrants and the Alchemy of Race*. Cambridge, Mass.: Harvard University Press.

Jacoby, J. 2018. "Masterpiece Cakeshop Leaves a Tasty Morsel for the Travel Ban Case." *Boston Globe*, June 8, 2018. https://www.bostonglobe.com/opinion/letters/2018/06/07/masterpiece-cakeshop-leaves-tasty-morsel-for-travel-ban-case/HkZJlC19qalQao2rYUQRlJ/story.html.

James, H. 1907. *The American Scene*. New York: Harper and Brothers.

James, W. 1890. *The Principles of Psychology*. New York: Holt.

Jamil, U., and C. Rousseau. 2012. "Subject Positioning, Fear, and Insecurity in South Asian Muslim Communities in the War on Terror Context: South Asian Muslim Communities in the War on Terror." *Canadian Review of Sociology/Revue Canadienne de Sociologie* 49 (4): 370–388. https://doi.org/10.1111/j.1755-618X.2012.01299.x.

Jammer, M. (1954) 2013. *Concepts of Space: The History of Theories of Space in Physics*. 3rd ed. Mineola, N.Y.: Dover.

"Japanese Protest the Immigration Bill." 1924. *New York Times*, January 7, 1924.

Jaroszyńska-Kirchmann, A. D. 2015. *The Polish Hearst: Ameryka-Echo and the Public Role of the Immigrant Press. History of Communication*. Urbana: University of Illinois Press.

Jerald, M. C., L. M. Ward, L. Moss, K. Thomas, and K. D. Fletcher. 2016. "Subordinates, Sex Objects, or Sapphires? Investigating Contributions of Media Use to Black Students' Femininity Ideologies and Stereotypes about Black Women." *Journal of Black Psychology* 43 (6): 608–635. https://doi.org/10.1177/0095798416665967.

Jiwani, Y. 1995. "Helpless Maidens and Chivalrous Knights: Afghan Women in the Canadian Press." *University of Toronto Quarterly* 78 (2): 728.

———. 2009. "Race and the Media: A Retrospective and Prospective Gaze." *Canadian Journal of Communication* 34:735–740. https://cjc-online.ca/index.php/journal/article/view/2286/3017.

Johnson, A. 1921. "An Act to Limit the Immigration of Aliens into the United States." Pub. L. No. 4075, Section 5, 42 Stat. 8.

Johnson, I. 2005. "As Muslims Call Europe Home, Dangerous Isolation Takes Root." *Wall Street Journal*, July 11, 2005.

Johnson, J. 2015. "Trump Calls for 'Total and Complete Shutdown of Muslims Entering the United States.'" *Washington Post*, December 7, 2015.

Johnson, K. R. 1997. "The Antiterrorism Act, the Immigration Reform Act, and Ideological Regulation in the Immigration Laws: Important Lessons for Citizens and Noncitizens." *St. Mary's Law Journal* 28 (4): 833.

Jorae, W. R. 2009. *The Children of Chinatown: Growing up Chinese American in San Francisco, 1850–1920.* Chapel Hill: University of North Carolina Press.

Jung, M. H. 2005. "Outlawing 'Coolies': Race, Nation, and Empire in the Age of Emancipation." *American Quarterly* 57:677–701.

Kaczynski, A. 2016. "On Twitter, Michael Flynn Interacted with Alt-Right, Made Controversial Comments on Muslims, Shared Fake News." CNN, November 18, 2016. https://www.cnn.com/2016/11/18/politics/kfile-flynn-tweets/index.html.

Kanazawa, M. 2005. "Immigration, Exclusion, and Taxation: Anti-Chinese Legislation in Gold Rush California." *Journal of Economic History* 65 (3): 779–805.

Karim, K. 2011. "Covering Muslims: Journalism as Cultural Practice." In *Journalism after September 11*, 2nd ed., edited by B. Zelizer and S. Allan, 131–146. New York: Routledge.

Katz, Y. 1988. "Agricultural Settlements in Palestine, 1882–1914." *Jewish Social Studies* 50 (1/2): 63–82.

Kawai, Y. 2005. "Stereotyping Asian Americans: The Dialectic of the Model Minority and the Yellow Peril." *Howard Journal of Communications* 16 (2): 109–130. https://doi.org/10.1080/10646170590948974.

Kehaulani Goo, S., and J. Mitz. 2003. "U.S. Officials Warn of New Tactics by Al Qaeda." *Washington Post*, September 5, 2003, p. 2.

Kelley, N., and M. J. Trebilcock. 1998. *The Making of the Mosaic: A History of Canadian Immigration Policy.* Toronto: University of Toronto Press.

Kelsey, A. 2017. "Latest Version of Travel Ban Blocked by Federal Judge." ABC News, October 17, 2017. http://abcnews.go.com/Politics/latest-version-travel-ban-blocked-federal-judge/story?id=50541798.

Kemp, K. 2004. "Speaking Out Against Terrorism." 2004. *Washington Post*.

Kennedy, R. n.d. "Cartoon of the Day." *Harper's Weekly.* http://www.harpweek.com/09Cartoon/BrowseByDateCartoon.asp?Month=February&Date=18.

Kerber, L. K. 1997. "The Meanings of Citizenship." *Journal of American History* 84 (3): 833. https://doi.org/10.2307/2953082.

Khan, M. 1995. *Sahih al-Bukhari.* London: Darussalam.

Khan, Y. S. 2015. *Enlightening the World: The Creation of the Statue of Liberty.* Ithaca, N.Y.: Cornell University Press.

King, C. 2015. "Don't Sugarcoat the Islamic Threat." *Washington Post*, January 17, 2015.

Kirillova, K., A. Gilmetdinova, and X. Lehto. 2014. "Interpretation of Hospitality across Religions." *International Journal of Hospitality Management* 43:23–34.

Kirk, A. 2016. "Which Country Has the Most Immigrants?" *The Telegraph*, January 21, 2016. http://www.telegraph.co.uk/news/worldnews/middleeast/12111108/Mapped-Which-country-has-the-most-immigrants.html.

"Klan Letters Sent to Grand Jurors: Every Alderman Also Receives Message Defending Ku Klux Activities." 1922. *New York Times*, December 12, 1922.

Kleinfeld, N. R. 2001. "U.S. Attacked; Hijacked Jets Destroy Twin Towers and Hit Pentagon in Day of Terror." *New York Times*, September 12, 2001. https://www.nytimes.com/2001/09/12/us/us-attacked-hijacked-jets-destroy-twin-towers-and-hit-pentagon-in-day-of-terror.html.

Kohler, M. 1924a. "Aspects of Pending Immigration Legislation." *New York Times*, January 7, 1924.

———. 1924b. "Aspects of Pending Immigration Legislation." *New York Times*, January 14, 1924.

———. 1924c. "Some Aspects of Immigration Legislation." *New York Times*, January 25, 1924.

Kohut, A. 2015. "In '60s, Americans Gave Thumbs-up to Immigration Law That Changed the Nation." Pew Research Center. http://www.pewresearch.org/fact-tank/2015/02/04/50-years-later-americans-give-thumbs-up-to-immigration-law-that-changed-the-nation/.

Kornelsen, J., A. Kotaska, P. Waterfall, L. Willie, and D. Wilson. 2010. "The Geography of Belonging: The Experience of Birthing at Home for First Nations Women." *Health & Place* 16 (4): 638–645.

———. 2011. "Alienation and Resilience: The Dynamics of Birth outside Their Community for Rural First Nations Women." *International Journal of Indigenous Health* 7 (1): 55.

Koser, K. 2007. *International Migration: A Very Short Introduction*. Oxford: Oxford University Press.

Kraut, J. R. 2012. "Global Anti-anarchism: The Origins of Ideological Deportation and the Suppression of Expression." *Indiana Journal of Global Legal Studies* 19 (1): 169–193. https://doi.org/10.2979/indjglolegstu.19.1.169.

———. 2020. "Threat of Dissent: A History of Ideological Exclusion and Deportation in the United States." Cambridge, Mass.: Harvard University Press.

Kuakkanen, R. 2003. "The Responsibility of the Academy: A Call for Doing Homework." *Journal of Curriculum Theorizing* 26 (3): 61–74.

Kurzban, I. 2008. "Democracy and Immigration." In *Keeping Out the Other: A Critical Introduction to Immigration Enforcement Today*, edited by D. Brotherton and P. Kretsedemas. New York: Columbia University Press.

"Labor Shortage Found to Be Increasing." 1922. *Wall Street Journal*, June 28, 1922.

Lamon, M. 2018. "After 'Disparaging' Comments on Black Students, Amy Wax Barred from Teaching First-Year Course." *Daily Pennsylvanian*, March 13, 2018. https://www.thedp.com/article/2018/03/penn-law-dean-ted-ruger-professor-amy-wax-removed-racial-conservative-graduate-upenn-philadelphia.

Landauro, I., M. Dalton, and A. Entous. 2015. "Paris Attacks." *Wall Street Journal*, November 14, 2015. http://www.wsj.com/articles/paris-attacks-syrian-migrant-was-among-the-bombers-1447547354.

Lardner, G. 2003. "Congress Funds INS Registration System but Demands Details." *Washington Post*, February 15, 2003. https://www.washingtonpost.com/archive/politics/2003/02/15/congress-funds-ins-registration-system-but-demands-details/34c392bf-942e-4cf3-865a-bce9fe98ac1f/?utm_term=.f88df07a82d9.

Lashay, C. and A. Morrison, eds. 2000. *Search of Hospitality: Theoretical Perspectives and Debates*. Oxford: Butterworth-Heinemann.

Lavery, C. 2016. "Situating Eugenics: Robert DeCourcy Ward and the Immigration Restriction League of Boston." *Journal of Historical Geography* 53:54–62. https://doi.org/10.1016/j.jhg.2016.05.015.

Lavie, S. and T. Swedenburg, eds. 1996. *Displacement, Diaspora and Geographies of Identity.* Durham, N.C.: Duke University Press.

Law, J. 1999. "After ANT: Complexity, Naming and Topology." *Sociological Review* 47 (S1): 1–14.

Lawrie, P. R. D. 2016. *Forging a Laboring Race: The African American Worker in the Progressive Imagination.* New York: New York University Press.

"Lawyer Urges Judge to Free Detained Muslim." 2002. *New York Times,* August 24, 2002. https://www.nytimes.com/2002/08/24/us/lawyer-urges-judge-to-free-detained-muslim .html.

Lazarus, E. 1882. *Songs of a Semite.* New York: Office of the American Hebrew.

———. (1882) 2002. "The New Colossus." In *Emma Lazarus: Selected Poems and Other Writings,* collected by G. Eiselein. New York: Broadview.

Lee, C. 2010. "'Where the Danger Lies': Race, Gender, and Chinese and Japanese Exclusion in the United States, 1870–1924." *Sociological Forum* 25 (2): 248–271. https://doi.org/10 .1111/j.1573-7861.2010.01175.x.

Lee, E. 1969. "A Theory of Migration." In *Migration,* edited by J. A. Jackson. London: Cambridge University Press.

———. 2003. *At America's Gates: Chinese Immigration during the Exclusion Era, 1882–1943.* Chapel Hill: University of North Carolina Press.

———. 2019. *America for Americans: A History of Xenophobia in the United States.* New York: Basic.

———. 2020. "Yes—the Echoes of the Past Are Loud and Clear Today." Twitter, January 31, 2020. https://twitter.com/prof_erikalee/status/1223273354918010881?s=20.

Lee, M. 2008. "Congressional Controversy over the Federal Prohibition Bureau's Public Relations, 1922." *Public Relations Review* 34 (3): 276–278. https://doi.org/10.1016/j .pubrev.2008.03.023.

Lee, T. 2016. "Trump Supporter: Internment 'Precedent' for Muslim Registry to 'Protect America.'" NBC, November 17, 2016. https://www.nbcnews.com/news/asian-america/ trump-supporter-cites-internment-precedent-muslim-registry-n685131.

Leibowitz, A. H. 1969. "English Literacy: Legal Sanction for Discrimination." *Notre Dame Law Review* 45 (1): 7.

Lenning, A. 2004. "Myth and Fact: The Reception of the *Birth of a Nation*." *Film History* 16 (2): 117–141.

Leonard, T. C. 1986. *The Power of the Press: The Birth of American Political Reporting.* New York: Oxford University Press.

Leschnitzer, Adolf A. 1971. "The Wandering Jew: The Alienation of the Jewish Image in Christian Consciousness." *Viator* 2:391–396.

Levenstein, H. A. 1968. "The AFL and Mexican Immigration in the 1920s: An Experiment in Labor Diplomacy." *Hispanic American Historical Review* 48 (2): 206–219. https://doi .org/10.2307/2510743.

———. (1994) 2003. *Paradox of Plenty: A Social History of Eating in Modern America.* Berkeley: University of California Press.

Lewis, A. "Immigration Restriction." 1924. *New York Times,* January 13, 1924.

Li, A. 2016. "WVU Students Talk Post-Elections Fears and Hopes at Unity Circle." WV Public Broadcasting, November 15, 2016. http://wvpublic.org/post/wvu-students-talk -post-elections-fears-and-hopes-unity-circle#stream/0.

"Liberty's Place of Rest." 1884. *New York Times,* August 6, 1884.

"Liberty Unveiled." 1882. *The Sun.*

Librairie Larousse. 2020. *Dictionnaire Larousse poche 2021.* Paris: Larousse.

Lieu, T. 2015. "Congressman Lieu Statement on Donald Trump Muslim Travel Ban Proposal." House.gov, December 8, 2015. https://lieu.house.gov/media-center/press-releases/congressman-lieu-statement-donald-trump-muslim-travel-ban-proposal.

Light, I. 1974. "From Vice District to Tourist Attraction: The Moral Career of American Chinatowns, 1880–1940." *Pacific Historical Review* 43 (3): 367–394. https://doi.org/10.2307/3638262.

"Like-Minded or Well-Born?" 1924. *New York Times*, February 10, 1924.

Lim, S. J. 2006. *A Feeling of Belonging: Asian American Women's Public Culture, 1930–1960.* New York: New York University Press.

Lind, D. 2016. "Obama Just Made It Much Harder for Trump to Build His 'Muslim Registry.'" *Vox*, December 22, 2016. https://www.vox.com/2016/12/22/14053190/obama-nseers-trump-muslim.

Lipka, M., and C. Hackett. 2017. "Why Muslims Are the World's Fastest-Growing Religious Group." Pew Research Center, April 6, 2017. https://www.pewresearch.org/fact-tank/2017/04/06/why-muslims-are-the-worlds-fastest-growing-religious-group/.

Liptak, A., and M. Shear. 2018. "Trump's Travel Ban Is Upheld by Supreme Court." *New York Times*, June 26, 2018. https://www.nytimes.com/2018/06/26/us/politics/supreme-court-trump-travel-ban.html.

"Liquor Scandals Alarm Politicians." 1922. *New York Times*, January 9, 1922.

Livingstone, S. 1998. "Audience Research at the Crossroads: The 'Implied Audience' in Media and Cultural Theory." *European Journal of Cultural Studies* 1 (2): 193–217. https://doi.org/10.1177/136754949800100203.

Lowell, B. L. 2001. *Some Developmental Effects of the International Migration of Highly Skilled Persons.* Geneva, Switzerland: International Labour Office.

Lowell, B. L., and A. Findlay. 2001. "Migration of Highly Skilled Persons from Developing Countries: Impact and Policy Responses." *International Migration Papers* 44:25.

Lukermann, F. 1964. "Geography as a Formal Intellectual Discipline and the Way in Which It Contributes to Human Knowledge." *Canadian Geographer/Le Géographe canadien* 8 (4): 167–172.

Lüthi, B. 1999. "Migration and Migration History." *History* 14 (1): 5–11.

Lynch, P., J. G. Molz, A. Mcintosh, P. Lugosi, and C. Lashley. 2011. "Theorizing Hospitality." *Hospitality & Society* 1 (1): 3–24.

Maalouf, A. 1998. *Les Identités Meurtrières.* Paris: Grasset. Translated by B. Bray. 2001. *In the Name of Identity.* New York: Penguin.

Maghbouleh, N. 2017. *The Limits of Whiteness: Iranian Americans and the Everyday Politics of Race.* Stanford, Calif.: Stanford University Press.

Mahler, S. J., and P. R. Pessar. 2006. "Gender Matters: Ethnographers Bring Gender from the Periphery toward the Core of Migration Studies." *International Migration Review* 40 (1): 27–63.

Mahtani, M. 2001. "Representing Minorities: Canadian Media and Minority Identities." *Canadian Ethnic Studies Journal* 33, no. 3 (Fall): 99–133.

———. 2015. *Mixed Race Amnesia: Resisting the Romanticization of Multiraciality.* Vancouver: University of British Columbia Press.

Maldonado, A. 2017. "Suffering Islamophobia? Try Bassem Youssef's 'Muslim Morning After Kit.'" *Salon*, August 21, 2017. https://www.salon.com/2017/08/21/suffering-islamophobia-try-bassem-youssefs-muslim-morning-after-kit/.

Malone, D. 2008. "Immigration, Terrorism, and Secret Prisons." In *Keeping Out the Other,* edited by D. Brotherton and P. Kretsedemas, 44–63. New York: Columbia University Press.

Mangiafico, L. 1988. *Contemporary American Immigrants: Patterns of Filipino, Korean, and Chinese Settlement in the United States.* New York: Praeger.

Manji, I. 2007. "Muslim Melting Pot." *Wall Street Journal,* June 4, 2007. https://www.wsj .com/articles/SB118090620007623006.

Mara, R., and J. Phoenix. 2020. "Wet Markets Breed Contagions like the Coronavirus. the U.S. Has Thousands of Them." *Washington Post,* April 21, 2020. https://www .washingtonpost.com/outlook/2020/04/21/mara-phoenix-wet-market-animal-cruelty/.

Marchetti, G. 1993. *Romance and the "Yellow Peril": Race, Sex, and Discursive Strategies in Hollywood Fiction.* Berkeley: University of California Press.

Martínez Cobo, J. R. M. 1986. *Study of the Problem of Discrimination against Indigenous Populations,* vol. 1–5. United Nations Economic and Social Council. https://digitallibrary.un .org/record/768953?ln=en.

Mattelart, T. 2009. "Globalization Theories and Media Internationalization: A Critical Appraisal." In *Internationalizing Media Studies,* edited by D. K. Thussu, 48–60. London: Routledge.

"Max James Kohler Papers." 1888–1935. Collection, identifier P-7. Center for Jewish History. https://archives.cjh.org/repositories/3/resources/13251.

Mazumdar, S., F. Docuyanan, and C. M. McLaughlin. 2000. "Creating a Sense of Place: The Vietnamese-Americans and Little Saigon." *Journal of Environmental Psychology* 20 (4): 319–333.

McAdam, D., S. Tarrow, and C. Tilly. 2003. "Dynamics of Contention." *Social Movement Studies* 2 (1): 99–102.

McAuliffe, M. 2017. "The Nexus between Forced and Irregular Migration: Insights from Demography." In *Demography of Refugee and Forced Migration,* edited by G. Hugo. New York: Springer Berlin Heidelberg.

McChesney, R. W. 2015. *Rich Media, Poor Democracy: Communication Politics in Dubious Times.* New York: New Press.

McCombs, M. E., and D. L. Shaw. 1972. "The Agenda-Setting Function of Mass Media." *Public Opinion Quarterly* 36 (2): 176–187.

McCrummen, S. 2017. "Love Thy Neighbor?" *Washington Post,* July 1, 2017. https://www .washingtonpost.com/national/in-a-midwestern-town-that-went-for-trump-a-muslim -doctor-tries-to-understand-his-neighbors/2017/07/01/0ada50c4-5c48-11e7-9fc6 -c7ef4bc58d13_story.html.

McGee, T. G. 1977. "Rural-Urban Mobility in South and Southeast Asia: Different Formulations, Different Answers." In *Human Migration Patterns and Politics,* edited by W. H. McNeill and R. S. Adams, 199–224. Bloomington: Indiana University Press.

McGurty, F., and N. Frandino. 2017. "Tens of Thousands in U.S. Cities Protest Trump Immigration Order." *Reuters,* January 29, 2017. https://www.reuters.com/article/us-usa-trump -immigration-protests/tens-of-thousands-in-u-s-cities-protest-trump-immigration-order -idUSKBN15D15H.

McKeown, A. 2004. "Global Migration 1846–1940." *Journal of World History* 15 (2): 155–189.

McKinnon, S. 2010. "Inhospitable Publics." In *Public Modalities,* edited by D. Brouwer and R. Asen. Tuscaloosa: University of Alabama Press.

Mecklin, J. M. 1924. *The Ku Klux Klan: A Study of the American Mind.* New York: Harcourt, Brace.

"Media Advisory: Final Presidential Debate of 2020 Draws 63 Million Viewers." 2020. Nielson Ratings, October 23, 2020. https://www.nielsen.com/us/en/press-releases/2020/ media-advisory-final-presidential-debate-of-2020-draws-63-million-viewers/.

Melendy, H. B. 1985. Review of *Chinese in the Post–Civil War South: A People without a History*, by L. M. Cohen. *American Historical Review* 90, no. 3 (June): 760–761. https://doi .org/10.1086/ahr/90.3.760.

"Melting Pot Fails." 1921. *New York Times*, February 3, 1921.

Meltzer, D. J. 2013. "The Human Colonization of the Americas: Archaeology." In *The Encyclopedia of Global Human Migration*, edited by P. Bellwood, 61–70. London: Wiley-Blackwell.

Metrick-Chen, L. 2012. *Collecting Objects/Excluding People: Chinese Subjects and American Visual Culture, 1830–1900*. Albany: State University of New York Press.

Miller, R. J., L. Behrendt, J. Ruru, and T. Lindberg. 2010. *Discovering Indigenous Lands: The Doctrine of Discovery in the English Colonies*. Oxford: Oxford University Press.

Miller, S. C. 1969. *The Unwelcome Immigrant: The American Image of the Chinese, 1785–1882*. Berkeley: University of California Press.

———. 1971. "An East Coast Perspective to Chinese Exclusion, 1852–1882." *Historian* 33 (2): 183–201. https://doi.org/10.1111/j.1540-6563.1971.tb01154.x.

Mink, G. 2009. "Meat vs. Rice (and Pasta): Samuel Gompers and the Republic of White Labor." In *Racially Writing the Republic*, edited by B. D. Baum, 145–162. Durham, N.C.: Duke University Press.

Minnick, S. S. 1988. *Sam Fow: The San Joaquin Chinese Legacy*. Fresno, Calif.: Heritage West.

Miščević, D. D., and P. Kwong. 2000. *Chinese Americans*. Southport, Conn.: Hugh Lauter Levin.

Mitchell, L. 2017. "Civil Society During the Trump Years." *Huffington Post*, January 2, 2017. https://www.huffingtonpost.com/lincoln-mitchell/civil-society-during-the_b_13929112 .html.

Mitchell, M. N. 2008. *Raising Freedom's Child: Black Children and Visions of the Future after Slavery*. New York: New York University Press.

"Mob Law in Wyoming." 1885. *New York Times*, September 19, 1885.

Moloney, D. 2012. *National Insecurities: Immigrants and U.S. Deportation Policy Since 1882*. Chapel Hill: University of North Carolina Press.

Monroe-Sheridan, A. R. 2018. "Frankly Unthinkable: The Constitutional Failings of President Trump's Proposed Muslim Registry." *Maine Law Review* 70 (1): 1–34. https:// digitalcommons.mainelaw.maine.edu/mlr/vol70/iss1/1.

Monson, I. T., ed. 2003. *The African Diaspora: A Musical Perspective*. New York: Routledge.

Montejano, D. 1987. *Anglos and Mexicans in the Making of Texas, 1836–1986*. 1st ed. Austin: University of Texas Press.

———. 1999. "The 'Mexican Problem.'" In *Major Problems in American History, 1920–1945: Documents and Essays*, edited by C. Gordon, 172–180. Boston: Houghton Mifflin.

Moore, S. T. 2014. *Bootleggers and Borders: The Paradox of Prohibition on a Canada-US Borderland*. Lincoln: University of Nebraska Press.

Morgan, E. 1975. *American Slavery, American Freedom: The Ordeal of Colonial Virginia*. New York: W. W. Norton.

Morgan, E. S. 2003. *American Slavery, American Freedom: The Ordeal of Colonial Virginia*. New York: W. W. Norton.

Morison, S. 1963. *Journals and Other Documents on the Life and Voyages of Christopher Columbus*. New York: Heritage.

Mufson, B. 2017. "This Statue of Liberty Drawing Became a Symbol of the 'No Ban, No Wall' Movement." Vice, January 30, 2017. https://creators.vice.com/en_us/article/8qvzw5/ jamie-hu-no-ban-no-wall-jfk-protestors-monday-insta-illustrator.

Murphy, C. 2005. "U.S. Muslim Scholars to Forbid Terrorism." *Washington Post,* July 28, 2005.

Murphy, C., and A. Cooperman. 2004. "Muslims in U.S. Begin PR Campaign Denouncing Terrorism." *Washington Post.* http://www.washingtonpost.com/wp-dyn/articles/A61654 -2004May27.html.

Murray, R. K. 1955. *Red Scare: A Study in National Hysteria, 1919–1920.* Minneapolis: University of Minnesota Press.

"Muslim Group Starts an Effort to Increase Voter Registration." 2002. *New York Times,* February 23, 2002. https://www.nytimes.com/2002/02/23/us/muslim-group-starts-an -effort-to-increase-voter-registration.html.

Mutz, D. C., ed. 2006. *Political Persuasion and Attitude Change.* Ann Arbor: University of Michigan Press.

Myre, G. 2015. "The Migrant Crisis." NPR, September 8, 2015. http://www.npr.org/sections/ parallels/2015/09/08/438539779/the-migrant-crisis-by-the-numbers.

Naff, A. 1993. *Becoming American: The Early Arab Immigrant Experience.* Carbondale: Southern Illinois University Press.

Nast, T. 1882. "Justice for the Chinese." *Harper's Weekly.*

Navasky, V. 2011. Foreword to *Journalism after September 11,* edited by B. Zelizer and S. Allan. New York: Routledge.

"Negro and Chinaman." 1882. *New York Times,* March 9, 1882.

"New Plea to Wilson in Typhus War Here." 1921. *New York Times,* February 14, 1921.

Ngai, M. 1999. "The Architecture of Race in American Immigration Law: A Reexamination of the Immigration Act of 1924." *Journal of American History* 86 (1): 67. https://doi.org/ 10.2307/2567407.

———. 2014. *Impossible Subjects: Illegal Aliens and the Making of Modern America.* Princeton, N.J.: Princeton University Press.

Noel, M. C. 2016. "Des cours de langues qui ne profitent pas à des réfugiés." *Le Journal de Montreal,* March 13, 2016. http://www.journaldemontreal.com/2016/03/13/des-cours-de -langues-qui-ne-profitent-pas-a-des-refugies.

Nord, D. P. 2001. *Communities of Journalism: A History, 1690–1960.* New York: Macmillan.

Oberly, J. 1995. Review of *The Political Economy of Slavery: Studies in the Economy and Society of the Slave South,* by E. D. Genovese. Humanities and Social Sciences Online, October 1995. https://networks.h-net.org/node/16806/reviews/18633/oberly-genovese-political -economy-slavery-studies-economy-and-society.

Odzak, L. 2011. *"Demetrios Is Now Jimmy": Greek Immigrants in the Southern United States, 1895–1965.* 1st ed. Durham, N.C.: Monograph.

"Of One Mind." 1882. *San Francisco Chronicle,* March 5, 1882.

Okihiro, G. Y., and M. H. Jung. 2014. *Margins and Mainstreams Asians in American History and Culture.* Seattle: University of Washington Press.

Olzak, S. 1989. "Labor Unrest, Immigration, and Ethnic Conflict in Urban America, 1880– 1914." *American Journal of Sociology* 94 (6): 1303–1333.

Omi, M., and H. Winant. 2015. *Racial Formation in the United States.* 3rd ed. London: Routledge.

"141 Infested Aliens." 1921. *New York Times,* February 18, 1921.

"The Only Objection." 1886. *New York Times,* November 1, 1886.

"Opposes Literacy Tests." 1924. *New York Times,* January 18, 1924.

Osnos, E. 2013. "Reading 'Gatsby' in Beijing." *New Yorker,* May 2, 2013. https://www .newyorker.com/news/daily-comment/reading-gatsby-in-beijing.

"Ottawa et Vancouver cessent temporairement l'accueil des réfugiés." 2016. *Le Journal de Montreal,* January 19, 2016. http://www.journaldemontreal.com/2016/01/19/ottawa-et -vancouver-cessent-temporairement-laccueil-des-refugies.

Özden, Ç., C. R. Parsons, M. Schiff, and T. L. Walmsley. 2011. "Where on Earth Is Everybody? the Evolution of Global Bilateral Migration 1960–2000." *World Bank Economic Review* 25 (1): 12–56.

Palmer, A. M. 1920. "The Case against the 'Reds.'" *The Forum.*

Panunzio, C. 1921. *The Deportation Cases of 1919–1920.* New York: Da Capo.

Park, R. E. 1922. *The Immigrant Press and Its Control.* New York: Harper and Bros.

Park, R. E., E. W. Burgess, and R. D. McKenzie. 1984. *The City.* Chicago: University of Chicago Press.

Parkins, N. C. 2010. "Push and Pull Factors of Migration." *American Review of Political Economy* 8 (2): 6–24.

Paul-Biron, P. 2016. "Les premiers Syriens maintenant chez eux." *Le Journal de Montreal,* January 7, 2016. http://www.journaldemontreal.com/2016/01/07/les-premiers-syriens-maintenant-chez-eux.

Pavlovitz, John. 2017. "The Christian Myth of America's Moral Decay." HuffPost. Last modified May 19, 2017. https://www.huffingtonpost.com/john-pavlovitz/the-christian-myth-of-americas-moral-decay_b_10022720.html.

Pearson, R. L. 1970. "Gatsby: False Prophet of the American Dream." *English Journal* 59 (5): 638. https://doi.org/10.2307/813939.

Peffer, G. A. 1986. "Forbidden Families: Emigration Experiences of Chinese Women under the Page Law, 1875–1882." *Journal of American Ethnic History* 6 (1): 28–46.

Pegram, T. R. 2011. *One Hundred Percent American: The Rebirth and Decline of The Ku Klux Klan in The 1920s.* Chicago: Ivan R. Dee.

Perlberg, S. 2017. "Wall Street Journal Editor: Stop Calling the Travel Ban Countries 'Majority Muslim.'" BuzzFeed, January 31, 2017. https://www.buzzfeed.com/stevenperlberg/wall-street-journal-editor-stop-calling-the-travel-ban-count?utm_term=.ou2ogEreE#.hvijOVP6V.

Perry, L. 2016. *The Cultural Politics of U.S. Immigration: Gender, Race, and Media.* New York: New York University Press.

Pessar, P. R., and S. J. Mahler. 2003. "Transnational Migration: Bringing Gender In." *International Migration Review* 37 (3): 812–846.

Peters, J. D. 1989. "Satan and Savior: Mass Communication in Progressive Thought." *Critical Studies in Media Communication* 6 (3): 247–263.

Pfander, J. E., and T. Wardon. 2010. "Reclaiming the Immigration Constitution of the Early Republic." Faculty Working Papers 40. Northwestern University School of Law, Chicago, Ill. https://scholarlycommons.law.northwestern.edu/facultyworkingpapers/40.

Phillips, A. 2018. "Why Mike Pompeo's Senate Confirmation Is Historic—and Not in a Good Way for Trump." *Washington Post,* April 23, 2018. https://www.washingtonpost.com/news/the-fix/wp/2018/04/23/why-mike-pompeos-senate-confirmation-is-historic-and-not-in-a-good-way-for-trump/?utm_term=.85b91929a84a.

Pickard, V. 2014. *America's Battle for Media Democracy: The Triumph of Corporate Libertarianism and the Future of Media Reform.* Cambridge: Cambridge University Press.

Pieklo, J. 2017. "Trump's Muslim Ban Inches Closer to the Supreme Court." Rewire, May 9, 2017. https://rewire.news/article/2017/05/09/trumps-muslim-ban-inches-closer-supreme-court/.

Piggott, S. 2016. "Trump's National Security Advisor's Twitter Account Shows Extent of anti-Muslim Beliefs." Southern Poverty Law Center, December 20, 2016. https://www.splcenter.org/hatewatch/2016/12/20/trumps-national-security-advisors-twitter-account-shows-extent-anti-muslim-beliefs.

Pohl, C. D. 1999. *Making Room: Recovering Hospitality as a Christian Tradition.* Grand Rapids, Mich.: W. B. Eerdmans.

Pompeo, J. 2017. "Upset in WSJ Newsroom over Editor's Directive to Avoid 'Majority Muslim' in Immigration Ban Coverage." Politico, January 31, 2017. https://www.politico.com/blogs/on-media/2017/01/wsj-editor-it-is-loaded-to-refer-to-majority-muslim-countries-in-trump-travel-ban-234430.

Pope, J. C., and S. Treier. 2011. "Reconsidering the Great Compromise at the Federal Convention of 1787: Deliberation and Agenda Effects on the Senate and Slavery." *American Journal of Political Science* 55 (2): 289–306.

Popenoe, P., and R. H. Johnson. 1918. *Applied Eugenics*. London: Palgrave Macmillan.

Portes, A. 1981. "13 Modes of Structural Incorporation and Present Theories of Labor Immigration." *International Migration Review* 15 (S1): 279–297. https://doi.org/10.1177/019791838101501515.

Post, L. F. 1923. *The Deportations Delirium of Nineteen-Twenty: A Personal Narrative of an Historic Official Experience*. Chicago: C. H. Kerr.

"Predicts a Record Immigration Rush." 1924. *New York Times*, January 27, 1924.

"Problems of Immigration." 1924. *Washington Post*, April 5, 1924. ProQuest Historical Newspapers.

"Proposes Suspension of Immigration." 1921. *Wall Street Journal*, December 12, 1921.

Proshansky, H. M., A. K. Fabian, and R. Kaminoff. 1983. "Place-Identity: Physical World Socialization of the Self." *Journal of Environmental Psychology* 3 (1): 57–83.

Qin, Y. 2016. *The Cultural Clash: Chinese Traditional Native-Place Sentiment and the Anti-Chinese Movement*. Lanham, Md.: University Press of America.

Quinn, M. 2007. *Looking for Jimmy: A Search for Irish America*. Woodstock, N.Y.: Overlook.

Quito, A. 2017. "A Photo of Two Dads Has Become the Icon of Muslim-Jewish Solidarity at US Airport Protests." *Quartz*, February 1, 2017. https://qz.com/900346/muslim-ban-airport-protests-the-photo-thats-become-an-icon-of-muslim-jewish-solidarity-at-us-airport-protests/.

Rajabi, S. 2018. "What It Feels like to Know Your Iranian Family Is Under Attack by Your Own President." *Bustle*, May 10, 2018. https://www.bustle.com/p/what-it-feels-like-to-know-your-iranian-family-is-under-attack-by-your-own-president-9045658.

Rashbaum, W., and K. Flynn. 2003. "Threats and Responses: Emergency Response; in New York, a New Array of Safeguards Take Effect." *New York Times*, February 8, 2003.

Rashid, Q. 2015. "Islam Backs Free Speech." *USA Today*, January 9, 2015. https://www.usatoday.com/story/opinion/2015/01/09/free-speech-islam-charlie-hebdo-column/21458257/.

Rathod, J. M. 2013. "Distilling Americans: The Legacy of Prohibition on US Immigration Law." *Hous. L. Rev.* 51:781.

Ravenstein, E. G. 1876. *The Birthplaces of People and the Origins of Migration*. London: Trubner.

———. 1885. "The Laws of Migration." *Journal of the Statistical Society of London* 48 (2): 167–235.

———. 1889. "The Laws of Migration." *Journal of the Royal Statistical Society* 52 (2): 241–305.

Rawley, J. A., and S. D. Behrendt. 2005. *The Transatlantic Slave Trade: A History*. Lincoln: University of Nebraska Press.

———. 2009. *The Transatlantic Slave Trade: A History*. Rev. ed. Lincoln: University of Nebraska Press.

Rawlings, W. 2016. *Second Coming of the Invisible Empire: The Ku Klux Klan of the 1920s*. Macon, Ga.: Mercer University Press.

"A Re-action." 1882. *Oakland Tribune*, April 20, 1882.

Reich, D., N. Patterson, D. Campbell, A. Tandon, S. Mazieres, N. Ray, and A. Ruiz-Linares. 2012. "Reconstructing Native American Population History." *Nature* 488:370–374.

Reimers, D. M. 1985. *Still the Golden Door: The Third World Comes to America*. New York: Columbia University Press.

"A Report Adverse to Chinese Immigration." 1882. *New York Times*, January 27, 1882.

"Reports of Anti-Asian Assaults, Harassment and Hate Crimes Rise as Coronavirus Spreads." 2020. Anti-Defamation League, June 18, 2020. https://www.adl.org/blog/reports-of-anti-asian-assaults-harassment-and-hate-crimes-rise-as-coronavirus-spreads.

"Resistance by the Chinese; Combined Movement to Overcome the Exclusion Act." 1892. *New York Times*, December 17, 1892.

Ribas, G., and M. Macaya. 2018. "'No Ban, No Wall, Justice for All': Protesters Call for an End to Trump Travel Ban." *Washington Post*, April 25, 2018. https://www.washingtonpost.com/video/politics/no-ban-no-wall-justice-for-all-protesters-call-for-an-end-to-trump-travel-ban/2018/04/25/c963764a-48f8-11e8-8082-105a446d19b8_video.html?utm_term=.53eafbccf8cf.

Robbins, K. 1989. "Reimagined Communities? European Image Spaces, beyond Fordism." *Cultural Studies* 3 (2): 145–165.

Robbins, L. 2017. "Even Before Trump Acts on Immigration, New Yorkers Protest." *New York Times*, January 26, 2017. https://www.nytimes.com/2017/01/26/nyregion/new-york-protest-trump-immigration-orders.html.

"The Rock Spring Troubles." 1885. *New York Times*, September 21, 1885.

"The Rock Spring Troubles; Government and Chinese Authorities Investigating the Outrages." 1885. *New York Times*, September 19, 1885.

Roediger, D. R. 1994. *Towards the Abolition of Whiteness: Essays on Race, Politics, and Working Class History*. London: Verso.

———. 1999. *The Wages of Whiteness: Race and the Making of the American Working Class*. London: Verso.

———. 2006. *Working toward Whiteness: How America's Immigrants Became White; the Strange Journey from Ellis Island to the Suburbs*. New York: Basic.

Rogin, M. 1985. "'The Sword Became a Flashing Vision': D. W. Griffith's the Birth of a Nation." *Representations* 9 (Winter): 150–195. https://doi.org/10.2307/3043769.

Roosevelt, T. 1917. "Review of *The Passing of the Great Race*." *Scribner's Magazine*.

Rosello, M. 2001a. *Postcolonial Hospitality: The Immigrant as Guest*. Redwood City, Calif.: Stanford University Press.

———. 2001b. "Protection or Hospitality: The Young Man and the Illegal Immigrant in La Promesse." In *Media and Migration: Constructions of Mobility and Difference*, edited by R. King and N. Wood. London: Routledge.

Rothschild, M. 2006. "The Worst Ruling of the Week." *The Progressive*, June 12, 2006. http://progressive.org/op-eds/worst-ruling-week/.

Rotman, A. 2011. "Buddhism and Hospitality: Expecting the Unexpected and Acting Virtuously." In *Hosting the Stranger: Between Religions*, edited by R. Kearney and J. Taylor, 115–123. New York: Continuum.

Rudolph, C. 2005. "Sovereignty and Territorial Borders in a Global Age." *International Studies Review* 7 (1): 1–20.

Sachs, S. 2002. "A Nation Challenged: Detainees; Civil Rights Group to Sue Over U.S. Handling of Muslim Men." *New York Times*, April 17, 2002. https://www.nytimes.com/2002/04/17/nyregion/nation-challenged-detainees-civil-rights-group-to-sue-over-us-handling-muslim-men.html.

Sawaie, M., and J. A. Fishman. 1985. "Arabic-Language Maintenance Efforts in the United States." *Journal of Ethnic Studies* 13 (2): 33.

Saxton, A. 1975. *The Indispensable Enemy: Labor and the Anti-Chinese Movement in California*. Berkeley: University of California Press.

Schaefer Riley, N. 2012. "Defining the 'All-American Muslim.'" *Wall Street Journal*, March 22, 2012. https://www.wsj.com/articles/ SB10001424052702304636404577297371335370072.

Schmemann, S. 2001. "U.S. ATTACKED; President Vows to Exact Punishment for 'Evil.'" *New York Times*, September 12, 2001. https://www.nytimes.com/2001/09/12/us/us -attacked-president-vows-to-exact-punishment-for-evil.html.

Schmitt, E. 2002. "Threats and Responses: Asian Arena; Muslim Rebels Are Blamed for Bombing in Philippines." *New York Times*, October 5, 2002. https://www.nytimes .com/2002/10/05/world/threats-responses-asian-arena-muslim-rebels-are-blamed-for -bombing-philippines.html.

Schwarz, H. 2017. "Life after 'Hope': Obama Poster Creator Shepard Fairey Reflects on Art and Politics in the Age of Trump." CNN, November 20, 2017. https://edition.cnn.com/ 2017/11/20/politics/shepard-fairey-obey-giant/index.html.

Schwarz, J. A. 2001. "'The Saloon Must Go, and I Will Take It with Me': American Prohibition, Nationalism, and Expatriation in *The Sun Also Rises*." *Studies in the Novel* 33 (2): 180–201.

"Seek Drugs and Find Chinese Stowaways." 1921. *New York Times*, October 15, 1921.

"Seeks Further Immigration Restriction." 1922. *Wall Street Journal*, November 25, 1922.

"Seek to Keep Out Reds and Disease." 1920. *New York Times*, November 17, 1920.

"Sees Rum Raiders Gaining Sympathy." 1922. *New York Times*, January 8, 1922.

Sheehan, J. 2005. "How History Can Be a Moral Science." Presidential Address, American Historical Association, October 1, 2005. https://www.historians.org/publications-and -directories/perspectives-on-history/october-2005/how-history-can-be-a-moral-science.

Sheikh, I. 2008. "Racializing, Criminalizing and Silencing 9/11." In *Keeping Out the Other: A Critical Introduction to Immigration Enforcement Today*, edited by D. Brotherton and P. Kretsedemas, 81–108. New York: Columbia University Press.

Sheridan, M. B. 2005. "Immigration Law as Anti-Terrorism Tool." *Washington Post*, June 13, 2005. http://www.washingtonpost.com/wp-dyn/content/article/2005/06/12/ AR2005061201441.html.

Shryock, A. 2004. "The New Jordanian Hospitality: House, Host, and Guest in the Culture of Public Display." *Comparative Studies in Society and History* 46 (1): 35–62.

Siddiqui, F., J. Zauzmer, and S. Pulliam Bailey. 2017. "Officials: 17-Year-Old Muslim Girl Assaulted and Killed after Leaving Virginia Mosque." *Washington Post*, https://www .washingtonpost.com/local/fairfax-loudoun-police-searching-for-missing-17-year-old -reported-to-have-been-assaulted/2017/06/18/02e379ac-5466-11e7-a204-ad706461fa4f _story.html.

Silverstone, R. (2006) 2013. *Media and Morality: On the Rise of the Mediapolis*. London: John Wiley.

Simons, M. 2002. "Behind the Veil: A Muslim Woman Speaks Out." *New York Times*, November 9, 2002. https://www.nytimes.com/2002/11/09/world/the-saturday-profile -behind-the-veil-a-muslim-woman-speaks-out.html.

Sinnar, S. 2017. "Trump Travel Ban: Head Back to the Airports and Bring Your Protest Signs." *USA Today*, November 30, 2017. https://www.usatoday.com/story/opinion/2017/ 11/30/trump-travel-ban-head-back-airports-and-bring-your-protest-signs-shirin-sinnar -column/903124001/.

Skalka, L. 2016. "Stamford Group Hosts Immigrants' Forum Ahead of Trump Presidency." *Stamford Advocate*, November 18, 2016. https://www.stamfordadvocate.com/news/

article/Stamford-group-hosts-forum-for-immigrants-in-wake-10621509.php#photo
-11823104.

Slayden, J. L. 1921. "The Mexican Immigrant: Some Observations on Mexican Immigration." *The Annals of the American Academy of Political and Social Science* 93 (1): 121–126.
https://doi.org/10.1177/000271622109300124.

Smith, M. M. 1997. *Mastered by the Clock: Time, Slavery, and Freedom in the American South.*
Chapel Hill: University of North Carolina Press.

"Smith Seeks Millions in Immigrant Fund." 1924. *New York Times,* February 6, 1924.

Snow, H., and N. Banks. 2017. *The Intersectional Impact of the Muslim Ban.* Accessed
August 5, 2018. http://muslimintersectionality.web.unc.edu/immigrants/.

Sobh, R., R. W. Belk, and J. A. Wilson. 2013. "Islamic Arab Hospitality and Multicultural-
ism." *Marketing Theory* 13 (4): 443–463. https://doi.org/10.1177/1470593113499695.

Soerens, M., J. Yang, and L. Anderson. 2018. *Welcoming the Stranger: Justice, Compassion & Truth in the Immigration Debate.* Rev. and expanded ed. Downers Grove, Ill.:
InterVarsity.

Sohrabji, S. 2017. "Obama Pulls the Plug on Muslim Registry." *India-West,* January 6, 2017.

Somin, I. 2018. "The Supreme Court's Indefensible Double Standard in the Travel-Ban Case
and Masterpiece Cakeshop." *Vox,* June 27, 2018. https://www.vox.com/the-big-idea/2018/
6/27/17509248/travel-ban-religious-discrimination-christian-muslim-double-standard.

"Speed Immigration Legislation." 1924. *Washington Post,* March 12, 1924. ProQuest Historical Newspapers.

Speri, Alice. 2018. "Detained, Then Violated." The Intercept, April 11, 2018. https://
theintercept.com/2018/04/11/immigration-detention-sexual-abuse-ice-dhs/.

Spiro, J. P. 2009. *Defending the Master Race: Conservation, Eugenics, and the Legacy of Madison Grant.* Lebanon, N.H.: University Press of New England.

Stack, L., and C. Mele. 2017. "Road Rage Is Cited in Killing of Muslim Girl in Virginia."
New York Times, June 19, 2017. https://www.nytimes.com/2017/06/19/us/muslim-girl
-murder-virginia.html.

Stannard, D. E. 1993. *American Holocaust: Columbus and the Conquest of the New World.*
New York: Oxford University Press.

Stephens, B. 2010. "Our 'Moderate Muslim' Problem." *Wall Street Journal,* August 17, 2010.
https://www.wsj.com/articles/SB10001424052748704868604575433214247852860.

Stephenson, G. M., 1926. *A History of American Immigration, 1820–1924.* Boston: Ginn.

Still, J. 2006. "France and the Paradigm of Hospitality." *Third Text* 20 (6): 703–710.

Stoddard, L. 1920. *The Rising Tide of Color against White World-Supremacy.* New York: Blue
Ribbon.

Strauss, A., and J. Corbin. 1998. *Basics of Qualitative Research: Techniques and Procedures for
Developing Grounded Theory.* London: Sage.

Strauss, D. A. 2010. *The Living Constitution.* New York: Oxford University Press.

Streissguth, T. 2009. *The Roaring Twenties.* New York: Facts on File.

"A Symposium: What Is Moderate Islam?" 2010. *Wall Street Journal,* September 1, 2010.
https://www.wsj.com/articles/SB10001424052748703369704575461503431290986.

Takaki, R. T. 1994. *Journey to Gold Mountain: The Chinese in 19th-Century America.* New
York: Chelsea House.

———. 2008. *A Different Mirror: A History of Multicultural America.* 1st rev. ed. New York:
Back Bay.

Taylor, J. 2015. "Trump Calls for 'Total and Complete Shutdown of Muslims Entering' U.S."
NPR, December 7, 2015. https://www.npr.org/2015/12/07/458836388/trump-calls-for
-total-and-complete-shutdown-of-muslims-entering-u-s.

Taylor, J. G. 1966. Review of *The Political Economy of Slavery*, by E. Genovese. *Journal of American History* 53 (1): 120–122. https://doi.org/10.2307/1893943.

Taylor, S. 2010. *Narratives of Identity and Place*. London: Routledge.

TGRANE. 2020. "First 2020 Presidential Debate." C-Span, September 29, 2020. https://www.c-span.org/video/?c4910673/2020-presidential-debate.

Thibodeau, R. 2002. "Foreign Students' Concern Grows." 2002. *Washington Post*, January 3, 2002.

"Thousands Hear Sunday in Booze Funeral Sermon." 1920. *Chicago Daily Tribune*, January 17, 1920.

Tilly, C. 2017. "From Mobilization to Revolution." In *Collective Violence, Contentious Politics, and Social Change*, edited by Ernesto Castañeda and Cathy Lisa Schneider, 71–91. London: Routledge.

Tilly, C. and H. Brown. 1967. "On Uprooting, Kinship, and the Auspices of Migration." *International Journal of Comparative Sociology* 8 (2): 139–164.

Tomlinson, J. 1999. *Globalization and Culture*. Chicago: University of Chicago Press.

Torres, S. 2005. "Television and Race." In *A Companion to Television*, edited by Janet Wasko, 395–408. London: Wiley.

"The Trouble at Rock Springs; General Manager Callaway Describes the Situation." 1885. *New York Times*, September 7, 1885.

"Trump Fills Three Key Positions; Trump's National Security Team Takes Shape; Immigration Groups Fear 'Muslim Registry.'" 2016. Aired November 10, 2016. CNN Newsroom.

Tucker, R. 1990. *Immigration and U.S. Foreign Policy*. Boulder, Colo.: Westview.

Turner Classic Movies. n.d. "The Birth of a Nation." Accessed July 1, 2022. https://www.tcm.com/tcmdb/title/5764/the-birth-of-a-nation/#overview.

Twitter. 2018. "#MyMuslimAmericanFamily." Accessed June 30, 2022. https://twitter.com/hashtag/MyMuslimImmigrantFamily?src=hash&lang=en.

"The Typhus Menace." 1921. *New York Times*, February 11, 1921.

UC Santa Barbara. 1880. "Republican Party Platform of 1880." American Presidency Project, June 2, 1880. https://www.presidency.ucsb.edu/node/273308.

———. 1884. "Republican Party Platform of 1884." American Presidency Project, June 3, 1884. https://www.presidency.ucsb.edu/node/273309.

Umar, M. 2018. "Islam Teaches Us That Life Is a Test. So Is This President." *New York Times*, January 20, 2018. https://www.nytimes.com/2018/01/20/opinion/sunday/islam-lessons-trump.html?rref=collection%2Ftimestopic%2FMuslim%20Americans.

"United Nations Declaration on the Rights of Indigenous Peoples" (UNDRIP). 2008. Published at the United Nations, March 2008. https://www.un.org/esa/socdev/unpfii/documents/DRIPS_en.pdf.

"The Unveiling of the Statue." 1886. *New York Times*, October 29, 1886.

Urgo, J. R. 1995. *Willa Cather and the Myth of American Migration*. Urbana: University of Illinois Press.

Van Meijl, T. 2007. "Beyond Economics: Transnational Labour Migration in Asia and the Pacific." *International Institute for Asian Studies Newsletter* 43:17.

Venne, S. H. 1998. *Our Elders Understand Our Rights: Evolving International Law regarding Indigenous Peoples*. Penticton, B.C.: Theytus.

———. 2012. "An Indian in Law: 'They Don't Know a Damn Thing about Us.'" *The Ring* 2, no. 16 (November 3, 1976): 5.

Veracini, L. 2010. *Settler Colonialism: A Theoretical Overview*. Hampshire, U.K.: Palgrave Macmillan.

———. 2014. "Understanding Colonialism and Settler Colonialism as Distinct Formations." *Interventions* 16 (5): 615–633.

"Vote Not Yet Reached on the Anti-Chinese Bill." 1882. *New York Times*, March 9, 1882.

"Wages Continue to Move to Higher Levels." 1922. *Wall Street Journal*, October 18, 1922.

Wald, M. 2002. "A Nation Challenged: Legislation; A Move to Release Money to Pay Terrorism Victims." *New York Times*, April 17, 2002. https://www.nytimes.com/2002/04/17/world/a -nation-challenged-legislation-a-move-to-release-money-to-pay-terrorism-victims.html.

Walsh, K. 2012. "Emotion and Migration: British Transnationals in Dubai." *Environment and Planning D: Society and Space* 30 (1): 43–59.

Wang Yuen, N. 2017. *Reel Inequality: Hollywood Actors and Racism.* New Brunswick, N.J.: Rutgers University Press.

"Wants Scientific Immigration Laws." 1924. *New York Times*, January 18, 1924.

Ward, L. M., E. Hansbrough, and E. Walker. 2005. "Contributions of Music Video Exposure to Black Adolescents' Gender and Sexual Schemas." *Journal of Adolescent Research* 20 (2): 143–166. https://doi.org/10.1177/0743558404271135.

Wasserman, I. M. 1989. "Prohibition and Ethnocultural Conflict: The Missouri Prohibition Referendum of 1918." *Social Science Quarterly* 70 (4): 886.

"Watch the Rascals." 1882. *Oakland Tribune*, May 13, 1882.

Watenpaugh, K. D. 2010. "The League of Nations' Rescue of Armenian Genocide Survivors and the Making of Modern Humanitarianism, 1920–1927." *American Historical Review* 115 (5): 1315–1339.

Weaver, D. H. 2007. "Thoughts on Agenda Setting, Framing, and Priming." *Journal of Communication* 57 (1): 142–147.

Weinryb Grohsgal, L. 2014. "Chronicling America's Historic German Newspapers and the Growth of the American Ethnic Press." National Endowment for the Humanities, July 2, 2014. https://www.neh.gov/divisions/preservation/featured-project/chronicling -americas-historic-german-newspapers-and-the-grow.

Welskopp, T. 2013. "Prohibition in the United States: The German America Experience, 1919–1933." *Bulletin of the German Historical Institute* 53:31–53.

West, T. 2014. "Remembering Displacement: Photography and the Interactive Spaces of Memory." *Memory Studies* 7 (2): 176–190.

"What the Klan Did in the Oregon Elections." 1922. *New York Times*, December 3, 1922.

"White Man Lynched." 1929. *Reading Times*, May 18, 1929.

Wilkerson, I. 2011. *The Warmth of Other Suns: The Epic Story of America's Great Migration.* New York: Vintage.

Wills, J., D. Kavita, and J. Evans, eds. 2010. *Global Cities at Work: New Migrant Divisions of Labour.* London: Pluto.

Wilson, K., and E. J. Peters. 2005. "'You Can Make a Place for It': Remapping Urban First Nations Spaces of Identity." *Environment and Planning D: Society and Space* 23 (3): 395–413. https://doi.org/10.1068/d390.

Wilson, S. H. ed. 2012. *The U.S. Justice System: An Encyclopedia.* Santa Barbara, Calif.: ABC-CLIO.

Wise, A. and E. McPike. 2015. "Republican Ben Carson Compares Syrian Refugees to 'Rabid Dogs.'" *Reuters*, November 20, 2015. https://www.reuters.com/article/us-usa-election -carson-idUSMTZSAPEBBJ2WMEHQ20151120.

Wolf, R. 2018. "Supreme Court Shows Support for President Trump's Immigration Travel Ban." *USA Today*, April 18, 2018. https://www.usatoday.com/story/news/politics/2018/ 04/25/supreme-court-support-president-trump-immigration-travel-ban/547495002/.

Wolfe, B. 2021. "Indentured Servants in Colonial Virginia." Encyclopedia Virginia, November 10, 2021. http://www.EncyclopediaVirginia.org/Indentured_Servants_in_Colonial_Virginia.

Wolfe, P. 1999. *Settler Colonialism and the Transformation of Anthropology: The Politics and Poetics of an Ethnographic Event.* London: Cassell.

———. 2006. "Settler Colonialism and the Elimination of the Native." *Journal of Genocide Research* 8 (4): 387–409. https://doi.org/10.1080/14623520601056240.

Women's March. 2017. "Immigrants Make America Great." Twitter, January 26, 2017. https://twitter.com/womensmarch/status/824407523188994048.

Wong, K. S., and S. Chan, eds. 1998. *Claiming America: Constructing Chinese American Identities during the Exclusion Era.* Philadelphia: Temple University Press.

World Health Organization (WHO). n.d. "Archived: WHO Timeline—COVID-19." Accessed August 6, 2021. https://www.who.int/news/item/27-04-2020-who-timeline---covid-19.

———. 2020. "Statement on the Second Meeting of the International Health Regulations (2005) Emergency Committee regarding the Outbreak of Novel Coronavirus (2019-nCoV)." January 30, 2020. https://www.who.int/news/item/30-01-2020-statement-on-the-second-meeting-of-the-international-health-regulations-(2005)-emergency-committee-regarding-the-outbreak-of-novel-coronavirus-(2019-ncov).

"World's Muslim Population More Widespread Than You Might Think." 2017. Pew Research Center, January 31, 2017. https://www.pewresearch.org/fact-tank/2017/01/31/worlds-muslim-population-more-widespread-than-you-might-think/.

"Would Amend Immigration Laws." 1922. *Wall Street Journal*, March 4, 1922.

Wu, E. D. 2008. "America's Chinese': Anti-communism, Citizenship, and Cultural Diplomacy during the Cold War." *Pacific Historical Review* 77 (3): 391–422. https://doi.org/10.1525/phr.2008.77.3.391.

"The Wyoming Massacre; White Miners Determined to Drive Out the Chinese." 1885. *New York Times*, September 6, 1885.

"The Wyoming Troubles." 1885. *New York Times*, September 9, 1885.

Yahr, E., and B. Butler. 2016. "Late-Night TV Hosts React to Trump's Presidency with Disbelief, Lots of Jokes." *Washington Post*, November 10, 2016. https://www.washingtonpost.com/news/arts-and-entertainment/wp/2016/11/10/late-night-tv-hosts-react-to-trumps-presidency-with-disbelief-lots-of-jokes/?utm_term=.fb690d8c9253.

Yang, G. 2003. "China's Zhiqing Generation Nostalgia, Identity, and Cultural Resistance in the 1990s." *Modern China* 29 (3): 267–296.

———. 2016. *The Red Guard Generation and Political Activism in China.* New York: Columbia University Press.

Yang, P., and K. Koshy. 2016. "The 'Becoming White Thesis' Revisited." *Journal of Public and Professional Sociology* 8 (1): 1–25.

Yasin, H. 2018. "The U.S. Is Still Harsh to Muslims, No Matter How The Travel Ban Case Goes." *Washington Post*, May 15, 2018.

Yelsey, R. 2015. "The Chinese Exclusion Act Raised the Price of Becoming an American." *Humanities* 36, no. 1 (January/February). https://www.neh.gov/humanities/2015/januaryfebruary/feature/the-chinese-exclusion-act-raised-the-price-becoming-american.

Young, J. 2017. "Making America 1920 Again? Nativism and US Immigration, Past and Present." *Journal on Migration and Human Security* 5 (1): 217–235.

Yung, J., G. H. Chang, and H. M. Lai, eds. 2006. *Chinese American Voices: From the Gold Rush to the Present.* Berkeley: University of California Press.

Zelizer, B. 2016. *What Journalism Could Be.* Cambridge: Polity.

Zelizer, B., and S. Allan, eds. 2011. *Journalism after September 11*. 2nd ed. Abingdon, U.K.: Routledge.

Zertal, I. 2005. *Israel's Holocaust and the Politics of Nationhood*. Cambridge: Cambridge University Press.

———. 2014. "Interview with Prof. Idith Zertal about Her Book: Israel's Holocaust and the Politics of Nationhood." Center for Comparative Conflict Studies, July 27, 2014. YouTube video, 13:10. https://www.youtube.com/watch?v=5SV_V_ir_jQ.

Zimmerman, L. 1995. Review of *God Is Red*, by Vine Deloria, Jr. *Plains Anthropologist* 40 (153): 298–299.

Zinzius, B. 2005. *Chinese America: Stereotype and Reality; History, Present, and Future of the Chinese Americans*. New York: Lang.

Zolberg, A. R. 2006. *A Nation by Design: Immigration Policy in the Fashioning of America*. New York: Russell Sage Foundation.

Zolberg, A. R., A. Suhrke, and S. Aguayo. 1992. *Escape from Violence: Conflict and the Refugee Crisis in the Developing World*. New York: Oxford University Press.

Zuhur, S. 2008. *Precision in the Global War on Terror: Inciting Muslims through the War of Ideas*. Carlisle, PA: Strategic Studies Institute.

Index

Page numbers in *italics* refer to figures.

White racial hierarchy, 84
White supremacy, 2, 43, 45, 52
WHO. *See* World Health Organization
Williams, Brian, 133
Wilson, Woodrow, 92
Wolfe, Patrick, 56
women: Asian men as sexual threat to, 50;
 Chinese, as sex workers, 55; Chinese, as
 threat to American family, 7, 50; vulner-
 ability of, in forced displacement, 155
Women's March (2016), 152
work ethic, 2, 81
working class, 51
Workingmen's Party, 45
World Health Organization (WHO), 39

World War I, 79–80, 84, 93
World War II, 84, 120, 121; Japanese intern-
 ment and, 148, 149
Wu, Ellen, 66

xenophobia, 3, 6, 114, 115, 140, 152

Yellow Peril, 50–51, 56, 65; Mongolian invasion trope, 50
Youssef, Bassem, 143

Zertal, Idith, *Israel's Holocaust and the Politics of Nationhood*, 21
Zimmerman, L., 28
Zionist Organization of America (ZOA),
 147

About the Author

NOUR HALABI is an assistant professor of media and communication at the University of Leeds. Her research examines the interactions between mobility, social movements, and media. She received her doctorate from the Annenberg School for Communication at the University of Pennsylvania, masters from the London School of Economics, and bachelors from Paris (IV) Sorbonne.